Strategic Organization Development

Managing Change for Success

D1354546

A volume in
Contemporary Trends in Organization Development and Change

Series Editors:
Therese F. Yaeger and Peter F. Sorensen
Benedictine University

Contemporary Trends in Organization Development and Change

Therese F. Yaeger and Peter F. Sorensen, Series Editors

Global Organization Development (2006)
edited by Therese F. Yaeger, Thomas C. Head, and Peter F. Sorensen

Strategic Organization Development (2009)
edited by Therese F. Yaeger and Peter F. Sorensen

Strategic Organization Development

Managing Change for Success

edited by

Therese F. Yaeger and Peter F. Sorensen
Benedictine University

Information Age Publishing, Inc.
Charlotte, North Carolina • www.infoagepub.com

Library of Congress Cataloging-in-Publication Data

Strategic organization development : managing change for success / edited by
Therese F. Yaeger and Peter F. Sorensen.
    p. cm. — (Contemporary trends in organization development and change)
    Includes bibliographical references.
    ISBN 978-1-60752-210-2 (paperback) — ISBN 978-1-60752-211-9 (hardcover)
1. Organizational change. 2. Organizational effectiveness. 3. Strategic planning.
I. Yaeger, Therese F. II. Sorensen, Peter F.
    HD58.8.S7594 2009
    658.4'06—dc22

                                      2009024389

Printed in the United States of America

CONTENTS

PART III:
BUILDING AND IMPLEMENTING STRATEGY

PART IV:
GLOBAL ISSUES

FOREWORD

Tim Goodly

It is with considerable pleasure that I am able to provide the foreword to this much-needed book. This book represents the best thinking on a major issue confronting organizations today: *management* and *organizational development* (OD). Over the last 15 years, I have had the privilege of being in an ideal position to observe the tremendous changes that have occurred in the world. These changes make the transition from OD to strategic OD not just a possible consideration, but an imperative. Contributors to this book include a group of scholars from leading OD academic programs, and OD leaders from major *Fortune 100* corporations. Current thinking on this evolution is documented through discussions and descriptions of the evolution of the field; current thinking on effective strategies, including the coming of age of OD being partners "at the table" with management; to building successful strategies for the future. In addition, it addresses one of the truly important issues for our field, the successful collaboration and the building together of OD and human resource management for our organizations' most important resources—our human capital. Indicators of successful strategic organization development are provided, including a number of award-winning papers and projects, as well as a number of classic and timely illustrations, incorporating a greater understanding of the importance of leadership, especially

Strategic Organization Development: Managing Change for Success
pp. vii–viii
Copyright © 2009 by Information Age Publishing
All rights of reproduction in any form reserved.

global leadership, and the importance of talent management and management succession. This is a book whose time has come. In fact, it is overdue.

INTRODUCTION

PART I: PAST, PRESENT, AND FUTURE
OF STRATEGIC ORGANIZATION DEVELOPMENT

Part I, the Past, Present and Future of Strategic Organization Development, includes three chapters. These chapters provide an historical perspective on the development of the field and how organization development (OD) has entered into a partnership with management in determining a successful future, and how strategic OD evolved from its early roots. The first chapter by Yaeger and Sorensen traces the development of strategic OD beginning with the classic chapter by Jelinek and Litterer written 20 years ago, on the need for OD to become more strategic, to an identification of current issues related to this new definition of OD.

The second chapter, *The Future of OD and its Alignment to the Business Strategy* by Linda Sharkey again addresses the evolution of the field, this time from the author's extensive experience as a practitioner. The author addresses the changing global environment of business, the need for global leadership, and effective talent management.

In the third chapter, *A Failure of True Organization Development*, author Thomas Head presents a provocative argument in contrast to the position of the previous author who argued that strategic OD evolved out of the success of "traditional" OD. Head argues that OD has always been strategic and that the term "strategic OD" has evolved out of the failure to recognize it as such, and to effectively use it as a strategic process. In

Strategic Organization Development: Managing Change for Success
pp. ix–xii
Copyright © 2009 by Information Age Publishing

summary, these first three chapters draw on a combined experience of more than 100 years as scholars and practitioners in the field, and a first-hand view of the history and promise of the discipline.

PART TWO: PERSPECTIVES AND STRATEGIES

This second section, Perspectives and Strategies, consists of four chapters including two chapters based on award-winning projects. The first chapter, "The Chief Executive's Role in Strategic Change: Lessons from U.S. Presidents," by Thomas Head and Peter Sorensen is based on an award-winning paper presented at the Academy of Management. In the chapter, the authors compare the leadership styles of four U.S. Presidents—Jefferson, Washington, Polk and Roosevelt. The authors use their analysis of U.S. Presidents in order to provide a better understanding of the role of the chief executive officer and implications for strategic OD and the strategic OD consultant.

In the second chapter by Nazneen Razi, "Global Leadership and Succession Management," the author expands on the theme of leadership—leadership within a global context. The author discusses the new competencies for global leadership and consequently for global succession planning, and provides four exceptional cases to illustrate the critical need for effective global succession planning and provides the reader with a framework for integrated talent management.

"Strategic Organization Development: An Invitation to the Table" by Philip Anderson, presents thinking based on another award-winning project; namely, the Best OD Project of the Year Award by the O.D. Institute. Anderson brings to his chapter extensive experience in managing OD operations for a global *Fortune 100* organization. He discusses what it means to be strategic, the role of values, ways of being "invited to the table," and ways of developing an OD strategy. The final chapter in this section provides the reader with a perspective on strategic OD from Scandinavia by two members of the Copenhagen Business School. The authors draw on their extensive academic and practitioner experience to present the reader with a discussion of "drivers" for strategic effectiveness. In summary, the authors in this section present the reader with background for the issues provided in the next section, Building and Implementing Strategy.

PART THREE: BUILDING AND IMPLEMENTING STRATEGY

Part III, Building and Implementing Strategy, includes six chapters which range from the relationship between strategic OD and strategic human resource management (HRM), to a discussion of how OD can potentially contribute to other management disciplines, to the application of strategic OD in a specific field such as health care. The first chapter by Jim Dunn addresses some of the history of HRM, recent literature in the field, and ways of bringing OD and HRM together in a much-needed alliance.

The chapter by Susan Sweem deals with one of the important questions in strategic OD—the relationship between strategic OD and strategic HRM. She reviews a number of approaches to the integration of OD and HRM as well as citing a number of cases related to the implementation of combined OD and HRM strategies. The next chapter by Jimmy Brown proposes and explores the opportunity for integrating OD with other approaches to management.

The following three chapters deal with strategic OD specific to health care. Barry Halm in his chapter, "Strategic Organization Development: A Change Approach for Health Care Delivery," provides an overview of research and alternative approaches to OD in health care delivery.

In the following chapter, Jason wolf draws on his experience as a director of OD for a hospital organization. He presents an informed argument for replacing the model of best practices with an approach which he calls *discovering strength* through rigorous research and the application of positive change methods. His chapter is enriched by illustrations from Healthco.

The final chapter in this section is another award-winning project, the Impact Award for Outstanding OD Project of the Year by the Chicago OD Network. Here Roxanne Ray and Eric Sanders present the process and results of a hospital cultural transformation providing a powerful example of one of the key elements in the role of strategic OD—the creation of organization cultures in alignment with and capable of delivering on the identified strategy for the organization.

This third section sets the stage for Part IV, the final section that deals with one of the most important and difficult issues of our time; namely, globalization and the role of Strategic OD.

PART FOUR: GLOBAL ISSUES

This section is comprised of four chapters. Four of the five are written by executives or internal OD consultants. The chapters range from broad based chapters which review the relevant literature on the topic, personal experiences and case studies involving organizational change within a global context. The first chapter by Robert Kjar presents a review of the literature and cases drawn from his own experiences as a member of a Japanese multinational pharmaceutical firm. Based on his international experiences, Kjar provides clear examples of the need for deep contextual understanding of national cultural differences.

In the second study, Paul Eccher and Thomas Head report the results of a study involving a multinational, medical equipment manufacturing company. This impressive study introduces a new concept, the concept of the "translator" a new management role with knowledge of both the home country corporate culture and the local country culture, a role which serves to "translate" corporate strategy within the context of the local culture.

The third chapter by Mary Lou Kotecki provides the reader with additional insights into the implementation of global strategic OD. The author presents several cases well integrated with an understanding of OD concepts and their applications.

Richard Babcock and Bertha Du-Babcock, authors of the fourth chapter, present an important perspective on an increasingly important topic in global strategic OD: OD in China. The paper presents a three-stage model of organization development contrasting OD practices in traditional and progressive small Chinese family firms.

But rather than elaborate further, we feel it best to let the contributors and their chapters speak for themselves, for without their work this book would not be possible.

PART I

PAST, PRESENT, AND FUTURE
OF STRATEGIC ORGANIZATIONAL DEVELOPMENT

CHAPTER 1

A BRIEF LOOK AT THE PAST, PRESENT, AND FUTURE OF STRATEGIC ORGANIZATION DEVELOPMENT

Therese Yaeger and Peter Sorensen

The nature and content of the field of organization development (OD) has clearly changed over the years. It has become more corporate, more global, and yes, more strategic. It seems like only yesterday when such icons in the field such as Larry Greiner, Marianne Jelinek and Joseph Litterer, along with numerous others were calling for OD to become more strategic, and a partner with management. This call for OD to become more strategic is illustrated by Jelinek and Litterer's article which appeared more than 20 years ago (1988) in Woodman and Pasmore's *Research in Organizational Change and Development*, titled "Why OD Must Become More Strategic."

In 1989, in the fourth edition of Cummings and Huse introductory OD textbook, strategic change was represented by seven pages entirely based on Noel Tichy's classic work on strategic change focusing on managerial tools (mission and strategy, organizational structure, and human resources management), and managerial areas (cultural systems, political

Strategic Organization Development: Managing Change for Success
pp. 3–7

systems and technical systems). Tichy's work continues to provide a valuable road map for today's strategic OD. In the 1989 edition there was also no reference to either global or international organization development. today in Cummings, and now Worley, there are almost 100 pages devoted to strategic change interventions and 35 pages devoted to global and international OD.

WHAT IS STRATEGIC OD?

In the Jelinek and Litterer article, strategic OD is defined in terms of group process, job design, team building, group decision making, helping teams cope with stress, and an emphasis on socio-technical—all mainstream interventions at that time. Now 20 years later, we have a number of additional approaches which can be considered as strategic. Some of these approaches include, for example, Worley's integrated strategic change (ISC) model which combines traditional OD with strategic management. Clearly, many of the large group interventions would be cited as approaches to strategic OD including the search conference, future search, real time strategic change and ICA strategic planning process (Bunker & Alban, 1997). More recent strategic interventions include social construction and Appreciative Inquiry related approaches such as Thatchenkery's *Appreciative Sharing of Knowledge (ASK): Leveraging Knowledge Management for Strategic Change* (2004), and the integration of classic OD methods such as action research and strategy presented by Coghlan and Rashford in *Organization Change and Strategy* (2006).

Probably the most comprehensive classification of approaches to strategic OD can be found in Cummings and Worley (2009). Under strategic OD interventions one finds the inclusion of ISC, mergers and acquisitions, alliance interventions, network interventions, organizational transformation, culture change, self designing organizations, and organizational learning and knowledge management. We would also include Cummings and Worley's strategic OD as it relates to international strategic orientation, global strategic orientation, multinational strategic orientation and transnational strategic orientation. Additional areas for strategic OD include alliances between human resources management (HRM), organization design, and positive change management.

STRATEGIC OD AND HRM

A major role for strategic OD is gaining alignment between the strategic mission of the organization and its ability and competence to fulfill its mission. Again returning to our comparison between the OD text of 20 years ago with the textbook of today we see an important expansion in the role of HRM in terms of developing and sustaining organization capabilities. Performance management in terms of goal setting, appraisal and reward systems have received increasing attention, along with career planning and the addition of workforce diversity (Cummings & Worley, 2009). However, closer consideration needs to be given to the relationship between Strategic OD and HRM as the field also works to become more strategic. How is Strategic OD different from Strategic HRM? Where do the two come together and how?

STRATEGIC OD, THE ROLE OF POSITIVE CHANGE, AND GLOBAL OD

The concept of positive planned change is an additional concept which appears in the present today, but not in past OD textbooks. The most influential and frequently cited illustration of positive planned change is appreciative inquiry. As a major new approach to organization development it has implications and application for each of the areas of strategic OD previously mentioned. It has been applied and used successfully in a number of strategic OD applications. For example, it has been applied in the most rapidly expanding areas of strategic OD—in the global and international arena. It has been applied to transcultural strategic alliances between U.S.-India biotech alliances (Miller, Fitzgerald, & Murrell, 2004); it has also been used to create positive change in such global organizations as World Vision (Mantel & Ludema, 2000). At a more fundamental level, it has begun to address such basic issues as convergence versus divergence in national cultures, or whether the world is becoming more or less diverse. It has begun to address the question of basic human values with findings pertaining to highly consistent experiences surrounding peak work experience across such highly diverse cultures as China, Japan, Brazil, Sweden and the United States. Appreciative inquiry has also been used in such additional strategic OD activities as executive team building and accelerated team development with highly diverse groups. The possibility of identifying common universal work-related values and experiences has tremendous implications and potential for international and global strategic OD.

DISCUSSION

Twenty years ago, there was considerable concern that OD needed to become more strategic. This concern was illustrated best by the voices from such icons in the field as Larry Greiner, and Jelinek and Litterer. It is quite clear that OD has become more strategic. This chapter has reviewed the evolution of OD from the concerns voiced 20 years ago to today's reality. We have reviewed definitions of what it means to be strategic and have reviewed the key changes in the field which reflect the key characteristics of strategic OD. These key areas include references in the literature to strategic OD, references to international and global OD, the role of HRM, organization design, and positive change. One of the ways of assessing changes in these areas is to review the changes in content of one of the major introductory texts in the field, past and present, as well as work published over the decades in Woodman and Pasmore's (1988) *Research in Organizational Change and Development*. Such a review provides significant increases in the number of references to strategic OD, global and international and positive change.

Each of these areas represents important changes in the field. OD has increasingly played a more significant role in the development and implementation of corporate strategies as indicated by the number of executive positions reflecting OD in their title. At the same time human resources management is becoming more strategic. However, there is little in the literature which indicates how OD and HRM have defined their respective roles, which remains critical in that HR clearly shares with strategic OD the responsibility for alignment of organizational capabilities with strategy and mission. Although there is increasing evidence in the literature in the form of calls for greater integration and collaboration between OD and HRM, there appears to be little reported evidence on how or even if this is being done.

Organization design and organization culture are two areas which have received considerable attention in the literature and are major aspects of strategic OD in terms of alignment of the organization with mission. There appears to be increasing evidence that these areas are in fact playing a major role in the practice and implementation of strategic OD. The role of the strategic OD practitioner in terms of supporting corporate global initiatives appears to be a relatively new one. This impression is reinforced by the fact that references to global and international OD did not, in fact, receive reference in basic OD texts in the past. This has changed significantly but one is still left with the impression that this is an emerging area of strategic OD practice.

The work in positive change also has important implications for global and international strategic OD. It has major implications, for example, in terms of the divergence/convergence question and the existence of common human values. There can be no question that OD has in fact become strategic. OD has a place at the table. It is a place that it has earned. If past is prologue to the future then there is little question that OD will sustain its place at the table, and of course, will continue to earn it.

REFERENCES

Bunker, B., & Alban, B. (1997). *Large group interventions.* San Francisco: Jossey-Bass.

Coghlan, D., & Rashford, R. (2006). *Organization change and strategy.* London: Routledge.

Cummings, T. G., & Huse, E. F. (1989). *Organization development and change* (4th ed.). St. Paul, MN: West.

Cummings, T., & Worley, C. (2009). Organization development and change (8th ed.). Mason, OH: Southwestern.

Jelinek, M., & Litterer, J. A. (1988). Why OD must become strategic. In W. A. Pasmore & R. W. Woodman (Eds.), *Research in organizational change and development* (Vol. 2, pp. 135-162). Greenwich, CT: JAI Press.

Mantel, M. J., & Ludema, J. D. (2005). From local conversations to global change: Experiencing the Worldwide Web's effect of appreciative inquiry. In D. Cooperrider, P. Sorensen, T. Yaeger, and D. Whitney (Eds.), *Appreciative inquiry: Foundations in positive organization development* (pp. 457-470). Champaign, IL: Stipes.

Miller, M., Fitzgerald, S., & Murrell, K. (2005). The efficacy of AI in building relational capital in a transcultural strategic alliance: Case study of a US-India biotech alliance. In D. Cooperrider, P. Sorensen, T. Yaeger, & D. Whitney (Eds.), *Appreciative inquiry: Foundations in positive organization development* (pp. 493-521). Champaign, IL: Stipes.

Pasmore, W. A., & Woodman, R. W. (1988). *Research in organizational change and development.* Greenwich, CT: JAI Press.

Thatchenkery, T. (2004). *Leveraging knowledge management for strategic change.* Chagrin Falls, OH: Taos Institute.

CHAPTER 2

THE FUTURE OF ORGANIZATION DEVELOPMENT AND ITS ALIGNMENT TO THE BUSINESS STRATEGY

Linda Sharkey

Organization development's position in the workplace and literature has dramatically changed over the years. On the scholarly front, the research has become much more quantifiable and the results more scientifically based. The application of organization development (OD) in the workplace is more solidly aligned with business results. OD has always been focused on leadership and building leadership capability. Now however, corporations do not have to be convinced that leadership, not management, is critical to execute the business strategy and hence, enterprise survival. Previously, OD was relegated to action learning, team building and T-groups—all important and a good foundation, but not fundamental to business success (or at least not proven so). Today OD interventions and analysis are much more a common part of the business DNA and the impact of these interventions are quantifiable and statistically relevant.

Strategic Organization Development: Managing Change for Success
pp. 9–22

This chapter will trace the evolution of OD from this author's perspective and experience; discuss the current landscape, and offer a formula for OD's relevance in the future. Also, included are specific interventions and practices such as talent management, executive assessment and measurement methods. These interventions will be particularly important to scholars and practitioners alike to further the impact of OD on organizations and help these organizations drive sustainable change.

EVOLUTION OF ORGANIZATION DEVELOPMENT

Early experiments in organization development that had a strong impact on the workplace were in the labor/management arena. General Motors, City of Jamestown and the coal mines in England were breeding grounds for adversarial union/management relationship. Many will remember the bloody battles between the UAW and GM in Lordstown, Ohio. The strikes that ensued changed the dynamics between GM and the UAW Labor Union forever. Both parties were willing to examine the fabric of the relationship and to develop ways to improve. General Motors turned to OD and were early adopters of OD interventions. General Motors established one of the first known OD departments headed by Dutch Landon. Through this department the first efforts in establishing "quality of work life", a joint labor and management process aimed at building cooperation, began. Quality of work life, as it came to be known, focused on building common ground between labor and management where they worked together to solve work related (non-contractual) issues. OD offered team and trust building as well as a focus on leadership and decision making—welcome notions at the time. To both practitioners and scholars a like it became clear that adversarial relationships in the 1970s and early 1980s benefited no one. The costs in terms of human capital and an organization's ability to perform effectively were huge. The long-term impact of deep distrust consumed energy otherwise available for productive, interesting and challenging work. These early experiences in OD centered on quality of work life initiatives had the potential to demonstrate solid business impact if the fabric of the labor/management relationships could indeed change.

Quality of work life (QWL) efforts from the private sector were being applied to the public sector; a newer entrant to the labor management and collective bargaining experience. New York State decided that it wanted to try to change the relationship it had with the state unions and started a QWL project. A small team of consultants was established, patterned after the GM/UAW experience to try and drive cooperative relationships between the public sector unions in New York and the

Governor's Office of Employee Relations. While this was an interesting and educational experience, neither organization was mature enough to see the benefit of cooperation or sustain the behavioral change necessary for success. Ultimately, the experiments ceased and both parties went back to business as usual. However, through this experience, the relationships with the unions did improve and skill sets were developed on both sides that lived on in terms of using cooperative tools.

Through this experience though, participants were fortunate to be associated with the Work in America Institute and meet such venerable individuals as Eric Trist. The union and management leadership learned firsthand of Trist's cooperative labor/management experiments in England in the coal mines and meet Stan Lundine who was instrumental in turning around the City of Jamestown in Upstate New York. The Jamestown experiments were focused on turning around a bankrupt city through partnership with the local unions and city government. Lundine ultimately became the lieutenant governor of New York State due to his notoriety and success with the Jamestown experiment. It was during this period (1970s and early 1980s) that many of the handbooks on facilitation, team building and collaborative interventions came into the public domain. These experiences, experiments, and tools left a lasting mark on the workplaces of America and internationally that would not be reversed. These experiments were substantially changing the fundamentals of the employee/employer contract. Managers needed to exhibit more leadership and managers needed to change the way they interacted with the workforce.

Subsequent to the QWL era, a plethora of literature and experiments were launched in the area of participative management. Ken Blanchard and others were making the executives' bookshelves with quick reads like *The One Minute Manager. Theory Z* by Ouchi was all the rage. More emphasis was being placed on corporate culture and scholars such as Terrence Deal and Kennedy were examining the impact that culture had on productivity. With the decline of the labor represented employees, the labor management arena was changing but the need for gaining market success through an engaged and empowered workforce did not go away. More and more businesses were embracing the values of OD as a long-term viable route to creating healthy and productive workplaces where all stakeholders could be successful. Marvin Weisbord's work relative to *Productive Workplaces*, Peter Block's notion of stewardship, and Edgar Schein's work on process consultation, was fast becoming "must reads" in certain corporations and among many human resource (HR) professionals. These authors spoke, wrote, and taught about the fundamental changes in the employee/employer contract and offered more profound interventions that uncovered deeper values, behaviors and norms that aided productivity or got in the way of productivity. Human resource professionals' skill sets were beginning to change from pure employee relations, policy and benefits administration, to being able to facilitate, develop teams, provide feedback and create better approaches to develop leaders.

During this period, attitudes were changing about how organizations should be managed and led; however, these attitudes were definitely not mainstream. Places like AT&T, IBM, Xerox, and of course, GM seemed to be on the cutting-edge with deeply rooted OD work. However, these companies struggled at some juncture in spite of these OD efforts. The perception of OD during the early 1980s and 1990s ran the spectrum, from essential, to a business' success, to a "flash in the pan" outcome. Often OD was associated with those "touchy feely types" (in fact, it still does suffer from that perception in many places today).

However, in spite of the above, OD has had a profound effect on the workplace. From my own experience, let me cite a few examples and stories.

- When I first started out we had to teach people what the word "facilitation" meant. I will never forget walking into a meeting suggesting we "brainstorm" some ideas and everyone stared at me not knowing what to do. This would never happen now. More collaboration, and the understanding of the tools for collaboration, is now by and large a significant part of American business approaches, and growing more so worldwide. In fact, if you do not engage employees in dialogue, you generally will hear about it in employee discussions and surveys.

- There is a proliferation of books, materials, and consultants to assist in building high performance teams, understand corporate culture, and develop the "softer side" of leaders. Most companies spend significant dollars teaching managers leadership skills, how to engage employees, and develop themselves through feedback and observation. Most corporate education centers have programs on team building, and whole businesses have been built around creating team-building events for leadership teams.

- Employee attitude surveys are now common. In fact, it is hard to think of a company that does not conduct some kind of employee feedback mechanism in the form of a survey. Twenty years ago this was a rarity, and one had to do deep research to identify models prevalent in the workplace. Now there are big businesses around survey feedback and correlation analysis. Action planning to improve the organizations based upon the survey data is central to building high performance companies, and there are very few companies that do not use employee surveys to capture the "pulse" of the company. Companies like GE use this data regularly and track progress toward improving the culture to become an "employer of choice."

• We now take for granted that feedback and coaching make a difference, and the quality of the feedback is much more constructive than it was years ago. GE uses a process called *new manager assimilations* to help bond new leaders with their team. This process has been widely benchmarked and used by other HR professionals outside of GE. Leaders also regularly get feedback at GE, and use a process called *executive assessments* that essentially traces the life of the leader and his/her personal transitions to gain insights into their strengths and development needs.

• Many tools from OD are simply ingrained into the day-to-day operation of a business—so much so that they are no longer identified as "OD Interventions." Team assimilation processes are common. Action learning is the norm. GE has a change acceleration process (CAP) that was started by Steve Kerr, former president of the Academy of Management. This process is just part of doing business at GE.

• Assessing the culture of a company to be acquired is considered a best practice. Cultural assessments, while still not as mainstream as employee attitude surveys, are starting to come into their own right. There is greater recognition and research that indicates that culture clash, and/or compatibility, can dramatically impact the success or failure of an integration.

These are just a few examples of how mainstream OD has become. So, in my years of experience, OD has come an incredibly long way in enabling organizations to be healthier for all concerned—customer, employee, shareholder and the communities in which they reside. All of the examples and historic progress discussed, has been about changing how we lead, listen, build relationships and make profitable organizations. The contribution has been significant. Practitioners see the change in the workplace and see how OD can advance change in constructive ways—particularly with the advent of David Cooperrider's appreciative inquiry model as a new construct for driving whole systems change. Practitioners understand the acceleration of the rate of change in the workplace because they live it every day. Change is upon us at the most rapid pace we have experienced yet. With the advancement of technology, the flattening of the world as Tom Friedman (2006) points out, the global nature of companies, the need for organizations to constantly be changing their business models to compete, and the virtual nature of the workplace put nothing but change on the tables of practitioners, and hence on the research tables of scholars. The values of OD have not changed; in fact, they are more of an imperative for business. The need for more open communication, engagement and trust is clearly obvious as employees leverage communication channels more quickly and in ways we never dreamed of previously. The question becomes "can OD interventions drive change more rapidly and effectively to keep organizations competitive?" We need more rapid methodologies to define strategy, prepare leaders for the road ahead, and build virtual teams. Clearly this look back has demonstrated that OD is now an accepted discipline for organizations. But where are we now relative to the business dynamics and what does that mean for OD in the future?

THE CURRENT LANDSCAPE

The landscape of today's business environment has become increasingly more competitive—companies must drive out fat to survive. The war for talent is front-and-center on most chief executive officer's minds. Globalization is a fact of life—many Fortune 100 companies secure the bulk of their revenue's off shore, and in many cases such as GE, Honeywell, Pfizer, IBM—have substantial numbers of their employees who do not reside in the United States. Politics and politicians have less and less impact on world economies. Governments have turned over, the Iraq war continues, yet the global economy is strong until recently. The recent turn down does demonstrate though how entwined global economies have become. The answer to why, according to Nikos Mourkogiannis in his book *Purpose and Lectures*, is that global companies are the primary investment vehicles in the world. Increasingly, Mourkogiannis (2006), Friedman and others assert that more and more economies will be impacted by global companies because of the need for these companies to find ready labor and new markets. We can see that in the case of Ireland, India, Poland, Costa Rica, China, and soon-to-be Africa, where conglomerates are investing and the economies are now progressing. These investments are beginning to create a middle class; starting to level the playing field worldwide; wages are going up, more people have jobs and can afford more than the basics; and this trend is likely to continue. Another interesting supporting point is that economies are becoming more and more interrelated. The recent housing meltdown in the United States which could be perceived as a local event 20 years ago is now impacting investments worldwide (see, Wolf, 2007). This incredible growth and economic interrelationship is putting pressure on the need for the best talent. The war for talent in emerging countries is intense. Turnover rates for some companies doing business in emerging markets are as high as 30% (Corporate Leadership Council, n.d.). Employees can move in nine months from one company to another and improve their income and get to a higher position. This movement holds companies hostage. The companies either need to continue investing because the business model from a customer perspective works, or they need to move to the next fertile low-cost employment ground and hope they are enough ahead of the curve to maintain an advantage.

Technology is making the dream of a truly global marketplace a reality today and information is readily available at a speed no one could imagine years ago. The impact of private equity cannot be ignored. Private equity is changing the business equation in ways we cannot yet anticipate. Global markets and fluctuating currency has created liquidity not seen before—until very recently. Finally, the need for CEOs to balance the tension between efficiency and short-term profit and long-term growth is now essential. Described above are only some of the many complicated issues that companies are dealing with—the list could certainly be expanded. But the above makes the point that the changes facing today's corporations and their leaders is deep as well as broad. The question becomes, "what do OD professionals need to do to address this landscape and to remain current in this ever-changing environment?"

IMPLICATIONS FOR ORGANIZATION DEVELOPMENT

These realities put OD front and center in the business equation. This is going to require another dramatic shift in the skill sets of HR professionals. I have long said that the skills required of HR professionals will be weighted more heavily towards OD skills than the traditional focus of HR. The real value added of HR in businesses today is their ability to be catalysts of organization change. The fundamentals of HR are often outsourced like benefits, staffing, and so forth. In fact, there are whole businesses being built around providing those outsourced services to corporations. Change management, or change leadership and organization strategy, are the biggest areas that draw on a HR/OD professional's time. In my experience, HR and OD at the senior leadership level are blurring and the HR professional must be a deep OD professional. There are three things in my view that will require major focus over the next decade and they all require OD skills.

1. Increased focus on HR/OD as a driver of business strategy, as opposed to being the once sought after business partner. HR/OD must be business professionals who shape two of the most key

aspects of an organization—its leaders and its culture. If you are a human resource professional who is still trying to get a seat at the table and be a business partner, you have lost the game.

2. Increased focus on leadership. Leadership has always been a strong business concern, but now more than ever we need leaders who know how to truly operate in a global economy, understand the fundamentals of business beyond the balance sheet and are the chief talent officers of the company; with an increased focus on talent management. They also understand the impact of culture on performance and the types of culture that their leadership behaviors drive.

3. CEO's are recognizing more than ever that their real competitive advantage is to have the best players on their teams. Many CEO's believe that when you have the best players you can feel and visibly see the difference in your company's performance. Talent is the key to success—not just talent, but the best talent. Everyone is fighting to attract and retain top talent.

Let me elaborate further on these three points.

HUMAN RESOURCES

Human resource professionals will need deeper OD and change leadership skills. They are no longer in the game of change management, but must know how to lead change and help other leaders drive change. HR/OD will need a more profound understanding of the business fundamentals, need to be able to explain interventions and approaches in the context of the business strategy, and be able to explain the impact these approaches will have on the business results. They will need to quantify results in a way that clearly shows how certain organization cultural elements, or leadership gaps, directly impact the ability of organizations to execute its strategy.

Human resource professionals have to understand the workforce in deeper ways. What are the current demographics of the workforce, what are the true costs, is the business spending it dollars on the right people and job families, or is the bell-shaped curve skewed to populations that are not as relevant to the future business imperatives? How does the workforce impact revenue and the gross margins and how can it be shaped to have greater business impact. Here you need to be able to breakdown your workforce, determine job families and skills, determine what job families are most important to the business, and analyze if the right families are getting the right compensation. Then it is important to know what your total cost of the workforce is, and compare that to your revenue and gross margin to ensure you have the right productivity equation. Once you understand this, you can understand where you need to spend your dollars; what effect your cost of payroll has on your bottom line; and what the right mix of employee cost-to-revenue should be. With this information in hand, you can then design your workforce to better reflect your business marketplace. Few companies, in my experience, are this analytical about their workforce mix—most tend to look at head count rather than overall costs, skill sets and real retention needs. Only looking at head count can skew your view and bloat your ranks. The next questions to ask are: is the workforce located in the most strategic locations to drive growth? What is the organization design? Is it flexible to surge with the market, or do you have fixed costs that are slow to change? Workforce planning in this manner will become a critical skill of HR/OD professionals. This is the financial end of workforce planning. Without this financial rigor employed by HR/OD, companies run the risk of repeating the bloat of the 1970s and 1980s that is at least one factor impacting such venerable companies as GM and Ford. New start-ups, like Infosis, the Indian technology powerhouses operate more cheaply—not only because it is in India (although it is building facilities in the U.S.) and Toyota because they actively understand and manage the employee cost equation to product costs. This area of financial understanding has often been in the backyard of finance professionals. I contend that HR/OD must be well-versed in this area and lead these types of workforce analytics to continue to be relevant. While this equation is important, it is equally important to understand in a deep way the skill set needs and shifts.

Human resource and OD professionals have always talked about understanding skills sets and competencies. But now we have to understand skill sets in light of the future business strategy and start building talent for what the future will be and not what it is today. They have to know where the best talent is in the world for these skills sets and create talent pools in these locations. They have to think about organization design models that work in a global company, that are efficient but also enable employees to feel a sense of community and career growth. These professionals must know the total business fundamentals in ways they were not called upon before to understand. Understanding how money is made, how the supply chain works, what the financial picture is, and how the people fit is critical. HR/OD professionals must be business leaders in their own right. They must be able to use data and statistics to tell the story and demonstrate improvements. If you are not comfortable with the numbers and how to correlate cause and affect data you will need to get comfortable to be credible going forward. A good example is being able to know the critical skill sets that differentiate top performers from mediocre performers and know which specific skills in fact drive results. This can be done through data collection on current skills and using statistical tools to isolate the critical factors. We have to get away from arguing for competencies (HR/OD jargon for most managers) and make a concrete business case for key skill development. If one can do this, the argument is eliminated as to where or whether a company needs development programs or not. It will be obvious.

Let us delve further into the discussion of culture. Understanding how to assess company culture, and provide a clear picture of how culture will drive or inhibit execution of a company's strategy, will be essential. Providing a simple and crisp cultural analysis that is statistically correlated to performance will definitely buy you a strong place in the management ranks. The question of organization culture is now proven to be a key component of organization success. A study conducted by a Fortune Twenty conglomerate reviewed the causes of why acquisitions failed and found four key elements that contributed to the inability of acquisitions to meet the pro-forma of the initial deal: ineffective understanding of the leadership capability; lack of understanding of the cultural capability; not replacing or focusing the HR/OD efforts on leadership and cultural fit early, and finally, not instituting strong financial controls. This study underscores the need for strong leadership assessments and cultural assessments and having the HR/OD professionals that are capable of conducting these types of assessments.

Today, HR/OD professionals must have the ability to assess leaders, isolate the core behaviors that will drive the business forward, or keep it from progressing. Factor analysis and other social science statistics can help businesses understand the behaviors that most contribute to high performance and most contribute to strong leadership. Sadly though, of the studies conducted of numerous Fortune 100 companies they are still focusing solely on the behaviors of results to the exclusion of the other critical skills of global leaders. Robert Cooke, CEO of Human Synergistics through his research on leadership behaviors and their impact on organization cultures, has proven that certain behaviors create positive or negative organization results. HR/OD professionals must be able to conduct these types of studies and use this data to help senior executives understand what they need to do in quantifiable terms to drive performance. The science is to such a stage that one can isolate a specific set of behaviors and see the correlations to organization performance and culture. We now have the hard evidence that links what we believed in the last century about leadership behaviors and values to real organization performance and impact. How many HR/OD professionals can use this data to have business conversations with CEOs in the language of business so that they can see the financial return of focusing on culture?

To summarize HR/OD professionals must be business strategists, comfortable with numbers, strategic thinkers, cultural experts, community builders, and talent assessors and developers. This requires deep understanding of:

- company cultural elements and how to shape the culture to best fit the new business realities;
- employee development strategy and how to keep the employee vitality strong; and
- how to develop and engage employees to drive high performance.

It is essential to do this with rigor and analytics that reflect the language of business and not of OD or HR. Daunting but exciting for those who feel passionately about building strong organizations that thrive financially, are great for the people who work there, and contribute to the communities in which these companies reside.

GLOBAL LEADERSHIP

What is changing for leaders? Leaders now must know how to operate globally. This means, to be successful, they must understand not only country cultures, but organization culture. They have to understand global and regional economics and the various different operating models around the world. They have to be able to engage and energize employees even though they may be managing teams that span the globe. They have to be able to lead teams with diverse perspectives and attract and develop diverse talent. Successful leaders maximize people differences and maximize technology to do so.

Additionally, leaders now must understand many more facets of the business than ever before. It is not enough that they understand the business financial fundamentals. Often leaders of the past, like Jack Welch former CEO of GE, came from one or two frames of reference—engineering and operations. He made GE lean and efficient, but it really was the financial arm of GE that drove the double digit profits of the 1990s. His frame of reference was manufacturing. Jeff Immelt, current CEO of GE, views GE through a different frame of reference which is sales and marketing. His emphasis is much more on growth. He has launched a brilliant eco-imagination campaign to help market GE as green. He sees GE through the customer's eyes and is less focused on the operational areas. The point here is that according to Hambrick (1996) leaders shape their companies through their own functional experience. If the functional experience is financial, they tend to focus on that end of the business to drive success. Today however, leaders must understand human resources like never before, and these implications globally. They have to understand various business models and have deep expertise in more than one functional area. In fact, the ideal would be deep expertise in at least sales, marketing, operations, supply chain and how to globally leverage technology. They have to view their enterprises from a variety of lenses. They have to understand most areas of a company and what multiple levers are needed to pull in order to drive efficiency and growth. This means that leaders with potential must be identified earlier in their careers, and companies need to put in place orchestrated ways to grow talent so they have broader experiences to draw upon. Career development then becomes much more critical to business—it is not just nice to have, but essential to get talent ready for larger leadership roles. Careers must be better planned and less happenstance. As I interview leaders, I am amazed how some have meandered through their professional lives.

Younger workers coming into the market place want to know what career opportunities they have. Career development is a key differentiator for employers today. As salaries and benefits become more uniform around the world, the elements to keep employees in a tight market are clear career paths and advancement opportunities. How well a company orchestrates career advancement is a big differentiator. Management associate programs that bring talent in early in their careers and develop them for future roles, is a must. We are now seeing a proliferation of these types of initiatives. People have choices of where they want to work and good talent can move around more readily.

TALENT MANAGEMENT

Finally talent management is front and center today of any business's success. According to Ready and Conger (2008) in a study they conducted of 40 companies around the world, virtually, all of those companies lacked successors for their leaders and had insufficient pipelines. If you scratch the surface of many succession plans, you will find that the successors are really not individuals that are placed in the identified roles if someone leaves or moves on. Succession planning is often a corporate exercise that amounts to little development and change. They also point out that those companies have processes and systems in place to assess talent and develop pipelines, but they are not aligned to where the company is heading. Companies need to have a better way to assess the talent they currently have with real data so they have a true inventory of existing skills. Most companies rely on their own internal assessment of their talent and it is usually the employee's manager who does the assessment. More rigorous assessments should be put in place that are behavior-based and have some independent judgment. This will provide the company with a truer point of view on the gaps and what they need to do to develop their leaders. Not having robust talent management leaves a company extremely vulnerable when they need to deploy talent fast to get a strategic advantage. Recruiting from outside the company costs a lot of money in terms of time and recruiting fees. Often outside talent can't make the cultural adjustment to the new company environment. Home grown talent understands the culture and how to make things work. Additionally, you cannot be sure that you have the best talent if you bought it rather than developed it internally.

In particular, organizations will need to analyze the future of the business and map the talent to that future to realize the gaps. The data from the gap analysis becomes the basis of creating a talent plan that looks as detailed and focused as a business plan and provides a true baseline from which improvement can be effectively measured. A deep understanding of existing talent is essential. Without this understanding it will be very difficult to get the talent to the right places quickly enough to win.

Leaders should become their own chief talent officer aided by their human resource colleague. Together they need to fully understand the depth and breadth of their talent and they need to have a road map that builds successors and pipelines. This cannot be left to chance. Rigor is required and candid assessments and feedback is central so people understand where they stand and what they need to do to grow and remain competitive. Leaders must be willing to invest in people's development earlier in their careers so that they have the global talent needed within their companies to sustain growth. Great leaders attract, retain, and develop great leaders.

CONCLUSION

All three of the factors discussed above—great human resource professionals with deep OD skills, well rounded leaders that can operate sophisticated businesses globally, and development of the best talent—are interrelated and fundamental to business success going forward. Organizations that have the best HR/OD business leaders that are catalysts for change, the best leaders that understand all aspects of the business and can operate globally, and the best talent in all their jobs, will win today and tomorrow. This will be OD's legacy of the future.

What to Do Next

The next step is to assess yourself as a practitioner or a scholar in the area of OD and ask yourself the following questions:

- Can you analyze business problems effectively, apply analytics and practical solutions?
- Do you know how to develop leaders with practical and state of the art techniques?
- Can you candidly and accurately assess talent?
- Can you create workforce plans and talent road maps that make a difference?
- Do you understand the business and how it makes money and can you speak the language of the business?
- Do you have the scholarly underpinnings to advise and drive the changes discussed above?

If your answers are "yes" to all of these questions, you are ready for the future. If your answers are "no"—get a career plan and get ready.

REFERENCES

Corporate Leadership Council (n.d.). Retrieved January 15, 2008, from https://www.clc.executiveboard.com/Public/CurrentResearch.aspx#ibl

Friedman, T. (2007). *The world is flat 3.0: A brief history of the twenty-first century*. New York: Picador.

Hambrick, D., & Nadler, D. (1997). *Navigating change: How CEOs, top teams, and boards steer transformation*. Cambridge, MA: Harvard School Press.

Mourkogiannis, N. (2006) *Purpose: The starting point of great companies*. New York: Palgrave MacMillian.

Ready, D., & Conger, J. (2008). Enabling bold visions. *Leadership and Organization Studies, 49*(2), 70-76.

Wolf, M. (2007, October 4). Britain faces its own housing risk. *Financial Times*.

CHAPTER 3

STRATEGIC ORGANIZATION DEVELOPMENT

A Failure of
True Organization Development?
Part Two

Thomas C. Head

First, let me make one thing perfectly clear. True organization development, by definition, is *strategic*. There are no ifs, ands, or buts, about this. The problem is that most practitioners seem to have forgotten this, or never learned it in the first place. It is this sad fact that prompted my notorious *Strategic Organization Development: A Failure of True Organization Development* (Head, 2007) article that has created such a stir lately, and has forced me, purely out of self-defense, to pen this follow up. So at this point I ask you to please put away your tar, feathers, ropes, effigies, and matches, and please read the paper. If you feel like using these implements afterwards, my sense of social justice will not get in your way. However I will try to make it difficult for you to catch me.

Strategic Organization Development: Managing Change for Success
pp. 23–42

This tome will be in two parts. The first is a restatement here of what I said in the first place that made so many of you angry. The second part is where I will look to the strategic management literature to identify the elements that are required before something can earn the title "strategic." By doing this, I hope to show that there really is no difference between what organization development is supposed to be and what is being called strategic organization development. If you accept this logic, you (hopefully) will come to the same conclusion as I, that the use of strategic organization development is clearly a failure of traditional organization development—either through its absence or malpractice.

PART I: THE RESTATEMENT

Strategic organization development a failure? Quite the contrary, as there are plenty of well documented case studies where clearly strategic organization development has proven highly successful. Rather, this author believes it is time that we recognize that strategic organization development is the result of an organization failing to use the age-old traditional methods of the field, as they were originally intended, that necessitates the need for strategic organization development. (Head, 2006).

This is the quote that started all the trouble. What I am trying to say is that the way strategic organization development is currently approached, it is intended to serve as a "cure," a corrective action for truly significant problems. However, had the organization utilized "regular" organization development techniques it wouldn't have found itself in trouble in the first place. In fact, knowing that there exists a "cure" might be the exact thing that causes the organization to engage in risky behaviors. To use a comparison that I truly hope does not offend, look to the AIDS/HIV epidemic. The knowledge that a cure does not exist has driven millions to take preventative measures in order to avoid contacting the disease. These practices have also had the beneficial side effects of reducing other sexually transmitted diseases and unwanted pregnancies. But what might happen on that truly blessed day when a cure will be found for this dreaded plague? It is quite possible that, with the knowledge that a cure exists, the masses will abandon the proven, and healthy, preventative measures.

Cummings and Worley (2005) define strategic organization development as "efforts to improve both the organization's relationship to its environment and the fit between its technical, political, and cultural systems" (Cummings & Worley, 2005, p. 12). They continue by adding "that strategic change involves multiple levels of the organization and a change in its culture, is often driven from the top by powerful executives, and has important effects on performance" (p. 12).

It is important to note that only truly large-scale disturbances trigger the implementation of strategic organization development. Experts suggest these disturbances can involve forces such as: changes in federal regulations, a new chief executive officer (CEO) charged with transformation, or a technological breakthrough. To this list add: a basic change in an industry's competitive makeup, movement to the next level in a product's life cycle, or a dramatic increase or decrease in the number of employees (Tushman, Newman, & Romanelli, 1986). If one looks at these disturbances/triggers closely it becomes clear that the need to change is much less a cause for change than it is the serious and long-term neglect of management. In all these situations the use of traditionally defined organization development practices would negate the forces impelling the need for "strategic organization development."

If this seems unreasonably harsh, please examine these so-called triggers. For example, we must remember that changes, particularly significant ones of regulatory requirements, do not happen rapidly, or without warning. Governments don't operate on whims, rather deregulation requires a long battle between various stakeholder groups in very public forums. Even in those cases where regulations are altered through a court decision, the action is neither fast nor private. Managers are given plenty of time to study, analyze and develop plans for appropriate action. If they fail to do so clearly problems existed in the organization's structure, culture, or management systems long before the deregulation occurred. The deregulation didn't cause the need for strategic change–it simply made the problems obvious.

The second trigger, a new CEO being hired and charged with transforming the entire organization, by definition signals the true problem lay with the previous executive. It isn't the CEO's replacement that initiates the strategic organization development process; instead it is the charge for the transformation from the board. Boards are notoriously, and legally, conservative and they will never demand a new CEO completely reinvent the business unless they perceive the company is facing serious and dire problems. You might recall a mass of studies on executive demographics in the early 1980's that indicated when companies are running smoothly, boards will attempt to find a "clone" to replace a CEO, but when there are significant problems they will search for a very different candidate. Clearly the old CEO placed the organization in a precarious position through a history of bad decisions and/or poor practices. Had these never happened, or the organization acted quicker, strategic organization development would not be required.

There is no question that technological breakthroughs can occur with little, or no, advance warnings and force the need for change upon an entire industry. However, it is only when the organization finds it difficult or impossible to adopt the necessary changes that strategic organization development would occur. It is the existence of possessing an overly bureaucratic/mechanistic structure (Burns & Stalker, 1966; Head, 2005) when organic elements are required that forces one to engage in the revolutionary process of strategic organization development. Those with an organic structure would be able to implement the requisite changes with relative ease.

It is virtually inconceivable that a well functioning organization could find itself in a position needing to completely reengineer itself due to changes in the industry's competitive mix. First, if the organization possesses the appropriate degree of adaptability in its structure the changes necessitated by such an occurrence could be made naturally and in a timely manner. Second, it would only be in the complete absence of boundary spanning activities, or the failure to acknowledge the information they generate, which could lead an organization to be caught off guard. Clearly the true problem lies with the organization rather than the so called "force for change."

Movement along the product life cycle is natural, and never happens over night. We have also long known (Greiner, 1972; Quinn & Cameron, 1983) exactly what changes are required to meet the new stage's set of demands.

> So the question arises: "if the demands created by product/organizational maturation are universally known, and the appropriate adaptation methodologies are equally well known, how could such changes require a total organizational transformation, rather than simply a series of "surgical" interventions? Once again, there must be something fundamentally wrong with the organization that was present long before the change in life stage that prevented the company from recognizes the need to take appropriate action. (Head, 2006, p. 24)

If one recalls that organization size is measured by the number of employees there are only two possibilities that could impose the need for strategic organization development, a merger/acquisition or a large scale layoff. Small natural growth or shrinkage could never lead to strategic change if management maintains even a modicum of vigilance over the years. There is no question that downsizing creates the need for restructuring (Cascio, 1993), but equally true is the fact that the need for large scale layoffs is only due to long-term, large-scale managerial incompetence. Either they have failed to make the "right" decisions over the years, or they have consistently failed to act. This leaves only the significant growth or shrinkage due to acquisition or sell-off for us to consider. Healthy organizations will not sell off healthy divisions. Unhealthy organizations (due to poor management) will sell off healthy divisions. Healthy organizations will sell unhealthy divisions, which will be bought by other businesses who believe a change in management (from bad to good) will "do the trick." There is also no question that an acquisition could impose the need for significant structural/cultural changes. However, astute managers will have known this going into the merger and have incorporated it into their plans. If one looks at the class cases of merger failure (Gong & Head, 2002) it is almost always due to management failing to recognize the cultural/structural incompatibilities in the acquisition.

In summary:

> "There is no doubt that strategic organization development, as we currently define it (system-wide, multiple level, long-term, alteration to realign the organization to its environment) is a necessary process for many cases. Organizations do face problems that require massive actions. The techniques and interventions used in strategic organization development have proven completely effective from small non-profit organizations to large global corporations" (Sorensen, Head, Scoggins, & Larsen, 1985; Sorensen, Head & Stotz, 1985). "At the same time it is clear that the underlying cause for strategic organization development is the failure of the executives to exercise proper preventative actions. They either failed to recognize serious (but manageable) problems before they escalated to near fatalness or they made poor plans and/or mistakes in implementation." (Head, 2006, p. 25)

How does using all of this information, and placing a slight twist on the traditional perspective of strategy, that of proactively formulating and implementing plans in order to ensure organizational competitiveness, than another view of strategic organization development is possible. It becomes the use of well-timed and executed smaller scale interventions to prevent the misalignment between the environment and the organization, or correct small misalignments before they become significant—in other words, the original conceptualization of organization development.

Look at Rensis Likert's diagnostic three variable model. The causal variables (culture, structure, management) lead to the intervening level (those which reflect the internal state of health) and those, in turn, establish the end-result variables (organization measures of efficiency and effectiveness). Central to Likert's model is the concept of "lead-time." Likert noted that it takes time before issues at the causal level impact the intervening, and yet more time before the intervening level troubles negatively affect the end-result. Therefore, Likert advocated constant monitoring at the causal and intervening levels in order to allow organizations to identify problems and implement solutions before they impact the end-result. Action research presents another example—a cyclical approach of diagnosis, intervention and evaluation, which is actually a new diagnosis to evaluate the potential need for further action. The ultimate purpose of action research is to eventually transfer the entire process to the client organization so that it can proactively identify and correct problems on its own, well before they grow to require large scale changes.

I'll end this section's diatribe by presenting the six aspects of this revised perception of strategic organization development (Head, 2006) in which most will recognize an uncanny resemblance to traditional organization development:

- Regular and systemic "theory-based" data collection.
- Avoid packaged assessments and interventions.
- Participation and involvement from all stakeholders.
- Adopt a "change is good value" into the culture.
- Never rest on one's laurels, continued vigilance is the key for true success.
- Make sure constant vigilance is paid to environmental scanning.

PART II: WHAT DOES THE STRATEGIC MANAGEMENT LITERATURE TELL US

So far we have looked at this issue through organization development's eyes. It appears clear that strategic organization development is reactive—only needed when the organization has failed to exercise true organization development, which would prevent any serious issues from occurring. When one considers that organization development was also designed to "turn around" problem organizations, the question that begs to be asked is "why is there a need for the strategic label?"

To answer this question, in either the affirmative or negative, possibly the strategic management literature can shed some light upon the situation. Specifically, I have taken nine tenets from the strategy fields that appear particularly relevant to the current issue. Each will be analyzed in terms of what its implication would be for organization development—strategic or otherwise. I also take the liberty of presenting a personal observation based assessment of organization development's "current state of the practice" with regards to each. The outcome will, I believe with a fair amount of confidence, support my convictions that traditional organization development is "strategic," but that we need "strategic organization development" because most in the field really aren't practicing organization development.

Tenet One

"A strategy is a set of related actions that managers take to increase their company's performance relative to its competitors (Hill & Jones, 2007, p. 3). Daft (2005) defines it this way, "strategic management is the set of decisions and actions used to formulate and implement specific strategies (plans of action focusing on attaining goals) that will achieve a completely superior fit between the organization and its environment so as to achieve organizational goals" (p. 528).

There are two clear implications for "strategic" organization development with this definition. The first is that it consists of a set of related actions, not just one, and not a bunch of unrelated actions, all coordinated leading to a common objective. All too often today, the practice of organization development is anything but a set of related actions all directed towards accomplishing a competitive organization. Rather, it is a collection of independent interventions aimed at accomplishing "micro" goals—employee satisfaction here, less turnover there, stress reduction way over there, and the like. It is not unheard of for a large organization to employ multiple consultants at once working on a myriad of problems, in addition to having its own organization development staff. This cacophony of independent actions might reflect how organization development is, but historically what is it supposed to be like? Woodman (1993) in critiquing organization development's practice addresses this in terms of the change agents' desire to engage in a lot of seemingly unrelated process activities: "these interventions are way-stations, not the destination. For example, the goal of the organization is not to have effective teams; rather, effective teams are needed in order for the organization to attain its goals. This distinction is subtle, but crucial, for effective change agentry" (p. 428).

The second implication is that our ultimate goal is intended to be improving company performance, specifically as a concept that is considered in relation to one's competition. The purpose of strategic organization development must be aimed at what we call the "bottom line," rather than being buried in the "feel good" rhetoric—the focus must be on the results level, and not reaction level.

At a recent conference on management consulting Kurt Motamedi (Davidson, Motamedi, & Raia, 2007) suggested that a significant problem the field is facing is the lack of meaningful evaluation. A lively discussion ensued. Everyone agreed that one should evaluate their consulting, but the fascinating thing was the differences in "why." Some did acknowledge that it was to clearly establish that the intervention helped the client.

However many more, particularly those working in consulting firms, suggested evaluation should be done by the consultant for the consultant's own purpose, as a process to learn from one's actions, and there is no reason to share this information with the client. Others did question the need to evaluate at all, a feeling that is rife in the appreciative inquiry camp. At the 2005 Academy of Management conference when one presenter had the nerve to say AI consultants needed to provide "proof" for their claims, one individual (clearly representing the majority opinion among the audience) was "Why? My client keeps hiring me back. Isn't that proof enough?" There is no evidence here of a concern for establishing the intervention has made a positive impact upon the client's competitive position. In fact there isn't any evidence that those consultants are concerned about having an impact on the client at all.

If this critique appears too harsh, listen closely to professionals present their material. Most will discuss how they "got" the job, they will tell you what they did, but very rarely will they present evidence of what they've accomplished. In fact, I've actually heard organization development consultants claim that the employer owes it to the workforce to engage in organization development, even when it would clearly be to the financial detriment of the organization. Even with all of this lack of interest in the bottom line, some of organization development's "old-timers" have accused the field's youngsters of having "lost their values" because they show too much concern for the bottom line. David Jamieson wrote "The field has certainly grown and developed. Yet it can also be said that it has splintered and lost much of its foundation—core values that set it apart and started change down a different path" (2003, p. 40). In a direct response to this accusation, I (with Sorensen and Yaeger) (Head, Sorensen, & Yaeger, 2006) did a search of organization development's "founding fathers'" writings to find what the original attitude was in regards to this apparent "evil" bottom-line. With one single exception, Warren Bennis, focusing upon improving the client's competitive and financial positions appears to be a central theme of the early practitioners.

Clearly, organization development was originally designed (regardless of what some of the old-timers now say, to focus upon the organization's financial, as well as "spiritual" goals. While many, possibly most, in the field still maintain this viewpoint, obviously many also do not.

Tenet Two

Universally (Hill & Jones, 2007), it is maintained that the strategy process consists of two parts: (1) formulation, which is the selection of strategy and goals; and (2) implementation, which consists of the design and delivery of activities to support the strategy. It is safe to assume that any strategic organization development project must have, at its roots, the formulation stage. This means that the project must be clearly planned out ahead of time, complete with clearly defined objectives and directions established prior to the implementation. I will grant you, on this dimension, many of today's current organization development practitioners clearly engage in the formulation stage. Unfortunately, there are some who have taken the current "social constructionist" school of thought fad to a dangerous extreme. In their zealousness they prefer entering into a consulting situation with no preconceived notions including preestablished goals, objectives, or plans. Rather they trust to the belief that the "will of the masses" will provide all the guidance, direction, and objectives to lead the organization to success.

I'm sorry to disillusion these social constructionists, but even in "group therapy" the therapist is there to facilitate and provide direction to the group, all are very consciously aware of the desired end-results before entry, and there is a preestablished plan of some type to guide the group. If all this is needed for a collection of five or six individuals, why do we feel an organization of thousands requires any less? Look closely at any definition of organization development and you will see that it has always been meant to be a purposefully planned out venture. Take for example what most accept as the prototypical definition of organization development:

> Organization development is a system wide application and transfer of behavioral science knowledge to the planned development, improvement, and reinforcement of the strategies, structures and processes that lead to organization development. (Cummings & Worley, 2005, p. 1)

Need further convincing? Examine the conclusions Peter Sorensen arrived at 30 years ago when he reviewed the causes behind successful and unsuccessful organization development interventions. Among these he included: development of realistic expectations, custom designed solutions, and incremental approaches.

Organization development, strategic or otherwise, is meant to be a set of planned activities aimed at creating a truly effective and efficient organization. The fact that some among us don't currently practice it as such does not change this fact. All it does is establish why organizations will need to engage in strategic organization development—to repair those messes created by those not practicing true organization development.

Tenet Three

"Strategic leadership is concerned with managing the strategy-making process to increase the performance of a company thereby increasing the value of the enterprise to its owner—the shareholders" (Hill & Jones, 2007, p. 4). Once again, this clearly establishes the fact that anything using the label "strategic" must have as its central focus the financial and competitive well being of the organization. Clearly, all that we do must be aimed to improve the shareholders' positions.

This observation of Hill and Jones goes much deeper into the consulting relationship however. Remember, this quote is not about strategy as much as it is about strategic *leadership*, or the role of the top executive. The intervention's locus of control, meaning the decisions, must lie with the executive, not the consultant or low-level managers. For organization development to be considered strategic, entry and involvement must be at the top.

There's always a question of definition, but today many calling themselves organization development consultants will never even meet the chief executive, not to mention work with her/him. Some, if the project and their fee are low enough, might not even meet the functional vice-president. Others, working on truly significant issues, will meet with the chief executive, who will encourage the consultant, talk about how everyone is behind her/him, and will even write an e-mail to the employees introducing them to the consultant and stating how everyone is encouraged to support the change effort fully. The executive will walk out of the door and forget all about the organization development project. It is a sad fact that many organization development consultants are clearly "the pilot/captain" rather than the navigation as is intended.

At the recent Academy of Management global conference on management consulting in Denmark, the CEO of Tyco elucidated upon what he thought the proper CEO consultant relationship should be. Paraphrased, he stated "Don't tell me what my strategy is … don't tell me what best practices are. Those are my decisions. Give me good advice and suggestions, and I'll decide what the right thing to do is." This also summed up the relationship between consultant and client in most of the classic organization development case studies. The chief executive and consultant form a powerful partnership, working together to create successful change. The consultant is an expert on facilitation and intervention design, collecting and summarizing data, and the executive (or executive team) makes the decisions on what to do, and taking the clear figure head role in pushing the changes through.

Tenet Four

Hill and Jones (2007) lay out strategic planning as a six-step process:

1. Select the corporate mission (what and how the organization operates) and major corporate goals.
2. Scan the external environment to identify opportunities and threats.
3. Scan the internal environment to identify the strengths and weaknesses.
4. Select the strategies that will build upon the strengths, correct the weaknesses, take advantage of opportunities and accommodate the threats.
5. Implement the strategies.
6. It is essential to create a feedback loop.

There are many different implications for organization development embedded into this strategic process. The first is that step one clearly establishes that strategic organization development must be mission driven—and linked to the corporate goals. Daft (2005) reminds us that strategy involves a vision as well, one that is formulated around the company's core competencies, which is then incorporated into the mission.

It is safe to say that many of today's organization development consultants are not even aware of their client's mission or corporate objectives. They are hired to assist with a single issue, and that is their objective, and consequently their intervention's objective. They might believe that their project is in line with the company's strategy, or they may not actually care.

Refer back to Cummings and Worley definition of organization development provided earlier. Clearly organization development is to increase the organization's effectiveness and efficiency, as established through its mission. This is what organization development was always "supposed" to do.

> The application of organization development implies commitment to the values of underlying the processes and to the nature of organizations... our own formulation of this value base in as follows: ... 3) Seeking to increase the effectiveness of the organization in terms of all its goals. (Margulies & Raia, 1978, p. 137)

Steps two through four impose an additional burden on strategic organization development: its activities must incorporate the external environment into the change effort; must help the organization operate in its milieu, and; must involve both strengths (unlike the "problem-solving" model) and weaknesses (unlike the positivist appreciative inquiry advocates).

Many, particularly the large systems techniques, specifically incorporate representatives of external stakeholders. This is definitely the case in the Search Conference process, and such involvement is often encouraged in the open space tools that were spawned in the total quality management movement, However most organization development techniques do take a much more insulated viewpoint, ignoring the fact that one of contemporary management's driving assumption is that organizations operate as an open system (Daft, 2007), and therefore ignoring the fact that the client's systems must "fit" its environmental demands. This failure to acknowledge the environment's requirements could mean that the organization development intervention could actually be placing the client at risk, thereby requiring massive scale changes as outlined in strategic organization development.

The "implement the strategies" step specifically involves a coordinated combination of changes in the structure and culture to make sure they are both aligned in a supportive manner with the strategy. "Strategy implementation involves the use of organizational design, the process of deciding how a company should create, use, and combine organizational structure, control systems, and culture to pursue a business model successfully" (Hill & Jones, 2007, p. 413).

Many, if not most, organization development consultant's today don't even consider structure to be in organization development's realm, much less feel they are qualified to make such changes. A fascinating occurrence as organization theory is required in most contemporary MBA degree programs. We might also recall that most of our original tools, such as socio-cultural systems, Likert's four systems model, and Tannenbaum's influence graph, all focus upon the organization's structure as well as culture. Most, if not all, organization development advocates will agree cultural change clearly falls in the field's realm. But how many organization development projects today involve culture change, or even consider it as a part of the project's scope? Most are aimed at addressing single-issue topics and never even bother to look beyond the intervening level to the causal.

Our early leaders clearly established the fact that organization development must involve cultural and structural changes. Look at the definition again. What is involved in Lewin's third step, refreezing? Is it not ensuring that the structural supports, as well as the cultural values, are in place to prevent backwards movement to the old practices? The final stage in Kotter's (1996) model of strategic change management also demands the same type of changes. From the Topeka dog food plant to

Scandinavian Airlines and beyond, the true organization development projects have all ultimately altered the structure and culture. In fact, some in the field will not acknowledge an intervention is actually in the realm of organization development unless it includes alteration of these macro level elements.

The final implication, with regards to the strategic process, is the need to have a feedback loop introduced into the system. This permits the client to track the intervention's progress as well as monitor any unforeseen "side effects." The belief here is that strategic planning, and therefore strategic organization development, never ends. It is a process of change, evaluation, and change—constant and continuous.

At the aforementioned Davidson, Motamedi, and Raia (2007) session on consultation evaluation, a model outlining just such an approach to consulting was shown. A question was asked about how many actually evaluate their work (as opposed to the earlier reference where the issue was "should" evaluate), much less in such an "exhaustive" manner. Few, if any, raised their hand. I did mention that many of us in the academic arena evaluate at the end, as we need it to increase the odds of our manuscript being published in a quality journal. One participant asked how many in the audience actually went back to their client three to six months after the fact for a follow up visit. Two individuals indicated that their firm does this if the client has placed them on a retainer to be on call in case problems arise. Again, I volunteered that this is common among academics in the hope to improve their journal article. Other than these, it is clear that the consultants in the audience (all leaders in their areas from around the world) did not view their task in terms of anything other than a "single-shot" event. Contrast this with the understanding that most accept the action research model as the generally accepted model for organization development practice. Recall that the action, in action research, comes from the fact that the evaluation serves as a rediagnosis for continued intervention efforts. Organization development is supposed to be a continuous cycle of diagnosis, change, and rediagnosis. Enough said about this dimension.

Tenet Five

The organization's different functional areas must be coordinated for the common purpose, but they are each different enough as to require to be treated with a degree of individuality (Hill & Jones, 2007). Strategy recognizes that accounting is different than marketing, human resources is different from production, and so on. Therefore, a need exists for strategic mechanisms that permit differences in the functional areas while allowing them to operate in a coordinated fashion. I must admit, this is one dimension where clearly most organization development consultants have it right. I cannot think of a single case that would bring our profession dishonor on this point. I include it here as it is clearly a central point for strategy, and therefore strategic organization development. This is also a concept that was recognized early on as a critical issue for organization development. I refer, of course to the classic work of Lawrence and Lorsch (1967) around the dynamics of differentiation and integration. Lesser known to organization development, but very influential in organization theory, is the work of Perrow (1970) around the structural implications of differences in functional department level technology.

Tenet Six

When implementing strategies, executives must pay attention to laws, ethics, and internal and external stakeholders' satisfactions. Of course one can't always satisfy all the various stakeholders. When this happens the executive must identify those who are most important from the organization's perspective (Hill & Jones, 2007) and focus on their needs. A relatively recent development in strategy, but critical in understanding strategic organization development is the introduction of power and politics into the paradigm, just as we see here.

Everyone clearly recognizes that multiple stakeholders exist for any organization. Equally recognizable is the fact that at times these stakeholders' interests might conflict. When this occurs, and no amount of soul-searching and/or dialogue can find a mutually acceptable middle ground, the executive is left with a tough call: whom to please versus whom to tick off. Logic dictates approaching this in a completely rational manner. However, it appears unquestionably normal for organization development practitioners to ignore all stakeholders but management and employees. If there is a difference between these two more often than not the organization development consultant will take on the advocacy position for the employees. While this is probably a function of the consultant's background and practice, clearly it will not always be in the best interest of the client.

The fundamental values of organization development recognize our devotion to improving the organization through humanizing its operations. However, going back to the definition of organization development, as well as our codes of ethics (see for example the OD Network, ProChange International, and ASTD) is our obligation to always operate for the best interest of the client, which in the typical business enterprise refers to its owners. After all, the fundamental purpose of the for-profit organization is to maximize shareholder wealth. When all the stakeholders' needs are compatible there is no problem. However when these needs (and desires) are not "in-line" the executives, not the consultants, must make the tough call as to which stakeholders must take precedent. Recall that these same executives are legally obligated to first and foremost act in the best interests of the shareholders.

Tenet Seven

The Balanced Score Card (Kaplan & Norton, 1992) establishes that when evaluating organizational performance, from a strategic perspective, one must go beyond the financial indicators. It is critical to measure the indicators of competitive advantage as well: efficiency, quality, innovation and responsiveness to customers. Once again, here is one point on which organization development (strategic or otherwise) scores "full marks." If we do have one problem it is, as discussed earlier, our lack of embracing the financial indicators of financial performance.

Tenet Eight

Strategy " is important in the organization design process because it establishes the criterion for choosing among alterative organizational forms" (Galbraith, 2006, p. 565). Closely related to point four, this strategic requirement is included here as a separate point because it highlights another direction where strategy (and therefore what must be included in the definition of strategic organization development) and organization development's current practices part ways (at least for those few who pay attention to structure).

Clearly Galbraith's intention is that the organization structure must be established to support its strategy, even when this calls for a bureaucratic/mechanistic design. There is no question that organization development practitioners demonstrate a strong tendency towards favoring the organic structure. Organization development has also shown a strong penchant for creating new structures to facilitate modern management, starting with the matrix. In organization development's exuberance to push organizations away from traditional authority-based structures and encouraging them to adopt new participative designs, we have also been leading more clients down the road to extreme hardships. Many suggest that the matrix design was the root cause to both Shell's and Citi Corp's financial debacles. Several studies found that many organizations adopting the project management/collateral/parallel structural designs to meet the demands of Baldridge, ISO, and the like, have placed themselves into extreme hardship. The lesson to remember is that, as our early predecessors like Woodward, Burns and Stalker, and Miles and Snow, understood is the contingency approach to structure is to be taken seriously—meaning that sometimes the mechanistic/bureaucratic model is best for the client.

Tenet Nine

A fascinating study indicates that possibly up to 70% of business strategies never get implemented, mostly due to the complexity of their implementation (Corboy & O'Corrbui, 1999). I'll grant you that this really isn't a condition of strategy; it is a "factoid." However, I found it so interesting that I felt it was important to include here.

Imagine, all those organizations investing inconceivable amounts of time and resources to develop a strategy, only to find it cannot be implemented because it is too complex. I've never seen a similar study for organization development projects, but I wouldn't be at all surprised if it had the same results. I often find my client's try to develop grandiose plans full of unrealistic expectations. When this happens I try my hardest to "bring them down to reality," as I am very protective of my reputation for success. But no matter what one says to stress realism in planned activities it is very difficult to suppress "dreams of glory," particularly when using a technique such as appreciative inquiry. These dreams lead to developing plans that aim for the "stars and the moon." Unfortunately, when these dreams face the harsh light of reality, often the subsequent dose of reality will destroy any motivation, even for the realistically planned interventions. Remember, even NASA doesn't have the budget to aim for both the stars and the moon.

CONCLUSION

Hartman, Sifonis, and Kador (2000) developed a framework that suggests an approach for implementing strategy particularly relevant for the topic at hand. Their framework contains two dimensions: (1) the ease of project implementation (hard versus easy), and (2) the project's strategic impact (high versus low). Their specific recommendations with regards to the four situations are as follows:

A. Easy to implement and low strategic impact: incremental improvements, small wins, pursue for symbolic values of success.

B. Easy to implement and high strategic impact: simple changes that have high strategic impact—take action on these first.

C. Low strategic impact, hard to implement: difficult changes with little or no potential for payoff—these situations should be avoided.

D. High strategic impact, hard to implement: major changes, but with potential for high payoffs.

Due to the approaches typically found in organization development today, as opposed to what tradition mandates, I believe that most projects seem to fall into the C and A categories—either easy and of symbolic value only, or lofty and impossible. I'll assume most of you will have no problem with the former, but are decrying the later judgment. In my defense, I would simply point out that Edgar Schein suggests true organization culture change, that goal which we all should (at least publicly) acknowledge as our end result, will take several years to a decade plus, to accomplish. How many organizations are willing to wait this long, or pay the consultant over this time frame? For that matter how many of us (consultants) will live this long?

There is no question in my mind that organization development, true organization development that appears to be recently renamed strategic organization development, would benefit from examining the Hartman et al. model. Our current preponderance of activities focus upon the easy/symbolic value only, and/or the lofty but impossible sectors is what has always haunted the field. This is what has led to our reputation as "warm and fuzzy," good-natured, "cosmic navel gazers," who are to be tolerated for good employee relations. But when it comes to executives paying heed to "real consultants" their attention is drawn to the strategic, technology, finance, and marketing arenas.

What would organization development look like if we turned our efforts back toward the B (easy to implement, high strategic impact) and D (difficult to implement, high strategic impact) levels as Hartman et al (as well as organization development's definition) suggest? Obviously, the first implication is that once again organization development would find itself as a viable and desirable strategic tool for the client. The field would no longer be seen as the fun "fluff" that the organization must engage in now and then to demonstrate that it actually cares for its employees. Of course, this would also be the "death" of strategic organization development, as we would go back to our roots where all organization development was strategic.

Another positive consequence of focusing upon the high strategic impact spectrum is that our field's credibility, acceptance, and therefore marketability will sky rocket creating additional opportunities for all. Along with these opportunities the clients' managers will be more open and accepting of what we do, increasing the likelihood of smooth transitions by reducing resistance to change. By moving forward to the future by regaining what we are supposed to be doing, everyone wins. Isn't this what we're supposed to be in the business of doing?

The one final observation is that by moving organization development to the B and D zones, we end up actually attaining our conceptual paradigm elucidated by Kotter (1996). We operate sequentially, first addressing the small, easy, "quick fixes," that are nonetheless important. We then utilize the energy and momentum these "successes" bring to earn the loyalty and motivation from all groups in the organization to tackle the larger, more difficult dimensions of the change project. The ultimate result, of course, is by using organization development as it is meant to be used, we no longer require the concept of strategic organization development as we won't have "failures" (or at least as many), and we operate in the preventative, rather than reactive modes.

However, with these positive changes comes the need to redefine and/or redesign some of what we do. Personally, I find these changes healthy (particularly because they're in the right direction), but I also realize that many change consultants abhor the idea of change in their own paradigms. Change is fine for the client, but we don't have to do it ourselves. The amazing thing about these changes is they are necessary because the organization development practitioners have strayed from the right path and that they will take us "back" to what we're supposed to be doing—organization development.

I would like to finish this the same way I concluded that first paper. Hopefully this more complete essay has won you over, or at least made you think:

> Strategic organization development is the result of a failure, the failure of the organization to utilize the traditional organization development practices and processes in order to prevent problems from occurring. Therefore, in fitting with the spirit of the definition, as well as our founding fathers' collective wisdom, it appears best if we expand the concept to focus upon the prevention, through well timed, but relatively small-scale interventions. Therefore, building upon Cummings and Worley's (2005) definition:
>
>> Strategic organization development involves efforts to improve both the organization's relationship to its environment and the fit between its technical, political, and cultural systems. Such efforts can either be preventative or corrective in nature. Prevention requires constant monitoring of the internal and external environments to identify, and correct for, issues soon after they arise. Correction, in those cases where prevention was not exercised will involve large-scale transfor-

mations at multiple levels of the organization and a change in its culture. (Head, 2006, p. 27)

REFERENCES

Burns, T., & Stalker, G. (1966). *The management of innovation*. London: Tavistock Institute.

Cascio, W. (1993). What do we know? What have we Learned? *Academy of Management Executive*, 7, 95-104.

Corboy, M., & O'Corrbui, D. (1999). The seven deadly sins of strategy. *Management Accounting*, 77, 29-33.

Cummings, T., & Worley, C. (2005). *Organization development & change* (8th ed.). Mason, OH: Southwestern.

Daft, R. (2005). *The leadership experience* (3rd ed.). Mason, OH: Thomson-Southwestern.

Daft, R. (2007). *Organizational theory and design* (9th ed.). Mason, OH: Thomson-Southwestern.

Davidson, P., Motamedi, K., & Raia, T. (2007, May). *Evaluation competencies for management consultants*. Paper presented at the 2007 Academy of Management conference on management consulting, Copenhagen, Denmark.

Galbraith, J. (2006). Matching strategy and structure. In J. Galles (Ed.), *Organization development* (pp. 565-582). San Francisco: Jossey-Bass.

Gong, C., & Head, T. (2002). *What lessons have we learned from the merger and acquisition process?* Paper presented at the Midwest Academy of Management conference, Indianapolis, Indiana.

Greiner, L. (1972). Evolution and revolution as organizations grow. *Harvard Business Review*, 50, 37-46.

Hartman, A., Sifonis, J., & Dador, J. (2000). *Net ready: Strategies for the new economy*. New York: McGraw Hill.

Head, T. (2005). Structural changes in turbulent environments: A study of small and mid-size Chinese organizations. *Journal of Leadership & Organizational Studies*, 25, 82-93.

Head, T. (2006). Strategic organization development: A failure of true organization development? *Organization Development Journal*, 25, 21-28.

Head, T., Sorensen, P., & Yaeger, T. (2006). *Has organization development lost its way?: An investigation into the great values debate*. Paper presented at the National Academy of Management conference, Atlanta, Georgia.

Hill, C., & Jones, G. (2007). *Strategic management* (7th ed.). Boston: Houghton-Mifflin.

Jamieson, D. (2003). The heart and mind of the practitioner. *OD Practitioner*, 35, 40-45.

Kaplan, R., & Norton, D. (1992, January-February). The balanced scorecard—Measures that drive performance. *Harvard Business Review*, pp. 71-79.

Kotter, J. (1996). *Leading change*. Boston: Harvard Business School Press.

Lawler, E. (2006). Business strategy: Creating the winning formula. In J. Gallos (Ed.), *Organization development* (pp. 545-664). San Francisco: Jossey-Bass.

Lawrence, P., & Lorsch, J. (1967). High-performing organizations in three environments. *Organization and Environment*. Boston: Harvard Business School.

Margulies, N., & Raia, A. (1978). *Conceptual foundations of organization development*. New York: McGraw-Hill.

Perrow, C. (1970). *Organizational analysis: A sociological approach*. Belmont, CA: Wadsworth.

Quinn, R., & Cameron, K. (1983). Organizational life cycles and shifting criteria of effectiveness: Some preliminary evidence. *Management Science, 29*, 33-51.

Sorensen, P., Head, T., Scoggins, H., & Larsen, H. (1990). The turnaround of SAS: An OD interpretation. *Organization Development Journal, 8*, 1-6.

Sorensen, P., Head, T., & Stotz, R. (1985). Quality of work life and the small organization: A four year case study. *Group and Organization Studies, 11*, 320-339.

Tushman, M., Newman, W., & Romanelli, E. (1986). Managing the unsteady pace of organizational evolution. *California Management Review, 28*, 29-44.

Woodman, R. (1993). Observations on the field of organizational change and development from the lunatic fringe. *Organization Development Journal, 11*, 71-74.

PART II

PERSPECTIVES AND STRATEGIES

CHAPTER 4

THE CHIEF EXECUTIVE'S ROLE IN STRATEGIC CHANGE

Lessons From U.S. Presidents

Thomas C. Head and Peter F. Sorensen

Since before the classic Hovey-Beard case (Bavelas & Strauss, 1955) organization development has known about the critical role that the chief executive officer plays in the implementation of change, particularly those of a strategic nature. Everyone learns in the introductory organization development course that a major requirement for successful change is that the efforts must be top-down. But other than this nod, the executive's role as a change leader is really ignored by the organization development literature. This dearth of interest is even more fascinating as the organization behavior journals are overflowing with articles on transformational leadership. For example, Vas (2001) documented some essential transformational leadership traits, including (among others) courage, visionary, and the ability to manage complexity, uncertainty and ambiguity. Kotter (1996) outlined an eight stage model describing exactly what the transformational leader must accomplish to implement change, starting with establishing a sense of urgency among the employees and ending

Strategic Organization Development: Managing Change for Success
pp. 45–80
Copyright © 2009 by Information Age Publishing
All rights of reproduction in any form reserved.

with institutionalizing the changes into the organization culture. Daft (2005) suggest some of the roles the leader must undertake are managing the resistance to change, controlling the negative impact of change, and creating the proper environment (participative, open communication) in which it may occur.

The organizational behaviorists have given us a good start but it is about time that we in organization development begin to look long and hard at how the executive leader can facilitate the change process. It is in this spirit that this examination of four historical (three famous and one fairly obscure) executives approached the implementation of large-scale change efforts.

> A government must, therefore, find active among its members sufficient energy arising from biological, or from economic, political, or other social pressures, to serve its main purpose. This necessary energy may be very little, as in an isolated tribe located in a rich country, or very much, as in a nation with an itch for conquest; it may be sufficiently aroused by the pressures of physiological nature or of social tradition, with little interference of a political sort, or it may demand incessant and varied political activity. Whether simple or immeasurably difficult, the problem lies on the front doorstep of any government that, by whatever pressures may yield the most satisfactory net results, the energies sufficient to its main purpose be aroused among its members. (Dennison, 1932, p. 137)

From this quote one can see that a government agency, just like any other organization, must create energy within itself to accomplish its purpose for existence. The greater the purpose the more energy must be generated. This is particularly true with organizations trying to implement significant changes, either internally or externally. People have been looking to their government leaders for just as long, if not longer, than their employers, for initiating, guiding, and sustaining that energy. Therefore it could prove illuminating to see what can be learned about change management from examining the behaviors of four different United States' presidents known for spearheading significant changes: George Washington, Thomas Jefferson, James Polk, and Theodore Roosevelt.

The idea of looking at the governmental executive branch leaders to understand the intricacies of effective management is not new. Henri Fayol (1923), one of the founders of the classical management movement insisted that the prime minister has authority over the entire governmental enterprise. It is his duty to conduct the enterprise towards its objectives by endeavoring to make the best possible use of the resources at his disposal. In a suggestion that predated the learning organization by 70 years, Fayol recommended the formation of a "Council for Improvements" to assist the executive by constantly researching the organization's functioning in order to implement improvements in the enterprise and to carry them out under the auspices and authority of the director (prime minister).

Gulick (1937) examined organization and structural issues at the U.S. White House for ways to make the president (Franklin Roosevelt) a better manager. He, predating transformation leadership by 40 years, postulated that management practices leading toward authoritarian governance results in poor management systems as a "part of the diversion and scapegoat technique" (Gulick, 1937, p. 40).

Ironically, the United States' three branch system of government was created "to preclude the exercise of arbitrary power" (Schlesinger, 2003, p. 13) by the president. However a tripartite system has an "inherent tendency toward inertia and stalemate. One of the three branches must take the initiative if the system is to move. The executive branch alone is structurally capable of taking that initiative" (Schlesinger, 2003, p. 13). "For the most part, the president's job, as outlined the Constitution, is not one of dramatic decision-making and resolute action.... Nevertheless, from the Republic's beginning the presidency has been the institution of national government most capable of recognizing and responding to crisis" (Arnold, 1989, p. 37). The very structure designed to ensure congress would be the focal point of change basically forced the role upon the presidency.

Schlesinger (2003) clearly described the potential for transformational leadership in the executive role that the great presidents have all grasped the needs and dreams of the people and can lead the government in such a way as to lead the country toward reaching the dreams. He also points out "Throughout American history, the presidents have been the source of actions that have shaped the nation, its role in the world, and its citizens' understanding of themselves" (Arnold, 1989, p. 36).

Washington established the proactive nature of the presidency. Washington noted that the constitution gave the president the power to make treaties *with the advice and consent of congress*. So before he sent a negotiator to the Creek Indian Nation he went to the Senate for advice. The senators engaged in an extremely long and "inconclusive discussion and (after which they) finally asked to see the papers (proposed treaty). 'This defeats every purpose of my coming here!' Washington exclaimed ... (the session was postponed at that point, and) when the President returned to the Senate, he was overheard to say, after the business had been concluded, that he would 'be damned if he ever went there again' for such a purpose. No President has" (Brookhiser, 1996, p. 78).

The most nondescript and inconsequential presidents, such as Chester Arthur, have been able to act as a significant agent of change. Even his biographers admit he belongs to the group of presidents "whose historical reputation is neither great, nor terrible, nor remarkable" (Karabell, 2004, p. 2). And yet "by the time he left office, he had presided over a sea of change in the structure of government. Nixon went to China; Arthur reformed the bureaucracy" (Karabell, 2004, p. 10)." If an accidental, unwilling, unremarkable (yet intelligent and honest) president can implement significant organizational changes; imagine what can be accomplished by those who are highly driven, remarkably skilled, and significantly energetic.

Many consider George Washington's role the greatest in U.S. history, as he was the one to take the ambiguities of the constitution and create a workable executive branch. Literally everything he did as president involved implementing change, most of which have lasted over 200 years (Ferling, 1988). Although Washington truly believed in Congress's supremacy, he quickly realized (as in the case above) that it was up to him to act, and allow Congress (for the most part) to react (Johnson, 1984).

As stated earlier, much has been written about the transformational role of business executives in the organizational behavior literature. The literature describes what the role is, and what needs to be accomplished, but we have very few concrete examples of exactly how executives act to bring about change. For the most part the business executive's actions are conducted behind closed doors. However there is one executive leader whose every action and communication has been held up to close public scrutiny, the American president. Perhaps by examining the individual leadership styles (all very different) of Thomas Jefferson, George Washington, James Polk, and Theodore Roosevelt, we might learn valuable lessons on how executives should behave to implement change in even the most embedded bureaucracy.

THOMAS JEFFERSON

Even a superficial examination of Jefferson's life shows that while he was clearly a brilliant man, successful in many endeavors, in his executive roles (governor and president) he left much to be desired. Thomas Jefferson, quite simply, was never able to grasp the mechanics of executive transformational leadership. As Kennedy (2003) put it, "Thomas Jefferson was a greatly gifted teacher, but he failed to bring about the social transformation he laid before his nation of students as their great opportunity. He proclaimed two revolutions, one political and the other social. He had little to do with achieving the first and drew back from the second. He could start things but had difficulty finishing them" (p. 5). Jefferson's skills were in calling for change, explaining it, advocating it, convincing others to support it, but he could never lead an organization through the process.

If this judgment seems harsh, let us examine the conclusions of a biographer very favorable to Jefferson. Randall (1993) states "His two terms of governor of Virginia ended in failure only months before the final Franco-American victory of the American Revolution" (p. 312). Another historian commenting on Jefferson's presidency wrote "Once the prize was won and the best of him written into the first inaugural address, little is supposed to have remained to call forth superlatives. His Louisiana Purchase has been described as a fortuitous accident" (Brodie, 1974, p. 339). President Jefferson established his principal goals for the office in his first inaugural speech: peace, commerce and honest friendships with all nations. At his very first cabinet meeting Jefferson, with all but one secretary dissenting, ordered the navy to attack Tripoli without a declaration of war or consulting congress (Randall, 1993). Before Jefferson took office, the U.S. economy was booming with exports increasing 300% in 7 years. During the first 2 years of Jefferson's tenure exports dropped 40%.

In his second term tensions with the British increased. The British agreed to halt their hostile marine practices in exchange for U.S. neutrality in the British/French hostilities. However, because the treaty included a clause that nullified the contract if the United States honored Frances' naval blockade, Jefferson wouldn't let Congress consider it. "From that moment on, Anglo-American relations deteriorated (leading directly to the War of 1812)" (Randall, 1993, p. 574). He also began seriously considering a war with Spain in order to remove them from Florida. Jefferson, in his second term, called for a trade embargo with England and France. "In one year it destroyed eighty percent of all American trade and brought on the worst depression since the revolution" (Randall, 1993, p. 580). All of this occurring based upon Jefferson's goals of peace, commerce, and good relations with all nations.

Jefferson's Approach to Change

Jefferson's poor performance as an executive wasn't due to a nervousness about implementing change. Quite the contrary, as in everything else in life, he embraced change. For example, during his first term Jefferson pursued a "bloodless revolution" eliminating Federalists from every level of federal office, completely changing the executive branch that was only 12 years old, and only 4 years into the two-party system. "Not only did he oust the top elective officials but he removed the second tier as well by personal intervention or by wielding his power in congress to eliminate whole departments. He evicted 18 of 20 U.S. marshals ... sacking 15 of 16 revenue supervisors, 12 of 21 treasury inspectors and 50 of 146 customs officials" (Randall, 1993, p. 552). Jefferson's first message to congress called for repealing all internal federal taxes, abolishing the internal revenue system, reducing residency requirement for naturalization, slashing federal spending, and downsizing the navy by 67% (Randall, 1993). Jefferson's problems were that as an executive his choices, his ability for long-term commitment to decisions, and sometimes simply his timing, all left much to be desired. He succeeded in making sweeping changes, it is just that very few were "towards the good."

Jefferson's formal education emphasized three necessary qualities: caution, self-discipline, and patience. These qualities clearly led to Jefferson's scientific approach for most decisions, but they can also be seen as the roots of some of his leadership difficulties. One of Jefferson's definite leadership traits was to approach everything unemotionally. Jefferson's scientific approach can also be seen as the root for another less desirable trait of staying in the background and pulling the strings of change from behind the curtains.

If one needed a single metaphor to illustrate how Jefferson approached change it can easily be found in his residences. Jefferson had a lifelong passion for building, expanding, and changing his personal environment, starting around the age of 9 (Randall, 1993). Regarding his masterpiece, Monticello, a life-long friend, Anna Maria Thornton, remarked that he altered his plans so frequently that it looked like a house going to decay. Twenty years later it was noted that finally (although still not in a finished state) the house was truly a great residence. However the land around it had become very poor due to negligence (Kennedy, 2003). Jefferson loved change, but he often failed to think of the long term when creating plans or establishing goals. When asked by an English agriculturist why Virginians let their land deteriorate, Jefferson replied "We can buy an acre of new land cheaper than we can manure an old one" (Kennedy, 2003, p. 17). This short-term orientation (some might say practical could possibly be seen as Jefferson's greatest weakness as a leader.

Scholarly Approach

Jefferson almost always used scholarly principles and methods in his change attempts. Although extreme in its duration perhaps the best illustration of Jefferson's scholarly activism can be found in his efforts to reform Virginia's laws. Very early in Jefferson's law career he developed a loathing of the Virginia legal system. In 1768 he began to attempt a total system redesign using scientific order. When he turned the finished collection over to the Virginia Committee on Publications for public review in 1795 it was the most complete collection of law reports in the country. The collection was not published until 1829, 3 years after his death (Randall, 1993). While acknowledged as an incredible piece of scholarly research, Jefferson's work never, at least for 52 years from its inception, led to any desired changes.

"Amid the political turmoil brought on by the Stamp Act crisis, Thomas Jefferson made an auspicious political debut not as a fiery orator like his friend Patrick Henry but as a pragmatist.... Analyzing a problem, proposing a solution, and using the existing political system to bring about change" (Randall, 1993, p. 79). His first major success concerned a significant problem for the plantations (including his own). For years, because of a nonnavigable river, the planters had to ship their crops over land. Jefferson found the only barrier to water traffic was a short stretch with a very rocky bed. He spearheaded a public subscription to pay for removing the rocks. This straightforward solution provided the farmers with a cheap form of tobacco transportation and significantly improved the local economy.

As with any scholar Jefferson used his writing skills to bring about his primary change efforts. "Jefferson contributed to the Revolutionary cause the nucleating power of ideas, summoning a virtual—in the modern sense—convention of like-minded people on both sides of the Atlantic. Yet ... he made certain that no reader would take him and his fellows to be naïve about the realities of world politics" (Kennedy, 2003, p. 61). In writing the Declaration of Independence, Jefferson believed "It was not his task to educate, but to use the power of reasoning to argue, to persuade, and to justify a revolution, a tearing away from the womb of an empire that allowed the birth and survival of a new and sharply different type of nation" (Randall, 1993, p. 273).

Backroom Change Agent

It is fascinating to note that Jefferson's scholarly approach to change quite possibly led him to be a true force, but one that often acted behind the scenes. He started his revolutionary war change efforts by first studying everything he could find on the history and laws regarding colonies. With this knowledge base he then began to write clear and concise resolutions that often gained significant attention. However typically he would find more politically prominent individuals to actually sponsor his motions. It appears that he did this not out of a personal sense of fear, but because his review of Virginia's political environment made him rationally conclude giving someone else the sponsorship credit would significantly increase the odds of successful passage. While letting others take the lead on his proposals Jefferson would often support the changes through writing, and occasionally speaking, in favor of the bills (Randall, 1993).

As the U.S. Secretary of State, in response to the Alien and Sedition acts, Jefferson (with Madison) authored (in secrecy) the Kentucky Resolutions which that new state's legislature considered in 1799. The resolutions maintained that the state's had the right to nullify acts of congress, and implicitly suggested they had the right to secede, there by lying the philosophical rationale for the Civil War (Brodie, 1974).

Political Adeptness

Once, during the 1780s, Jefferson floated a suggestion for freeing Virginia's slaves at some time in the future. He was not, however, willing to be the sponsor for such a bill, although he would vote for it. After many years of no action on the issue some of his French friends asked why he didn't act more forcefully. His reply was "the moment of doing it with success was not yet arrived, and that an unsuccessful effort, as too often happens, would only rivet still closer the chains of bondage, and retard the moment of delivery" (Kennedy, 2003, p. 74). Jefferson's scientific and removed approach made for a clearly effective political approach to change, weighing all the options, looking at probabilities, and knowing when to hold them and when to fold them.

Jefferson's political approach, in all the contemporary meaning of the concept, was fully developed, and often effective. "Jefferson (as Secretary of State) had the deep deviousness that is given only to the pure of heart … Jefferson, who was too cagey to write anything for publication himself, kept a journalistic hatchet-man on the State Department Payroll" (Brookhiser, 1996, p. 81). This was decades, possibly even over a century, before the position of presidential press secretary was known.

It is difficult to imagine that the author of the Declaration of Independence would be timid about voicing support for change. "Jefferson admired Henry (for the sentiment and style of a dramatic speech denouncing the Stamp Act), but he was much too discreet ever to allow himself to emulate him" (Randall, 1993, p. 78). One could see this as a further example of a master politician—let others propose, and catch the heat for change, but follow up as a supporter in a far less visible manners.

Another political tool Jefferson utilized as an executive was engaging in delaying tactics, sometimes to wear down the opposition, sometimes to buy time for new ideas, but often simply hoping that the matter might just go away without the need for action. Jefferson proved a master of using bureaucratic mechanics for delay when he thought it was in his best interest. "But Jefferson was not only growing increasingly secretive as president, he was also making procrastination the chief virtue of his foreign policy" (Randall, 1993, p. 566).

One of the items of Adam's presidency that Jefferson objected most to was the sedition act, which he thought unconstitutional. Yet he had his people indict opponents for writing newspaper articles he considered "libels against the United States on the grounds they would 'sap the foundations of our constitution of government (more) than any kind of treason'" (Randall, 1993, p. 572). Jefferson didn't halt this prosecution until a Reverend Backus started subpoenaing individuals close to Jefferson for his public defense. Jefferson was politically astute enough to quickly realize that attacking enemies, even when using legal methods, can sometimes be more damaging to oneself rather than to one's enemies.

Short-Term Perspective

Perhaps Jefferson's greatest weakness as an executive branch change leader was his short-term perspective. Jefferson rarely, if ever, considered the consequences of his methods beyond his personal time frame. Without question Jefferson's greatest executive long-term achievement was the Louisiana Purchase. What is most surprising about this act is that it is actually the result of Jefferson's inability to achieve what he really wanted. The Louisiana Purchase first started as Jefferson's efforts in trying to stop the treaty that would turn Spanish Louisiana to France. He didn't really want the land; he simply didn't want the much stronger and potentially threatening country, France, to possess it. When he couldn't stop the transfer he thought it best to minimize Spain's presence and so he tried to buy Florida from Spain. When this plan didn't work, he finally commenced trying to obtain New Orleans (the port only, not the entire Louisiana Territory) from Napoleon. It was Napoleon who first suggested the possibility of the U.S. acquiring all of the territory (Randall, 1993).

Jefferson's short time perspective could have actually ruined his career. "Jefferson was determined to quit (the Continental) Congress and return to Virginia politics. He could not see into the future. To him, the Continental Congress ... (was) of little importance in the long run. Even if there were a permanent confederacy of states, it would be of far less importance than the reshaping of the weak old English colonies into strong independent countries" (Randall, 1993, p. 279). Jefferson actively campaigned against his own reelection to Congress, however Virginia did reelect him, as most did not believe he could actually want to return home and leave the center of power (Randall, 1993). Jefferson could not envision the nature of the government that he, himself, had helped to create.

Jefferson's inability to take a long-term perspective often came back to haunt him as an executive leader. For example, as a Virginia legislator Jefferson had worked to make sure the Governor had no real authority. Later, when he was governor, he found he had no power or ability to persuade the legislature to support any of his ideas or programs (Randall, 1993). His earlier dread of powerful executives led to his complete failure as an executive leader.

On the few occasions when Jefferson did seem to take a long-term perspective it appears that he got things wrong. For example, Jefferson often wrote on abolishing slavery, but believed it must involve resettling the emancipated slaves outside of Virginia. Toward the end of his life Jefferson wrote his most famous opinion on the subject, but most never heard the second sentence: "Nothing is more certainly written in the book of fate than that these people are to be free. Nor is it less certain that the two races, equally free, cannot live in the same government." (Randall, 1993, p. 305). Another such example involved Jefferson's trade embargo that crippled the U.S. economy. He first hoped to bring 20,000 to 30,000 American sailors home as well as 2,000 ships, thus removing them from impressment and confiscation. 30,000 sailors immediately unemployed, merchants requiring trade goods with nothing to sell; farmers whose cotton and tobacco for trade was their only source of income; all left with nothing. His idea was that American industry would develop to solve all these (but the sailors) woes. But where would they get the equipment, machines, and technical know-how on such a scale if couldn't get it from two industrial super powers of the time—England and France? "The Embargo was slower in hurting the British than the Bostonians. Even the textile manufacturers in English cities did not begin to go bankrupt as quickly as the cotton raisers in Georgia. Though many new factories sprang up in American ... commerce generally languished" (Brodie, 1974, p. 419).

Inconsistent Directions

Jefferson's lack of a long-term perspective resulted in today what would be seen as a major political character flaw. Jefferson often waffled on issues and could actually be accused as a flip flopper. For example, it has already been noted that Continental Congressman Jefferson strongly believed that the best approach to the United States would be treating each colony as a completely separate nation. Shortly after Yorktown, Peace Commissioner Jefferson, while waiting to travel to France: "studied the conditions in the United States ... (and developed) a deep fear that, unless the confederation of states was strengthened, the individual states would turn against each other and resort to civil war (Randall, 1993, p. 351). In less than 6 years Jefferson changed from being an unwavering supporter of a minimal national alliance to calling for a much stronger entity than the Articles of Confederation. President Jefferson, upset with the fact that the Supreme Court, (under control of his enemy Chief Justice John Marshall) established the court's power to declare acts of Congress void as unconstitutional, campaigned vigorously for an amendment permitting the removal of Federal Judges by joint act of president and Congress. He felt that the court's must be held accountable to the executive and legislative branches (Brodie, 1974). At the same time, however, Jefferson became the first president to claim what has now become known as executive privilege. Jefferson, ordered by the court to testify in Burr's trial for treason refused, reasoning "The president could not be independent of the judiciary as provided under the Constitution ... if he let himself be subject to the beck and call of every federal judge over the nation. He would send papers to the trial ... but the prerogative of choice among them must be his own" (Brodie, 1974, p. 410). Jefferson wanted to have his cake and eat it too—the presidency must have its constitutionally required independence, but the courts should not.

Jefferson was vehemently opposed to the sedition law passed under Adams' presidency. But four years later, in his second term, he grew tired of what the opposing press was saying against him. "The man who had become president by campaigning against a law that controlled the press now suggested that the states invoke their laws 'against falsehood and defamation'" (Randall, 1993, p. 572).

This is not the first time Jefferson has been accused of waffling on various issues. In his defense, Brookhiser, writes (1996) "When a great man is articulate and protean, like Jefferson, writing one thing one day and something slightly, or very, different the next, then the collected works are ransacked for bumper stickers, and real confusion ensures" (p. 192). Brookhiser's point is well taken. However, changing one's mind on (1) the nature and role of the federal government, and (2) the freedom of the press from sedition charges, are much more dramatic and of such a large scope, (particularly when in each case it was in his own self-interest at the time to change) that the waffling seems greater than conflicting bumper stickers and sound bites.

Summary

There is no way that anyone can deny that Thomas Jefferson was a truly successful change agent. However when one examines his successful change efforts it becomes quite evident that they all took place when he was a representative and not an executive. Jefferson was successful in almost everything he attempted with the possible exception of his tenures as president and governor. In this capacity he proved to be a very successful politician (in the contemporary definition), and took a very scientific approach to his actions, but ultimately these could be the reasons for his failure. As an executive Jefferson really couldn't pull the strings from behind the curtains, his preferred method of bringing about change, and his short-time frame often led his analytical process to the wrong conclusion (granted, this is with the benefit of hind-sight). Finally, his flip-flopping on major issues contradicts that central principal of transformational leadership—creating and maintaining a future vision.

GEORGE WASHINGTON

As with Jefferson, perhaps the best way to demonstrate George Washington's approach to executive leadership is to look closely at how he managed his personal property. While Jefferson took the normal attitude toward soil depletion and simply purchased more land, Washington took the long term strategic perspective. He did all he could to reinvigorate the soil at Mount Vernon, using manure, compost, and expensive chemical fertilizers. He also concluded that the true cause was the inefficiencies of the slave labor system. The laborers had no incentive to produce, much less increase effectiveness. In 1799 Washington announced his desire to parcel out much of his estates to "real farmers" and "expressed a preference that they work without slaves" (Kennedy, 2003, p. 17). He was one of the few great planters that recognized slavery removed the inducements needed for maximum productivity. More importantly, he actually tried to solve that problem with regards to his personal estates.

George Washington held three executive leadership roles in his life: Virginia plantation owner, commander of the U.S. armed forces, and first president of the United States. It is interesting to note that he had far more people working for him at Mount Vernon than the entire executive branch of the federal government (Brookhiser, 1996).

Leadership as a Duty

With the possible exception of Lincoln, clearly no president faced a greater challenge in assuming the role. Washington was well aware of the awesome responsibility he was given, to establish everything about how an elected executive branch should operate, and to do so with no real historic examples or role models for guidance (Ferling, 1988). Quite literally everything Washington did initiated change for he had to bring order and direction to a very loosely defined government. Washington took personal responsibility for the task and relied upon his character that had served him well in the past. In this, Washington has been credited as making the most significant presidential decision in U.S. history. "He chose to be an initiating leader, introducing proposals to Congress.... He also asserted the presidency's independence ... refusing Congress documents bearing upon the negotiation of the Jay treaty. He created the extralegal tradition of the president's cabinet" (Johnson, 1984, p. 37).

Perhaps the most unique aspect of Washington's change leadership style is that he clearly viewed it as a sacred duty that makes one responsible for, and yet accountable to, those he led. In 1782 a French philosopher wrote a portrait of the general. He felt that Washington's acquiescence to civil authority was truly at the heart of the man: "This is the seventh year that he has commanded the army and he has obeyed Congress: more need not be said" (Brookhiser, 1996, p. 40). This statement, so simple, was actually astounding. One must recall that almost everyone naturally assumed that Washington would eventually be named king of the new country. To willingly submit to the whims of a loose body of ineffective legislators was unheard of. Yet Washington never, as general or president, acted as a monarch. Washington clearly understood that the true source of a leader's power was to serve the people by guiding them.

It is fascinating that one of Washington's few writings on leadership dealt with how he felt one should behave towards the legislature. In a letter to a nephew Washington outlined his beliefs about how an executive should approach the legislature: "speak seldom, never exceed a decent warmth, and submit your sentiments with diffidence. A dictatorial stile [sic], though it may carry conviction, is always accompanied with disgust" (Brookhiser, 1966, pp. 65-66).

For Washington abusing one's power was unthinkable. As chair of the Constitutional convention he made only one speech to the delegation, a mild rebuke to the delegates reinforcing their previously established agreement of not discussing any of the proceedings to the press. As chair he felt it was essential that he remain neutral on all matters. He would voice thoughts and ideas privately, but never in his role of delegate. The context of the situation is what makes this behavior incredible. There was no question in anyone's mind that Washington would be the first president. As chair, Washington could have exerted incredible influence on shaping the powers of his future job. But he chose to remain silent.

Even when he whole-heartedly disagreed with the people's mandates he never failed to obey them. This is best in evidence when he was commanding the revolutionary army. As a result of political machinations, Congress ordered a court martial for Benedict Arnold (before his treasonable act). Arnold was found guilty on two minor charges. Washington was ordered to officially reprimand Arnold. Washington clearly did not support the decision, but he unquestionably followed the order. The general's reprimand began "The Commander in Chief would have been much happier in an occasion of bestowing commendations on an officer who has rendered such distinguished services to his country as Major General Arnold; but in the present case, a sense of duty and a regard to candor oblige him" (Brookhiser, 1996, p. 37). This rebuke illustrated Washington's view of leadership as a duty, but it also highlights another trait to be discussed later, his mastery of symbolic acts. Washington carried out the distasteful duty, but in a way that clearly praised Arnold for his significant accomplishments.

Brookhiser (1996) succinctly summarizes how Washington's sense of duty and responsibility effected his leadership approach to change: "When it was not necessary that he act, then it was necessary that he not act. But when the power to govern itself was challenged, then action on his part was required" (Brookhiser, 1996, pp. 83-84). Washington (with the loyalty of the military assured) was in a position to assume dictatorial powers. The fact that he only acted when clearly necessary, and then for only as long as necessary, speaks volumes about his approach to change—do what is necessary, when it is necessary, and make sure the path selected is the right one.

Honor and Ethics

Related to his belief that leadership was a duty was Washington's view that as an executive branch leader the true mechanism of change lies with the legislative branch. A review of his writings makes it clear that Washington hoped that slavery would end. Some have noted that as president he did nothing to end the institution. While true, the reason for the inaction is not hypocritical, as the critics would lead one to believe. In a letter he wrote to Robert Morris: "there is not a man living who wishes more sincerely than I do, to see a plan adopted for the abolition of it ... there is only one proper and effectual mode by which it can be accomplished, and that is by legislative authority" (Brookhiser, 1996, p. 179). Washington, as president, saw slavery's end as a legislative issue, one that had been clearly discussed and debated in both the Continental and Constitutional Congresses. In both cases the legislators understood his personal views.

To go beyond this would have violated Washington's beliefs in the separation of power. He had the right, as a citizen, for his representatives to know his thoughts. But as president it would have been a violation of his position to do anything to influence the representatives.

For Washington personal honor meant everything as a leader. Paraphrasing, a correspondence explains Washington's concept of honor: "Defeat posed a lesser threat to his (self-perceived) reputation than dishonor. It was bad enough to lose the Battle of Long Island; far worse to flee from Kip's Bay without making a stand" (Brookhiser, 1996, p. 132).

Washington's sense of honor could drive him to extreme behavior as a leader. At least twice during the futile attempt at defending New York the U.S. troops retreated in chaos. Washington placed himself between his fleeing troops and the pursuing British, in an unsuccessful attempt to reform the lines. He was so vexed at the routed troops that he literally had to be led away from the area for his own safety (Brookhiser, 1996).

In the time between his retirement as commander in chief and the constitutional convention Washington constantly lobbied visitors and friends to support a canal to the west. Washington truly felt it was in the nation's best interest to build such a canal, while he freely admitting he would personally benefit through speculations in western land. Such a public project is a natural for a sitting president to support and lobby congress for. However, because of the potential for personal gain, Washington never mentioned the canal after he took office.

One of the significant controversies Washington faced as president involved the fraudulent Georgian Yazoo land sale, where the Native Americans were conned out of a large amount of land. There was no question that legally the land grab should be voided. At the same time Washington realized repudiating the sale would cripple Georgia's commerce and slow the growth of the southern plantation system. From both a practical and political perspective Washington knew it would be prudent to let the deal stand. Washington never hesitated and forcefully repudiated the fraudulent land acquisition (Kennedy, 2003). Even the nation could not put anything above its honor, and as president it was his job to make sure it didn't.

While Washington felt duty bound to leave the slavery issue up to Congress, this did not stop him from acting upon his sense of ethics in his personal life. With regards to Mount Vernon, Washington stated "I am principled against selling Negroes, as you would cattle at a market" (Brookhiser, 1996, p. 182). From the late 1760s to his death Washington refused to sell a slave without the slave's own consent. As none ever consented to be sold, Washington never sold a slave. This policy resulted in a doubling of the number of slaves Washington owned between 1775 and his death, and actually created a significant economic hardship. In order to revitalize Mount Vernon, and humanely rid himself of the slaves, Washington acted to break up his beloved estate into four properties to be rented to farmers. Washington's idea was to free the slaves who had worked on each property, who would then be hired by the new farmer. Although he advertised this idea quite extensively (including Europe) he never found any takers. In his will, as the second item, Washington: freed all his slaves at his wife's death; provided for the old and orphans; and, stipulated that the children be taught to read and write. Martha Washington, agreeing with her husband's vision, actually released the slaves before she died.

Washington did make a symbolic act hoping to goad Congress to address the evils of slavery, but only when he felt it wouldn't put the executive branch in the role of dictating law. As he was leaving the presidency Washington freed most of the slaves that had served him at the executive residence. Washington found a way to maintain silence in the slavery debate, as he felt was his duty as president, but still act in a way to try to bring about its demise.

Personal Charisma

Washington was perhaps one of the greatest masters of using charismatic power to facilitate change and lead people. One example occurred relatively early in the war, immediately following his victory at Trenton. A majority of his army was about to disperse as their enlistment was expiring. It looked to be a long and difficult winter and the troops had already experienced significant hardships. Washington made a moving personal appeal to the troops and convinced the army to stay intact (Brookhiser, 1996).

Perhaps the greatest example of Washington's charismatic leadership occurred at the very end of the war. In 1783, after Yorktown, many of the army officers began to seriously talk of rebelling against Congress out of frustration for not being paid. Upon hearing of the possible revolt, Washington called for a meeting with the officers. Washington began the meeting by establishing his common ground with the officers, noting he was among the first to join their ranks, and in 8 years had never taken a furlough. Next he highlighted the army's justified pride in what they had done. Washington continued by establishing that Congress was not the army's enemy, and he even included a brief lesson on how such bodies work. He then asked the officers to maintain their honor and forget further talk of rebellion. Finally, to illustrate congress's good intentions, he wanted to read them a letter. Finding he couldn't make out the words, Washington asked "Gentlemen, you will permit me to put on my spectacles, for I have not only grown gray but almost blind in the service of my country." This simple admission from such a proud man, who the officers truly admired, brought most of the group to tears. Washington left the room and the officers voted unanimously to stop further actions (Brookhiser, 1996, p. 40).

Washington was also a master at using symbolism to facilitate action and change. Once, during a retreat the troops, under extreme pursuit from the enemy, had to pass over a very narrow bridge. Knowing the men could easily panic Washington sat unmoving upon his horse on the bridge all the while facing the enemy until the last of the troops crossed. This gesture kept the troops orderly by signaling that their leader would not quit his station until they were all safe (Brookhiser, 1996). Upon receiving the Declaration of Independence Washington immediately assembled the troops and had the entire document read aloud. Washington believed that the soldiers, many who had been serving from the beginning, would find the document an inspiration (Brookhiser, 1996). The gesture worked, as the men finally saw that they were truly fighting for independence.

Sometimes this desire for symbolism showed a truly historic/global scope. Washington received Congress's proclamation of the cease fire on April 13, 1783, in essence ending the war. Washington only had to issue the order not to fire on the enemy, and notify the British Commander of the order. He chose to wait 6 days, until April 19, to do so. That day was the eighth anniversary of when the fighting began at Lexington and Concord (Wensyel, 1992). This message was not mistaken by the soldiers, people, Congress, or Parliament. Other times Washington's symbolism, tied to his moral sense of right, led to very personal, but still long lasting, consequences. General Washington believed that something was needed to recognize exceptional soldiers, so he personally developed, and designed, two awards. The Honorary Badge of Distinction was a strip of white cloth appearing on the uniform's left cuff, one strip for each three years of service (this practice continues today in the U.S. Army's "hash marks"). The second was the Badge of Military Merit (a *purple heart* shaped patch) for singularly meritorious service, awarded after consideration by a special panel and requiring Washington's own approval. What made these awards more significant is that they were the first time in world history that such honors would be presented to enlisted personnel. Washington took the Purple Heart's symbolism even further, personally presenting the metal to those selected, recording the recipients' names in the special "Book of Merit" (since lost, possibly burned in the War of 1812), and requiring the recipients (regardless of rank) to receive salutes (Wensyel, 1992).

Another masterful use of symbolism, albeit one that was unintentional, was when Washington offered to serve as commanding general during the revolution without pay—having only his expenses reimbursed. "Rumor magnified his magnanimity: The Virginian, it was said, had proposed to outfit one thousand men at his own expense" (Brookhiser, 1996, p. 21). In a time calling for extreme sacrifice the fact that the only person serving in the army who would not be paid was the commander-in-chief ensured that Washington captured the hearts of most Americans. It is fascinating that Washington repeated this symbolic act. When he took office as the president there was no salary established for the position. Washington requested Congress not to give him a salary, and instead simply reimburse him for the job's expenses. Congress thought differently and provided him with a generous salary (Ferling, 1988).

One of Washington's major presidential roles was to establish political precedents. While scorned by some Americans for bringing too much pomp and circumstance into the presidency, most Europeans agreed with one of their own statement "What pomp there is in all this I am unable to discover" (Brookhiser, 1996, p. 77). For example, at his first presidential reception an aide shouted "The President of the United States" as Washington entered the room. This made the people in the room act as they would for a European monarch holding court. From that time on Washington made a point of being in the room prior to the start of the reception, allowing for an informal mingling type of event rather than the president holding court (Brookhiser, 1996).

Even Washington's last act of public life was rife with symbolism. After John Adams' inaugural ceremony a small problem emerged, who should exit the hall first. "Washington, in a symbolic gesture that had far more meaning than implicit good manners, insisted that first Adams and then Jefferson lead the way before him. So the nation passed its first test, the transference of power ... with exquisite courtesy" (Brodie, 1974, p. 305).

Strategic Perspective

Washington clearly approached change leadership with a strategic perspective. From "1776 to the summer of 1778, he fought seven battles and won only two of them. But during that time ... he managed to solve the strategic problem (using the great distance and cost of British reinforcements against them). Though by the end of 1778 he had not won the war, he had made it unwinable [sic] for the enemy" (Brookhiser, 1996, p. 25). Put another way, from the enemy's perspective "Cornwallis ... would find that winning battles was not conquering a continent, and that major engagements served to bleed him into ever debilitating weakness" (Brodie, 1974, p. 138).

Another example of his strategic leadership perspective can be seen in his response (as president) to the Whisky Rebellion. Washington chose a two sided strategy—he raised an army of 12,000, but at the same time he sent a group of commissioners to the area "to convince these people and the world of the moderation and the firmness of the government"—a show of mildness and a show of force (Brookhiser, 1996, p. 85). Washington's actions clearly were the primary reason for the rebellion's collapse. "by not reacting hastily, he had let the most extreme ring leaders work themselves into an untenable position" (Brookhiser, 1996, p. 89). Simply resolving the rebellion was only a part of what motivated Washington's actions. Washington wanted to send Europe a clear message about who controlled the area (Brookhiser, 1996).

Summary

Washington's leadership clearly brought about significant accomplishments, laying the groundwork that would allow the United States to grow into today's global super power. What is possibly most amazing is that he acted without any political machinations. Washington relied solely upon his own personal sense of honor, duty, and ethics, coupled with extreme charisma and use of symbolism, to lead and bring about changes. It is also fascinating to note that Washington, with little formal education, and no real training or examples, could take a very strategic perspective in all that he did.

JAMES POLK

Truman named Polk as one of the eight great presidents because Polk knew exactly what he was going to do, and he did it. Polk's low ranking of ninth in a 1962 survey of historians regarding presidential performance led Kennedy to remark that anyone who had not served in the office was unqualified to judge presidential performance. In a study of the 15 most significant U.S. presidential decisions, Polk's forcing war with Mexico was listed as number five (Arnold, 1989). "For four years there would be no rest for James Knox Polk. He was an obsessed workaholic, a perfectionist, a micromanager, whose commitment to what he saw as his responsibility led him to virtually incarcerate himself in the White House for the full tenure of his presidency. He rarely went out to visit. Sometimes he took a walk, usually to attend church with his wife.... He almost never attended a social function and took vacations only when Sarah (his wife) convinced him that his health demanded it" (Seigenthaler, 2003, p. 103).

Polk's accomplishments during his 4 years as president were incredible: "Somehow (Polk) is the least acknowledged among our presidents ...

which is somewhat mystifying. He boldly exerted the influence of the presidency in both foreign and domestic affairs. He threatened war with the British to take from them a major share of the Oregon Territory, waged war against Mexico to grab California and New Mexico, and increased the landmass of the country by a third ... reduced the tariff ... and created an independent Treasury that was viable for more than sixty years" (Seigenthaler, 2003, p. 1).

Polk's primary biographer, Seigenthaler (2003), suggests that it is not what he accomplished as president that places him in relative obscurity (as they are quite significant), but how he performed these tasks, citing the following observations of Polk's contemporaries about his managerial style: colorless, methodical, plodding and narrow; puritanical and inflexible; a stern task-master and a loner; not well-liked and a chilly demeanor; lack personal magnetism and developed no personal following; sometimes unscrupulous; no humor; a seeming lack of candor and forthrightness; secretive—even sly; lovable, or even likable, he was not.

Historians generally maintain that Polk lacked imagination, without any ability to think outside of the box, and was intellectually rigid. "To Polk, all politics was fiscal, deeply rooted in the early struggle between federalism and republicanism; Hamilton and Jefferson ... government had a role to play in providing economic justice for every working citizen —except, of course, women and slaves" (Seigenthaler, 2003, p. 29). As Andrew Jackson's protégé, he was definitely a Jeffersonian. However he was also extremely intelligent and logical, with a significant capacity to absorb facts and apply them to problems (Seigenthaler, 2003).

Stay Within the Boundaries

Polk's approach to change management was completely legalistic. Generally he never imposed his personal values, nor those reflected in public popular opinion, upon either how he acted, or goals he tried to accomplish as president. If an issue in question was not clearly within the rigid bounds of conservative constitution dogma he wouldn't even let it be discussed. For example, Polk experienced a great deal of political pressure to halt the Mormon Church's planned move to the Oregon Territory. He refused to act, not out of religious concerns or because of a personal sense of justice or ethics, but simply because the constitution would not permit the restriction (Seigenthaler, 2003). "After he became president, his position on Texas and slavery was that it was a matter for citizens of the new state to decide—which meant for white, male Texans to decide" (Seigenthaler, 2003, pp. 77-78).

Proactive

If Polk perceived a possible change was within the constitutional realm, he could easily become a pit bull with regards to implementation. Fully aware that he did not have power to declare war he devised a strategy to accomplish just that while staying completely within the constitution's parameters. "President James K. Polk was solely responsible for the war with Mexico in 1846. Without Congressional authorization, Polk ordered United States army units into a region claimed by Mexico—an act virtually certain to instigate hostilities. Predictably, Mexicans attacked the American soldiers, and war resulted" (Ferling, 1989, p. 15). As a rookie U.S. congressman, his voting pattern was strictly obstructionist, "Later (as Speaker of the House and President), ironically, Polk would exercise 'the influence of power' as ruthlessly and as manipulatively as Adams and Clay ever did" (Seigenthaler, 2003, p. 38). As president he pushed through his changes by completely controlling the executive branch. The Cabinet members were mostly ignored advisors. Polk single-handedly made all the managerial and policy decisions, not just for the White House, but for every executive department.

Refrain From Public Commitments

Another characteristic of Polk's approach to executive leadership was to, whenever possible, never publicly commit to anything. This included his entry into the presidential race. Polk took a very low key and back room approach, as demonstrated in the instructions he gave to his convention bound allies: "Bring just one delegate from every state ... to a meeting at Washington's Brown Hotel before they depart for the convention. Explain to them that the survival of the party is at stake. Move cautiously, without announcing to the public what you are at" (Seigenthaler, 2003, p. 81). Another example of this silence-is-golden approach is demonstrated in the active phase of his campaign. Possibly the greatest issue during Polk's presidential campaign were the very high tariffs that greatly helped northern factories at the cost of the southern agrarians. At first Polk simply said nothing about his thoughts on the tariff. After several weeks he finally made a statement when a senator convinced him that remaining silent would cost him the election. Polk, in a letter, tried to appease both sides of the issue: "I am in favor of a tariff for revenue, such as one that will yield a sufficient amount to the Treasury to defray expenses of the government, economically administered" (Seigenthaler, 2003, p. 90). While neither side was completely satisfied with the response, both saw the statement as supporting its own position.

Polk often took a very passive/aggressive approach to accomplishing goals. To avoid starting his presidency in controversy, Polk urged Congress to approve Texas statehood. However the Senate, not wanting to be rushed with the treaty's details around slavery, passed the annexation legislation (based to a great deal on Polk's support for the compromise) but requiring Polk to appoint a commission to work out the specifics. Polk saw nothing to be gained by taking an active role, so he simply refused to appoint the commission. After 3 years of inaction the Senate made Polk's deception public. Polk's reaction to the now open controversy was to simply refuse to respond, after all he had already won (Seigenthaler, 2003).

Most newly elected presidents have found that a very public goal statement, accompanied by political hoopla, a positive and strong mechanism for facilitating change. Polk, on the other hand, found his secretive, passive aggressive approach quite successful. Shortly after his election Polk privately shared his four goals initially only with his future Secretary of the Navy (Seigenthaler, 2003): lower the tariff, re-create Van Buren's independent treasury, acquire Oregon from the British, and acquire California from Mexico. Later, when he publicly announced his goals, they went, for the most part, unnoticed. Why did Polk choose such a low-key approach? Regarding the tariff, he had purposefully led the Northern voters to believe he would maintain it, but had no intention to do so. The other three issues were truly out of left field, never having really been presented to the public in any form. By keeping his goals low key he was able to pursue them without encountering resistance from political opponents. After all, one cannot debate when one doesn't know the issue.

Polk's secrecy was not an issue of self-doubt or uncertainty. Polk was convinced in the absolute righteousness of his goals and activities, so much so that he didn't see any need for discussion. Those that disagreed with him were obviously wrong. "He (Polk) did not need to make political enemies, as he assumed them (believing those who opposed him on an issue were vile enemies), accepted their opposition as natural, demonized them, sought to engage and defeat them" (Seigenthaler, 2003, p. 119). This approach was also applied to his colleagues. Polk ignored, and in some cases directly contradicted, the advice of his colleagues and mentors often turning them into fierce enemies. Several people asked why he pushed aside the suggestions (particularly the obviously excellent ones) of those close to him. He would simply reply "I will be my own president" (Seigenthaler, 2003). Polk once wrote about his closest advisors, the cabinet, "I have conducted the government without their (the cabinet members) aid. Indeed, I have become so familiar with the duties and working of the Government, not only in general principles but in minute details, that I find but little difficulty in doing this" (Seigenthaler, 2003, p. 121).

While the results of Polk's leadership have had long-term positive significant impact, there is no question that Polk lacked a strategic perspective. In fact, the only time Polk demonstrated an ability, or desire, to look into the future, he was right, but still proved very short sighted. If Polk's will prevailed in this case, the war with Mexico would have dragged on for unnecessary months. Polk was worried that General Zachary Taylor was actually too successful in fighting the Mexican Army as the victories could lead to a presidential nomination in the next election, an election that Polk had no intention to participate in. Polk therefore brought in Winfield Scott to lead a new wave of the fighting. Taylor was to be put on the shelf for the rest of the war. However Taylor continued to fight and he scored the critical victory over Santa Anna. Polk then tried to discredit Taylor by stating that by actually fighting, and routing the enemy's main army, had disobeyed orders. Most historians agree with Polk, but the U.S. population saw it differently (Casel, 1982).

Summary

There is no question that Polk was a very effective executive change agent when one examines his results. There is also no question that his methods for obtaining the changes were highly unusual and counterintuitive. He believed he was right and acted accordingly. He never felt the need to espouse a vision, nor did he court support or attempt to establish coalitions. His secrecy and personal control makes it very difficult to imagine how he actually accomplished his goals, other than to see that he was a master of the unimaginably diverse day-to-day machinations of the executive branch. In essence, by operating as a perfect example of the bureaucratic transactional leader, Polk was able to significantly move the United States further than most.

THEODORE ROOSEVELT

He had been a published author at eighteen, a husband at twenty-two, an acclaimed historian and New York Assemblyman at twenty-three, a father and a widower at twenty-five, a ranchman at twenty-six, a candidate for Mayor of New York at twenty-seven, a husband again at twenty-eight, a Civil Service Commissioner of the United States at Thirty ... Police Commissioner of New York City at thirty-six, Assistant Secretary of the Navy at thirty-eight, Colonel of the First U.S. Volunteer Cavalry ... at thirty-nine ...

Returning home a hero, Roosevelt had been elected Governor of New York within two weeks of his fortieth birthday.... Yet just when his momentum seemed irresistible, there had come that sickening sideways pull into the Vice Presidency. (Morris, 2001, pp. 6-7).

Roosevelt had to wait until his 46th year to become the President of the United States. Whatever else can be said of Theodore Roosevelt, it is obvious that he was a man of great achievements.

Most of these accomplishments occurred as a direct result of Roosevelt's innate ability as an executive change leader. Describing Roosevelt's effectiveness, Ferling (1989) writes "Eloquent, dynamic, by nature compelled to dominate almost everything he touched, he used the media and full panoply of resources afforded by his office to teach, sway, and bully a nation into following his lead" (p. 16). Two of Roosevelt's greatest accomplishments clearly illustrate his approach to the role of executive change leader. Roosevelt, a New York Republican, was the first president to attack the trusts head on. Roosevelt was thoroughly against the trusts complete freedom to act (Morris, 2001). Roosevelt's vision for economic reform grew from his observations on nature that species under fierce competition advanced best when controlled by laws of behavior and reasonable numbers. With this in mind he viewed his task as persuading the "Union League Republicans that perpetual mild reform was true conservatism, in that it protected existing institutions from atrophy and relieved the buildup of radical pressure (Morris, 2001, p. 34)." Roosevelt's actions as a leader were always grounded in his strong sense of morals and ethics. He was able to put these into action because of his political acumen and energetic proactive nature. He never sat back and waited, rather he always took the aggressive stance.

Another of Roosevelt's greatest change efforts involved leading the peace negotiations for the Russian Japanese War. He was not really a mediator. Roosevelt took direct leadership of the peace talks. He explained each other's positions, but he also cajoled the peace delegates, and at times he went secretly over the ambassadors' heads and communicated with the tsar and emperor in very undiplomatic terms in order to get them to come to an agreement.

The peace the President had made possible at Portsmouth was the result of ... an inexplicable ability to impose his singular charge upon plural power. By sheer force of moral purpose, by clarity of perception, by mastery of detail and benign manipulation of men he had become as Henry Adams (the famed historian who deplored Roosevelt) admiringly wrote him, "the best herder of Emperors since Napoleon." (Morris, 2001, p. 414)

Personal Ethics

Roosevelt used his strong personal sense of ethics and justice to drive all his actions. This moral impetus truly served as the base from which he used all his other leadership attributes. His ethics permitted him to clearly envision what the ideal goal state was, and his moral motivation gave him an unwavering drive towards achieving it. The fact that Roosevelt was a gifted orator, and an even better writer, proved invaluable, as he could communicate the vision and drive to others, bringing them into his proactive coalition.

Examine Roosevelt's accomplishments as an executive leader. We have already seen what lay behind his trust busting. As police commissioner he led the movement to eliminate corruption from New York City's force, actually prowling around in the middle of the night looking for cops on the take. He also insisted that the police enforce the law prohibiting liquor sales on Sundays. The law had never been enforced, but it was the law. The public, politicians, and even reporters held Roosevelt up to severe criticism, but he stated that his position required him to act: "I do not deal with public sentiment," he proclaimed, "I deal with the law" (Wert, 1982, p. 34). As both a Republican governor and president, he proved a forceful labor advocate, not to gain union support, but rather because he saw the need for workers to get a square deal. Racial based injustice was abhorrent to him, and although it caused him no end of political trouble, he not only had an African American as a lunch guest at the executive residence, he appointed many qualified blacks to positions of responsibility (even in the Deep South). He was the first president since Jefferson to take a real interest in the country's natural resources, but in Roosevelt's case it was because he believed that one had an obligation to future generations and not out of intellectual curiosity. Roosevelt expanded the U.S. Navy as no one before in order to make sure the country could "speak softly but carry a big stick." Even digging the Panama Canal, and covertly assisting with the revolution that made it practical, were both done because Roosevelt saw the long-term global need for such a water way.

Nothing could move Roosevelt from following his right path, not even personal relationships. J.P. Morgan had been a close personal friend of Roosevelt's father. However, as governor of New York, he denied Morgan tax breaks (Morris, 2001). George Perkins, one of Morgan's "Golden Boys," and the key player behind the Great Northern and Northern Pacific railroads merger, was one of Roosevelt's closest college friends. But this merger is what truly launched the anti-trust campaign (Morris, 2001) when Roosevelt had the attorney general (who was opposed to the action) file a federal antitrust suit against the merger.

Roosevelt's actions against racial injustice and hatred resulted in extreme political backlash throughout the country. The loss of political allies wouldn't quiet him, or move him from what he knew was right. Roosevelt was finally convinced to assume a low-key approach during the midterm elections of his second term after an Atlanta mob killed 20 African American men. Roosevelt saw that his actions were actually contributing to, not resolving, the violence. He did continue to call for racial justice, however through personal writings and subtle actions.

It is fascinating to note that what many consider Roosevelt's biggest mistake was due to his absolute commitment to follow his perceived right path, and it also directly involved racial hatred. There was an alleged shooting spree in Texas by a small number of black troops. There were very few facts, nothing was substantiated, and most of the evidence seems to have been planted. Roosevelt dismissed the entire unit of black soldiers from which the handful of alleged rioters belonged. The dismissals were not a punishment for the alleged event. Believing they would not receive a fair hearing the soldiers refused to talk to investigators. They were discharged for failing to obey orders to provide statements to the federal investigators. As a military officer, and as commander-in-chief, Roosevelt's sense of right could not tolerate such insubordination from military men. Therefore he had them dishonorably discharged (against the advice of every one of his advisors). This action, taking place immediately after his reelection, changed him from an angel to a devil in the black community (Morris, 2001). It is ironic that Roosevelt's stubbornness to always do what he thought was right actually underminded his efforts to promote social justice, one of his core moral tenets.

Master Politician

Roosevelt's strong sense of morality didn't prevent him from using the executive leader's political tools. He clearly understood the value of patronage to build political support, and used it frequently. Yet he was very cautious not to appoint anyone he believed would be inappropriate or unqualified for the position (although others might disagree with his criteria, for example when he would appoint Western law officers for their ability to shoot instead of their knowledge of the law) (Morris, 2001).

Racial injustice was quite possibly Roosevelt's greatest concern. Through the use of patronage it was an area where he made significant long-term changes. It was a struggle for Roosevelt to find a way to act without making the racial situation worse. A public letter he wrote praising the governor of Indiana for his actions to prevent a lynching actually negatively effected the midterm elections (Morris, 2001). Roosevelt finally recognized that he needed to take a quiet approach to correcting racial injustice. Roosevelt used patronage to make small steps towards progress, by appointing qualified African Americans.

Roosevelt was a master at political manipulation. His approach to the issue of railroad controls was summarized as: "Roosevelt saw no harm in encouraging political rhetoric more extreme than any he would use on Congress himself. Let Baker, Steffens, et al. do what advance guards had always done in battle: draw enemy fire from both sides while Caesar advanced down the middle" (Morris, 2001). Baker and Steffens were pushing for price controls and while Roosevelt opposed price controls, he wanted a law that would encourage growth but also impose discipline if competition was threatened. By encouraging the extremists he successfully accomplished his goal—the opposition was willing to settle for Roosevelt's lower key approach if it kept him from pushing for harsher intervention.

Cooptation was another of Roosevelt's favorite tools. For example Roosevelt very publicly asked Senator Hanna to manage his reelection campaign, just before Hanna wanted to initiate his own nomination campaign. Hanna, the only possible alternative nominee, was put in an untenable position. He could give many public reasons to refuse Roosevelt's request, but they would all preclude his ability to run for the office.

Roosevelt was an accomplished coalition builder, but possessed the unique ability to dominate the other members. When writing his first annual report to congress, Roosevelt planned to begin the fight for reform with a strong attack. He first consulted with key legislators who convinced him to water down his arguments. His final message was 80 pages long and included dozens of different requests, some large, some small, which literally took hours to be read aloud to Congress. Roosevelt was also wise enough to include positive elements, such as being the first president to praise the Smithsonian Institution and the Library of Congress. Most politicians, regardless of their beliefs, found parts of the message to object to, but they also found many items they fully supported. Roosevelt had consulted many different people when constructing the message, and often used their suggestions, word for word, in the text (Morris, 2001) thereby bringing them into the fold.

Embedded in the coalition building was another of Roosevelt's executive leadership traits, that of participation. Perhaps this is best demonstrated through his push for the Interstate Commerce Act. Some Western and Midwestern republicans wanted amendments far too liberal for Roosevelt. He planned a trip around these states to gain support for his more moderate bill. First, as he typically did, Roosevelt summoned six leading Midwestern republicans and asked what he should say and do, and what compromises might be possible. He incorporated some of their ideas while maintaining his own course. While the speeches were Roosevelt's, he made sure to incorporate material provided by his six consultants so that they could plainly see they did impact the final output (Morris, 2001).

First To Act

Roosevelt once summarized the building of the Panama Canal as "I took the Isthmus, started the Canal, and then left Congress—not to debate the Canal, but to debate me" (Johnson, 1984, p. 12). Perhaps Roosevelt's greatest trait as an executive change leader was his proactive nature. Unlike many of his predecessors, Roosevelt always tried to be the first to act, forcing others to play catch up if they could. Few were ever successful. For years Senator Hanna had dictated patronage jobs in the South. To facilitate his goal of racial justice Roosevelt asked Booker T. Washington, the African American founder of the Tuskegee Institute, to advise him on the matter of Southern patronage. A few days later his first Southern patronage job, a federal judgeship, opened up in Alabama. Washington recommended Thomas Jones, a former Democratic governor, who had an excellent record for promoting racial equality. Roosevelt made the appointment even before Hanna had a chance to make a recommendation (Morris, 2001). Hanna was never able to act fast enough to control the patronage during Roosevelt's presidency.

Roosevelt was possibly the most effective president in taking his case to the people. He would often meet with newspapermen in private and give select reporters exclusive stories. The reporters, all greatly honored, would write favorable and well-timed articles (Morris, 2001).

Perhaps Roosevelt's change with the greatest impact upon the nation was in forever increasing the president's power. A little over 2 years after assuming the office (elected only as vice-president), upon the Supreme Court's decision giving the president vast enforcement power over interstate commerce, the *New York Post* wrote they

> worried about placing such control in the hands of Theodore Roosevelt. He had already broadened the use of executive power in labor mediation, in foreign policy, and in federal patronage. Now he had dissolved the world's second-largest trust. Imagine the demagogue as president, armed with all the legitimate power of an office grown greater than man had dreamed possible. (Morris, 2001, p. 316)

Shortly later Congress was reviewing his bill to set up the American government in the Panama Canal Zone.

Roosevelt used his proactive nature to control the Republican Party, and therefore the future governmental infrastructure. His selection for Republican Party chairman, and a progressive agenda, was abhorrent to the party's old guard. But there could be no resisting Roosevelt without losing public support (Morris, 2001).

Long-Range Thinker

Roosevelt "was obviously an adroit politician. Speed was his most astonishing characteristic, combined improbably with thoroughness" (Morris, 2001, p. 82). However, unlike most who act quickly, Roosevelt demonstrated, possibly more than any other president, the ability to grasp the long-range implications of issues. When the Russian/Japanese war began most thought Russia would be victorious, but Roosevelt perceived Japan as the Great New Force. He also thought that should China develop itself as Japan "there will result a real shifting of the center of equilibrium as far as the white races (the Americas and Europe) are concerned." Roosevelt was not alarmed by such a possibility. He continued his thoughts "If new nations come to power ... the attitude of we who speak English should be one of ready recognition of the rights of the new comers, of desire to avoid giving them just offense, and at the same time of preparedness in body and in mind to hold our own if our interests are menaced" (Morris, 2001, p. 313). Roosevelt foresaw today's global environment as well as the key for peace in such a situation.

In 1897 Roosevelt posed the following question to the U.S. Naval War College: "Japan makes demands on the Hawaiian Islands. This country (U.S.) intervenes. What force will be necessary to uphold the intervention, and how should it be employed?" (Morris, 2001, p. 397). Later, as he was preparing for acting as the peacemaker, Roosevelt saw Japan's potential as a legitimate threat to the United States and "was even more convinced that the United States had to commission more warships, build them bigger, and launch them faster. Or, what had happened at Tsu Shima might happen in Pearl Harbor—and not too far ahead" (Morris, 2001, p. 397). Theodore Roosevelt accurately foresaw Pearl Harbor, and the need to have a proactive plan, long before World War II. Compare Theodore's vision to that of his distant cousin Franklin, who was also the Assistant Secretary of the Navy (during World War I), when shortly after the Great War, Franklin "abandoned his big navy views and criticized President Coolidge's recommendation to enlarge the fleet. The only possible naval foe was Japan, and 'there is no fundamental reason why our relations with

Japan should not be on a permanent and cordial basis' " (Freidel, 1990, p. 51).

Empathetic Leader

A final significant trait of Roosevelt that made him an effective change leader was that he inherently realized people require a personal touch from their leader. Roosevelt could give a speech to thousands of people, but sensing the need, would pull someone aside and in a one-on-one private meeting say or do just the right thing to inspire that person.

This natural empathy and personal attention is perhaps best illustrated in an incident that occurred at a critical time in the Panama Canal proceedings. Secretary of State, John Hay, suffered from chronic depression. When it appeared that the Columbian Congress was going to reject the treaty Hay had spent months negotiating his morale plummeted. Roosevelt met with Hay briefly, after which "whatever transpired, Hay returned to work as if galvanized" (Morris, 2001, p. 239). The next day Hay sent a cable to the U.S. minister to Columbia stressing that the Columbians invited the treaty talks and that the United States did have other options (which the U.S. Congress actually preferred). This bold move was at Hay's discretion. It was also totally out of character. The action was effective as it laid the groundwork for bringing the future revolutionaries to the front.

Roosevelt could also use his personal touch in creative ways to further his personal political agenda. Senator Hanna, the leader of the anti-Roosevelt movement in the Republican party, had been publicly shown up by Roosevelt in a series of events. Roosevelt sensed he had pushed Hanna too far, and as an accommodation to the Senator agreed to a private conference with a lobbyist. It was at this meeting that Roosevelt acknowledged that the United States would recognize Panama if it seceded from Columbia (Morris, 2001). By revealing this information Roosevelt enhanced Hanna's perceived (but not actual) role in the deliberations. Not only was Hanna temporarily mollified, but he had been unwittingly co-opted as well.

Even under the most severe circumstances Roosevelt never lost this empathetic personal touch. Upon the death of President McKinley, starting at midnight via a 5 hour open carriage ride in the rain, Vice President Roosevelt made a nonstop rush to Buffalo. From the carriage he immediately got on a train, and 13 hours later, which included a train accident, "Roosevelt was down the steps of his car before the wheels stopped rolling. An hour's rest had cleared the tiredness from his face, but his eyes were troubled (recall, he was now the acting president with all the pressures and problems of the roles) ... climbed into the waiting carriage. One of the policemen reached after him 'Colonel, will you shake hands with me?' Roosevelt recognized, and briefly embraced, a veteran of his regiment" (Morris, 2001, p. 11). It was acts like this, more than his speeches that caused diverse sets of people to follow his lead with extreme commitment.

CONCLUSION

It is clear that the executive plays the critical role in implementing strategic changes. This fact does not minimize the actions of anyone else (including the consultant), it simply recognizes the truth. This is the reason why one of the first lessons taught in any organization development class is that the change must be top down. Much has been written about the critical role the executive plays as a transformational leader, but for some reason there is little transference to organization development books and journals. Clearly, we in organization development need to start incorporating this critical player into our thinking—as a driving mechanism, rather than as the check signing client. This study sought to obtain further insights about how executives act to bring about change by examining four historical leaders. One could ask if it is fair to compare these presidents of the past to contemporary research-based knowledge. Certainly we cannot fault these individuals for not knowing facts that had not been discovered yet. However, we can certainly analyze the leaders' behaviors using this contemporary knowledge in an attempt to acquire examples of how to, and not to, act.

Jefferson, Polk, Washington, and Theodore Roosevelt all demonstrated very well defined, perhaps prototypical, approaches to change management. Their transformational leadership styles were very different, but three of the four (Jefferson was the exception) proved highly effective in implementing change. It is also interesting to note that three of the four will most likely be remembered for centuries, but most people today probably couldn't identify Polk as a president, much less tell you anything about his activities.

There are dozens of similarities and differences between the four individuals, but with regards to change management two dimensions emerge to shed some light. The first dimension reflects how they approached change: personal or political. The personal approach describes an executive who relied primarily upon his personal sources of power to implement the change. Both Washington and Polk acted as individuals, Washington's strong sense of ethics and charisma and Polk's single-handed mastery of the executive branch's complex bureau-

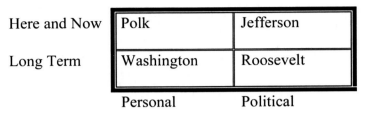

Figure 4.1.   The four president's approaches to change.

cracy allowed them to move the country forward. Jefferson and Roosevelt took a more political approach to change, proactively manipulating the press, people and groups, using patronage, and building coalitions to push their desired changes through to fruition. It is not surprising that Jefferson, one of the founders of the nation's two political party system, approached the presidency as an exercise in political manipulation. Roosevelt, who felt himself an ardent Republican party man, proved to be the party's greatest reformer. Jefferson completely understood political dynamics, letting the minions do the work while he sat back and pulled the strings. Roosevelt used his dynamic accomplishments and personal charisma as primary tools for winning the public's support for change, thereby forcing the congress to enact the desired legislation.

The second dimension classifies the four with regards to the time frame in which they approached change. Jefferson and Polk focused on the here and now, rarely looking beyond their immediate term. Washington and Roosevelt both considered the very long-term consequences before acting. Classifying Jefferson and Polk as tactical is not to say that these actors did not have long-term impacts. There is no question they did. Rather this is a categorization of how they perceived implementing change—for the present, instead of establishing precedents for the future.

With this framework in mind, what conclusions can we draw about how an executive should act to facilitate large scale changes? Examining the styles of the four presidents it becomes clear that the successful executive doesn't push the organization through the change, he pulls it. Polk, through total control of the executive bureaucracy, simply pushed the changes he wished through the channels. Change occurred, but Polk himself faded into obscurity. Jefferson also chose to push change, but in a different way. Jefferson drove key friends and associates ahead of him, acting as his front men to implement the desired changes. In essence he used these men as a plow that he drove ahead of himself and through the resistance.

Both Washington and Roosevelt acted as true change leaders—going far ahead of the organization, in essence to light the way for others to follow. They then proceeded to pull the bureaucracy to their desired outcomes. What did it take for these two to pull an entire nation to new heights? First, it took the ability to truly (and accurately) think strategically. Washington and Roosevelt both had the ability of using the current conditions to predict the desired future and then create a viable plan to reach it. Many have this ability, but Washington and Roosevelt linked it to the incredible energy that came from their complete certainty in the moral and ethical righteousness of what they wanted to accomplish. Roosevelt's astute grasp of political practices was essential for his success. Washington lacked this trait, but he really didn't need it—recall that if he had wanted it, he could have been king, or at least president for life. So, whereas President Washington was given much greater authority/position power, and was a master at its controlled use, Roosevelt was a skilled master of political machinations at both the individual and group levels. They both understood how to effectively use their different power bases to bring about change. Finally, Roosevelt and Washington's natural charismatic leadership cannot be discounted. The populace, and their elected officials, truly wanted to follow these two presidents and work to bring about a better future.

In a more advocacy frame of mind, the following are offered as some concrete suggestions that flow from this study:

- It is absolutely critical that the executive believes he/she is doing the right thing, right as established by what is best for the organization in the long-term. This rightness should unwaveringly guide the leader at all times. The rightness should also be clearly demonstrated by the leader through words and actions to all—both within and external to the organization.

- The leader must act, very visibly to all, as the leader. The executive must be, and appear to be, in change and ultimately is responsible for the change project. This requires much more than the typical e-mail introducing the consultant and telling everyone their cooperation is expected and appreciated. It is the executive, not the consultant, who is leading the change effort. He/she must be this most active person.

- In leading the change the executive must work with, and sometimes through, people. However it is critical that this is done in a mutually beneficial manner. No one is harmed through this interaction, or both are, but either way it is clear to all that it is necessary for the greater good.

- Unless one possesses near monarchical power (like Washington), the executive must be adept at, and willing to use, political tools to facilitate the change and proactively overcome resistance. It is absolutely essential that of the use of these tools be to advance the change, and therefore clearly in the organization's best interest (as opposed to the leader's personal interest). The executive must also exercise caution in selecting the right political tool. One should rely upon positive techniques such as image building, cooptation and coalition building, and avoid the negative, such as game playing and character assassination.

- The executive must be the leader—the individual who is ahead of the rest—the pioneer who is ahead of the rest on the path of change, thereby showing the followers the way.

- Avoid compromises, even in the face of great resistance, involving important elements of the change process. One should never sacrifice purpose for expediency. Rather than compromise try using collaboration, even if one must force the other party to do so.

- Actively use public opinion—create it, direct it, encourage it, then ride it like a surfer does a wave, just in front of the crest. Not only will this help to motivate the change supporters, and keep the change visible. It will force the wait-and-see fence sitters into active supporters.

- Keep the future good of the organization, and its members, foremost in all decisions, actions and statements. Don't just focus upon how this change will strengthen the organization—how will it possibly impact the members?

- The leader must know all the details—not just the big picture. This is not to say he/she should act as an omniscient autocrat, quite the contrary, it is simply saying one must be knowledgeable. The executive cannot afford to leave anything to chance, and this is exactly what happens when one operates without all the relevant information.

- The leader shouldn't be seen as a rule breaker, nor should she/he be seen as constrained by them. Remember, rules aren't made to be broken, but they are made to be changed. That is when the rule change is visibly obvious and needed for the organization's future good. Another important fact is that if no rule exists that says one *can't* do something, accept that as a perfectly good sight that one can do it. Don't be constrained by nonexistent barriers. Remember that change, by definition, is taking the organization into the unknown. One can't create a rule for something that is unknown—

one has to first experience the situation in order to establish what the rule should entail.

- Act fast. This is the only way to stay ahead of the race, which by definition, is exactly what a transformational leader does.
- Always remember that you must be a leader of individuals. Employees are not a faceless mass, rather they are individuals. It is critical that every single (or at least the vast majority) individual believes that the leader has his/her best interest at heart. The executive is someone who cares about them as individuals, not as simply a part of the larger group. In this light it is critical that the executive relies heavily upon symbolic acts that recognize the efforts of the little guy, again as individuals, as well as in groups or organizationwide.

What might the organization development consultant learn from this historical study? First, and foremost, they should see that they must let the executive be the change leader. This is the individual from whom all organizational members look to. The consultant (if external) is an outsider, and after every outsider's statement the employees will turn to their leaders for validation. If the change agent is an internal consultant, the members will still turn to the leader for confirmation of this peer's opinion.

This puts a whole different dimension on the client/consultant's relationship. The consultant must make sure the executive is aware of the demands of her/his role, and can execute them. Some executives will take to these requirements naturally, but many will probably require coaching. In the long run this could be the most important role for the organization development consultant with regards to strategic changes—coaching and mentoring the leader, rather than trying to be the leader.

ACKNOWLEDGMENT

An earlier version of this paper received the 2006 Paul Hershey Award for Best Leadership Paper from the Management History Division of the Academy of Management.

REFERENCES

Arnold, P. (1989). Fifteen presidential decisions that shaped America. *American History Illustrated, 24*(2), 36-42.

Bavelas, A., & Strauss, G. (1955). *Money and motivation*. New York: Harper & Row.

Brodie, F. M. (1974). *Thomas Jefferson: An intimate history*. New York: W.W. Norton

Brookhiser, R. (1996). *Founding father.* New York: The Free Press.

Casel, A. (1982). Old rough and ready's battle at buena vista. *American History Illustrated,* 17(6), 20-29.

Daft, R. (2005). *The leadership experience* (3rd ed.), Mason, OH: Southwestern.

Dennison, H. (1932, April). The need for the development of political science Engineering. *American Political Science Review, 26,* 241-255.

Fayol, H. (1923, September). *The administrative theory in the state* (S. Greer, Trans.). Presented at the Second International Congress of Administrative Science, Brussels.

Ferling, J. (1988). Defining the presidency. *American History Illustrated, 23*(2), 32-43.

Ferling, J. (1989). The evolving presidency. *American History Illustrated, 24*(2), 12-19.

Freidel, F. (1990). *Franklin D. Roosevelt: A rendezvous with destiny.* Boston: Little, Brown, and Company.

Gulick, L. (1937). Notes on the theory of organization. In L. Guilick & L. Urwick (Eds.), *Papers on the science of Administration* (pp. 1-46). New York: Institute of Public Administration.

Johnson, D. (1984). Three hats in the ring. *American History Illustrated, 19*(7), 12-17.

Karabell, Z. (2004). *Chester Alan Arthur.* New York: Times Books.

Kennedy, R. G. (2003). *Mr. Jefferson's lost cause.* New York: Oxford University Press.

Kotter, J. (1996). *Leading change.* Boston: Harvard Business School Press.

Morris, E. (2001). *Theodore rex.* New York: Random House

Randall, W. S. (1993). *Thomas Jefferson: A life.* New York: Henry Holt.

Schlesinger, A. (2003). The American presidency. In J. Seigenthaler (Ed.), *James K. Polk* (pp. 13). New York: Henry Holt .

Seigenthaler, J. (2003). *James K. Polk.* New York: Henry Holt.

Vas, A. (2001). Top management skills in a context of endemic organizational change. *Journal of General Management, 27,* 71-89.

Wensyel, J. (1992). The badge of military merit. *American History Illustrated, 17*(3), 26-31.

CHAPTER 5

GLOBAL LEADERSHIP AND SUCCESSION MANAGEMENT

Nazneen Razi

"Happiness is when what you think, what you say, and what you do are in harmony."

—Mahatma Gandhi

Global companies need effective global leaders in order to be successful. To remain successful, global companies need to ensure that their global leaders make succession management and the development of their key talent a top priority.

A well designed integrated talent management process that ensures the rigorous management of performance across the company is a significant source of a company's competitive advantage. It involves the development of strategies for identifying key talent and managing succession or vacancy risks globally. It is a consistent process that is deployed across geographies and drives superior performance. The process is integrated into the business strategic planning cycle with a rigorous annual review and evaluation of the company's top performers and the differentiation of talent that sorts out the top from the marginal performers.

Strategic Organization Development: Managing Change for Success
pp. 81–95
Copyright © 2009 by Information Age Publishing
All rights of reproduction in any form reserved.

The talent management process should start with the assessment of leadership, particularly at the senior executive level or the "Top of the house." The chief executive officer (CEO) of a global company should be aware and knowledgeable about the high-potential superior-performing executives within the firm; basically the top global leaders across the firm, and their strengths and areas for development. Developing strong global leaders and maintaining a solid global leadership pipeline are two critical success factors of a global business.

The objectives of this writing are twofold:

1. To define the characteristics of successful global leadership and
2. To lay out a process for building a strong succession bench of global leaders.

Examples of effective and ineffective succession scenarios will be used to illustrate the importance of a well developed and executed succession plan.

SUCCESSFUL GLOBAL LEADERSHIP

Over the past few years, the competition for global leadership talent has been unprecedented in its intensity. Leadership is perhaps among the most written about topics in management literature, yet the dynamics of global leadership continue to be the least understood due to the geographic and cultural complexities of managing in a multinational environment. Fueled by the wave of globalization, more and more leaders are being asked to live and work in countries outside their home country, organize global structures, build and maintain global technology platforms, and manage across multiple boundaries. Cross-border mobility is at its highest level and continues to grow at a phenomenal pace. Unfortunately, the failure rate of leaders on global assignments continues to remain high as evidenced by the early returns of expatriates to their home countries, low performance of leaders on global assignments, and high turnover within one year of repatriation (Black & Gergersen, 1999).

ASSESSING LEADERSHIP COMPETENCIES

The complexity of doing business internationally has provoked corporations to redefine their strategies and rapidly develop multicultural competencies that can effectively confront the powerful and pervasive challenges facing them. Human Resources functions are transforming their local attributes into global capabilities. Companies have spent millions of dollars either building leadership development programs in-house through their own corporate universities or buying leadership training from external experts. Leadership competency models range from the absolute generic that address general leadership skills to the highly customized that are intimately aligned with a company's brand, its strategic imperative or its employee value proposition.

The following are examples of some of the traditional competencies that have been used in assessing leaders:

- Strategic thinking;
- Results orientation;
- People management and development;
- Change management and leadership;
- Team leadership;
- Customer focus;
- Analysis and problem solving;
- Technical competence; and
- Financial and business acumen.

These competency frameworks have barely scratched the surface of the leadership challenges facing us today. Corporations are constantly scouting for successful leaders, especially those who can integrate effectively across countries, cultures and geographies and there is fierce competition for the global leader talent pool. Leaders who can handle with relative ease the demands of globalization and who can effectively motivate and inspire a team of people in any geographical context are the leaders of the future.

Based on a review of recent literature on global leadership, the following are the five key characteristics that distinguish a successful global leader from a successful business leader:

1. *Strong desire and propensity for learning*

    a. Exhibit a strong spirit of inquiry and curiosity
    b. Have a sense of adventure and risk taking
    c. Seek feedback and criticism
    d. Constantly seek to improve through experience, education or association

2. *Cultural sensitivity or adaptability*

    a. Work well with multiple cultures different from one's own
    b. Adapt style to meet local expectations, norms and values
    c. Forge collaborative relationships between multicultural groups
    d. Assess people in a culture-neutral manner

3. *Innovation and creativity*

    a. Create value through consistent focus on high growth strategies

    b. Create leadership passion to flame the creativity of people

    c. Promote idea generation from within the company

    d. Generate blockbuster ideas that can convert opportunities into revenue

4. *Global competence*

    a. Understand the complexity of a company's strategy and business operations within various geographies

    b. Have the ability and desire to grasp the economic, social and political landscape of the countries of operation

    c. Able to work with diverse people in diverse settings

    d. Seek out and welcome new and different work experiences

5. *Moral competence*

    a. Maintain his or her personal integrity at all costs

    b. Take responsibility when things go wrong

    c. Do the right thing even when personal consequences may be negative

    d. Be highly principled and speak up when necessary

Studies reflect that there is a strong correlation between a person's ability to learn and leadership potential. Research conducted by McCall, Spreitzer, and Mahoney (1994) with high potential and solid-performing international managers claims that the leader's development is directly a function of his ability to learn from an accumulation of experiences. Of all the competencies cited above, the one critical ingredient of success is the leader's desire to learn and grow. Studies reflect that there's a strong correlation between a person's ability to learn and leadership potential. For example, the Lominger research indicates that those employees with greater learning agility are more successful *after* they are promoted than others (Lombardo & Eichinger, 2000).

Assessing global leaders is just one half of the equation. Assessing the pipeline and grooming successors is equally important in the preservation of a company's human capital and its business viability.

GLOBAL SUCCESSION MANAGEMENT

Succession management is an organization's effort of safeguarding its leadership capabilities through planned replacement strategies for identified key positions and franchise players who are critical to the organization's business.

Why is succession management such a critical imperative for global corporations?

Effective succession planning at the senior executive level ensures a company's business continuity and sustainability in the face of an untimely or even planned departure of an executive. Conversely, history shows that a poorly planned or executed succession can result in the downfall or destruction of a company. Succession management should be viewed as a formal process that requires senior management's attention and involvement. It needs to be integrated into a company's overall talent management strategy. For global companies, the succession management process needs to be globalized to include key positions across geographies and the succession bench should consider high potential talent across regions and countries in which the company operates.

Despite the numerous events that have occurred where a CEO or senior executive had to be replaced due to an unanticipated event, succession planning remains a lower priority for many companies.

The following business situations are real examples that serve to illustrate effective and ineffective succession management practices. These are four case studies of high profile companies that implemented a succession plan with varying degrees of effectiveness and varying outcomes. Figure 5.1 plots these companies based on (a) the level of effectiveness and (b) planned or unplanned succession.

EFFECTIVE SUCCESSION MANAGEMENT/UNANTICIPATED SUCCESSION—THE McDONALD'S STORY

One of the best examples of a swift succession decision was McDonald's Corporation. On April 19 2004, Jim Cantalupo, the leader of McDonald's, the world's biggest fast food chain, died unexpectedly of a heart attack at the age of 60. Jim was attending a convention in Florida when he was stricken. Jim had only been the chairman and CEO since 2003, but had been with the company for 30 years in key positions and was instrumental in the rapid turnaround of the business in service, quality, and sales. McDonald's effective succession planning system allowed the company to announce Charlie Bell as the successor only a few hours after the demise of the leader. Charlie was 43 years old and started his career with the fast food chain in Sydney, Australia as a part-time crew member at the early age of 15. He became the youngest store manager in Australia at the age of 19, rose to vice president at the age of 27 and was appointed to Australia's board of directors at the age of 29. McDonald's talent management process identified him as a high potential leader very early on in his

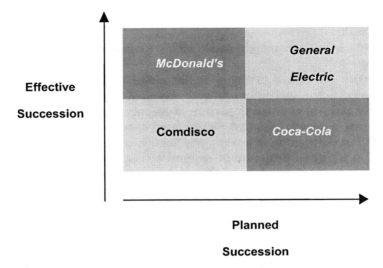

Figure 5.1.   Planned and effective succession management.

career and Bell rose rapidly to president of Europe and then of Asia and subsequently to chief operating officer and a member of the company's board of directors. He was being groomed for the CEO spot and was relied upon by Cantalupo for the turnaround that took place in the latter's CEO days. Charlie was a successful global leader recognized and accepted by analysts as McDonald's new CEO the very day he was appointed to the position (Hymowitz & Lubin, 2007).

Only a month after he ascended to the position of CEO, Charlie Bell was diagnosed with cancer and died on January 17, 2004, less than a year later. He was immediately succeeded by Jim Skinner, the company's third CEO in a year. Again, the swift succession decision was indicative of a powerful succession management process that circumvented any potential for business disruption and provided immediate reassurance to employees and shareholders that the fast food giant was quite capable of continuing on its growth and success trajectory. It short circuited any speculation or rumor that could have been harmful at a critical juncture for the company. More importantly, succession management was a global undertaking with executives from all over the globe on the successor radar.

EFFECTIVE SUCCESSION MANAGEMENT/
PLANNED SUCCESSION—THE GE STORY

Another succession success story is the famous well-orchestrated plan by Jack Welch who spent several years choosing his successor. Unlike the

McDonald's CEOs, Jack had the luxury of executing a well-thought out succession plan, but the company was always prepared for an untimely event should one occur. Jack was prepared to move very quickly to name a new CEO, if an emergency had rendered him unable to lead the company.

The human resources function under Jack Welch evolved from what he himself termed as "the health and happiness crowd" to one of two most important functions within the company. In the book *Winning* (Welch, 2005, pp. 98-99), Jack states "Without doubt, the head of HR should be the second most important person in any organization. From the point of view of the CEO, the director of HR should be at least equal to the CFO."

Bill Conaty, the chief of HR at GE, had a special gift for "picking out stars and phonies." According to Jack Welch, Bill "was a master at this. Whether it was with a handshake, a smile, or a way of talking about their family, job candidates were transparent to him" (Welch, 2005, p. 91). Bill's success could also be largely attributed to his strategic organization development and talent management initiatives, one of which was designing an intense succession plan that resulted in the selection of Jeff Immelt as Jack's successor, at the age of 44. Jack Welch, who was considered one of the world's most charismatic and successful leaders, departed the firm with little to no disruption, primarily due to his well thought out and executed succession. Jack had picked three potential successors who were to succeed him and knew that the two who were not selected had to be let go. Their succession was also orchestrated with similar diligence and finesse. He publicized his programmed plan which prompted Home Depot and 3M to pick up the two leaders who were released.

The GE and McDonald's stories are unique and attracted tremendous media attention due to their size and impact. They became the exemplar for other companies to emulate.

INEFFECTIVE SUCCESSION MANAGEMENT/UNPLANNED EVENT— THE COMDISCO STORY

Ineffective succession can have an equally dramatic impact on a highly successful global company and there have been instances where poor planning or execution of a succession is speculated to have caused a company's downfall or demise. Examples of such poor planning are Comdisco and TLC Beatrice International Holdings Corp.

A *Forbes* article stated that "Nicholas Pontikes (CEO of Comdisco), oversaw the swift demise of his dad's 30-year-old computer leasing firm." The successor "couldn't emulate his father's leadership style" (Gordon, 2001, p. 72). Comdisco, a successful Fortune 500 global company was run by Ken Pontikes, who built the company from a five-man operation to a highly successful leasing company. He died of cancer leaving the company in the hands of his friends and colleagues, including Jack Slevin as CEO. Ken's wish was to have Nick succeed him only when he had gained more experience. However, due to the earlier-than-anticipated retirement of Mr. Slevin, Nick took over the company at the age of 33. According to the Forbes article,

> Comdisco's swift fall from grace is the result of unchecked decisions by Pontikes. Perhaps fueled by a need to outdo his father's success, he set about transforming a fairly conservative computer leasing firm into a bold Internet player and provider of high-speed Internet access through digital subscriber line technology. The ideas seemed swell at the time, but Pontikes' timing was awful, coming right before both the Web and the DSL industry collapsed. (Gordon, 2001, p. 72)

Notwithstanding that opinion, it can be debated that the demise of the company was due more to the fact that the core leasing business had become irrelevant, and not because it was run by a successor whose leadership skills may not have been strong enough to survive the turbulence of the dot com era.

Another similar family succession that ended in the complete liquidation of a company was Beatrice International Foods Company, the only Black Enterprise 100 company to break the billion-dollar sales barrier. Similar to the Comdisco story, the founder Reginald Lewis' untimely demise from brain cancer, at a time when the company was at the zenith of its performance, was the beginning of its downfall that was to occur under the leadership of his brother and then his wife who succeeded him (Dingle, 1999, p. 117).

These are unfortunate cases of very successful companies that may have had an alternative fate under different succession scenarios. In both situations, the succession may have been based on sentiment rather than structure. Neither of the successors seemed to have had the benefit of a rigorous leadership development program that McDonald's and GE provided to their successor candidates.

INEFFECTIVE SUCCESSION MANAGEMENT/PLANNED SUCCESSION—THE COCA-COLA STORY

The final succession case study is about the succession of Coca-Cola CEO, Roberto C. Goizueta who died of lung cancer very shortly after he was diagnosed. It appeared that Coca-Cola maintained a succession pipeline and identified successors to the top executive; however, the succession outcomes were far from desirable. In 16 years, with CEO Goizueta at the helm, the company's market value grew 34-fold, from $4.3 billion to $147 billion. His successor, Douglas Ivester's tenure however, was very short. On his watch, Coca-Cola's earnings declined for two years running and he was asked to step down. Although Coca-Cola had a structured succession plan, the company suffered under an ineffective successor. Coca-Cola quickly remedied the situation by increasing the authority of three senior executives and strengthening the CEO succession bench (Hays 1999).

Daft was the chosen successor who retired within four years of taking over as CEO and was replaced by Neville Isdell who had originally retired from the firm. Although Isdell was not the board's first succession choice as Daft's replacement, he was identified as a result of his global experience and success within the firm both in Europe and Asia (Ward 2005).

Coca-Cola's succession story is different from the others in terms of a long-term succession outcome. However, similar to GE and McDonald's, the company managed succession on a global basis. Isdell, the current CEO, an Irishman by birth who worked in Europe, earned his reputation within Coca-Cola as head of the company's Philippine operation in the 1980s which brought him into the limelight (Ward 2005).

Effective succession planning for key executive positions is essential for the survival and viable sustainability of an organization. Effective succession planning involves a structured approach to identify, develop, and prepare high potential candidates for key positions. Effective *global* succession planning requires the CEO and HR to ensure that a wider net is cast in identifying the high-potential talent pool. As in the case of McDonald's, the Oak Brook-based company reached out to Sydney, Australia to build its senior talent pipeline. Similarly, GE and Coca-Cola's succession plans have a strong global reach.

THE INTEGRATED TALENT MANAGEMENT FRAMEWORK

Succession management should be incorporated into a company's talent management system. An example of a talent management process is depicted in Figure 5.2.

The five critical steps in a talent management process are as follows:

1. Step One: Assessing performance against preestablished competencies or business objectives.

As stated earlier, the process begins with the assessment of a company's top talent using a competency model that is aligned with the company's

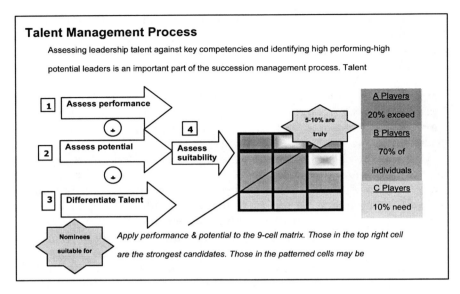

Figure 5.2.   Talent management process.

business objectives. For companies assessing global leaders, incorporating the five global competencies will further enhance and strengthen the talent pool.

2.   Step Two: Assessing leadership potential.

Assessing potential is also critical to the process as performance does not always predict potential. There are multiple ways of defining and assessing potential. Potential in the very basic sense is an individual's capacity or ability for future development or achievement. A person with demonstrable potential is one who is highly engaged and has a level of ability, determination, and tenacity for achievement and success.

An organization needs to establish what potential looks like at a particular level and what attributes are necessary for an individual to succeed at that level.

There are various tools that can be deployed to capture and compare talent across the firm. Lominger's CHOICES ARCHITECT® Dimensions describing learning agility provide a research-based validated instrument for defining potential. Their Performance-Potential Matrix (PPM), a nine-cell tool, is a method of placing value on a person in terms of long-term potential for significant growth in responsibility (Lombardo & Eichinger, 2000).

3. Step Three: Differentiating talent.

Stratifying the talent pool allows companies to recognize and distinguish its superior performers while addressing marginal performers. "Winning the war for talent isn't just about recruiting and retaining people. You've got to invest in A performers, raise the game of B performers, and-perhaps most difficult of all-deal decisively with C performers" (Axelrod, Handfield-Jones, & Michaels, 2002, p. 80A). Companies over time have forced the distribution of ratings to ensure that the mediocre or lower performing individuals are identified. Without a prescribed structure, managers may cluster ratings into the top and middle categories. Addressing marginal performers is as important as managing and recognizing the star performers.

A question often asked is whether an employee should be informed of his/her rating. It is good practice to let the strongest performing and high potential talent know how critical they are to the business and how the organization views them. However, it is equally important to let the "B" players know that they are appreciated. These are the company's "competent steady performers" who are "highly skilled, focused professionals." A company has to make sure it retains its B players. "Yet, many executives ignore B players, beguiled by stars' brilliance" (DeLong & Vijayaraghavan, 2003, p. 97).

Of equal importance is the process of weeding out the poor or marginal performers. These performers can weigh down an organization and erode its health and vitality, yet managers find it very difficult to let their marginal workers go for many reasons. It is also a more complicated and expensive process in certain countries due to local laws that provide protection to employees by installing costly severance and notice period requirements.

4. Step Four: Assessing suitability for position.

The fourth step in the talent management process relates to a person's upward mobility. Prior to promoting a leader to the next level, it is critical to ensure that he or she is suitable for the role identified. Developing a competency profile for each critical position allows the mapping of competencies of the successor against the preestablished competencies and identifying gaps that can be addressed over a period of time. The competency profile can also be used to evaluate the current incumbent and identify that individual's development needs for the position occupied. In a succession situation, suitability analysis has to be an iterative ongoing process to ensure that the leaders continue to remain suitable. This is particularly important in dynamic organizations that transform periodically either through restructure, organic growth or consolidation. Jack and Suzy Welch claim,

> People develop at different rates. A possible successor who starts in a blaze of glory might fade away over time, and a slow starter might take off. A CEO needs several years at least to see candidates in many jobs and differing economic environments before making a final call. (Welch & Welch, 2007, p. 19)

Therefore, it is critical that succession plans are reviewed and discussed annually.

5.   Step Five: Process of socialization.

Executive or top talent belongs to the organization. It is important that the senior executives or "top of the house" share their views about the people who are identified as top talent. As part of the talent management system, a socialization of the key attributes of people in key positions and their successors is as critical as the process itself. The CEO and the top executives need to take full accountability for strengthening the company's talent base. HR can facilitate the group discussion which often is a rich and robust dialogue around successors to key positions and strategies for maintaining continuity in key leadership. This socialization can take place at all levels and within multiple geographies to ensure an all-encompassing review of key individuals.

GLOBAL SUCCESSION MANAGEMENT

"You don't necessarily need a succession plan. You want one" (Welch & Welch, 2007, p. 20). As stated earlier, an effective succession plan is one that is an integral part of a company's talent management process. The following figure represents a simple succession planning process based on the Hewitt model.

Succession Planning and Management Enhancers and Pitfalls

Enhancers

1.   Refresh succession plans periodically. Jack and Suzy Welch claim, "People develop at different rates. A possible successor who starts in a blaze of glory might fade away over time, and a slow starter might take off. A CEO needs several years at least to see candidates

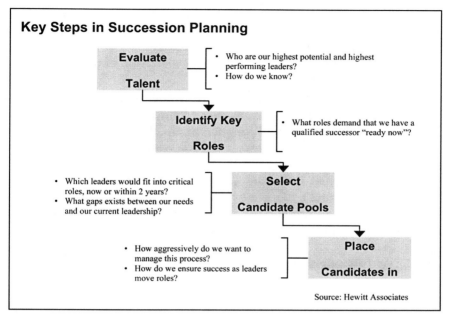

Figure 5.3.   Key steps in succession planning.

in many jobs and differing economic environments before making a final call" (Welch & Welch, 2007, p. 19).

2.   Identify at least two short-term successors for each key role where possible.

3.   Establish key metrics that measure the effectiveness of the succession management process. Examples of metrics to consider are:

   a.   Ratio of internal hires to external hires for key roles identified.
   b.   Percent of positions filled from the predetermined "successor pool."
   c.   Percent of key positions that have at least two successors identified.

4.   Evaluate an organization's key talent departure risk, particularly when the company may be most vulnerable for loss of talent, such as during a merger or acquisition, following a major transformation or restructuring, or during an economic downturn.

5.   Identify stretch/challenging assignments for key successors who may be tired of waiting on the bench for the position to open up.

6.   Identify retention strategies for successors not selected for key roles who could present a flight risk.

7. Identify a person or, in the case of large organizations, a function that is accountable for the mobility of key talent. This is most critical in global organizations where orchestration of moves could be quite daunting unless someone takes ownership of driving the process.

8. Determine the most optimal form of communication or the program's "degree of dissemination." This can range from being a "top secret" proprietary program to one that is broadly communicated to all individuals assessed. Most companies keep the process confidential to avoid problems with setting unrealistic expectations and to prevent information from leaking out to the competition (Rothwell, 2001).

9. Ensure the bench below a named successor is strong and can be relied upon to back fill with minimum disruption to the unit.

Pitfalls and Derailers

1. Do not assume successors are interested in advancing to the senior key role. Career discussions with key talent will help understand their interests and validate their succession plans.

2. Do not assume the successor on the bench will be always willing and able to take on the identified role, particularly if the role requires a cross-country relocation. Family situations change and can disrupt an individual's plans. Identifying multiple successor candidates will minimize the risk of an employee changing his or her mind at the last minute.

3. Do not identify more than three key roles for each successor. This dilutes the succession and development process, particularly if the roles have unique competency requirements.

4. It is not essential to have a successor for each key role. In some instances, it may be cost-prohibitive to maintain a deep succession bench, particularly for key staff roles. In these instances, it is best to identify an interim succession plan and an external replacement plan that can be executed rapidly.

5. Be careful of having too many rainmakers in successor positions for leadership positions as it could dilute the growth potential of the firm, and successful rainmakers do not always make successful business or people leaders.

6. Do not hoard key talent. Top talent belongs to the organization and should be considered for the "good of the firm."

CONCLUSION

An effective global talent management system produces strong leaders and maintains a fortified bench for the leaders in the event of their departure. Identifying and assessing global leaders is important but not complete in and of itself. Developing the global leaders, particularly those in the succession pipeline, is equally critical to ensure the right people are in the job and can effectively lead a country, region, business unit or even a company when appointed.

REFERENCES

Axelrod, B., Handfield-Jones, H., & Michaels, E. (2002, January). A new game plan for C players. *Harvard Business Review, 80*(1), 80-88.

Black, J. S., & Gergersen, H. B. (1999, March-April). The right way to manage expats. *Harvard Business Review, 77*(2), 52-63.

DeLong, T., & Vijayaraghavan, V. (2003, June). Let's hear it for B players. *Harvard Business Review, 81*(6), 96-102.

Dingle, D. T. (1999, September). TLC's final act—TLC Beatrice Holdig Internations Holding Inc.—Complete divestiture—Company profile. *Black Enterprise, 30,* 117.

Gordon, J. (2001). Geek tragedy. *Forbes, 167*(14), 72-73.

Hays, C. L. (1999, October 30). Coke assigns larger roles to 3 officers. *Business News*, p. C1.

Hymowitz, C., & Lubin, J. S. (2004, April). Lessons from McDonald's: Always have a succession plan. *Wall Street Journal, 243*(77), B1-B8.

Lombardo, M. M., & Eichinger, R. W. (2000). *The leadership machine*. Minneapolis, MN. Author.

McCall, M. W., McCall, J., Spreitzer, G. M., & Mahoney, J. (1994). *Identifying leadership potential in future international executives: A learning resource guide*. Lexington, MA: International Consortium for Executive Development Research.

Rothwell, W. J. (2001). *Effective succession planning: Ensuring leadership continuity and building talent from within*. New York: AMACOM.

Ward, A. (2005). Coke seeks to regain lost glory: Under CEO Neville Isdell the company is trying to bounce back from miscues. *The Chief Executive*. Retrieved December 2, 2005, from http://www.chiefexecutive.net

Welch, J. (2005). *Winning*. New York: HarperCollins.

Welch, J., & Welch, S. (2007, September 10). Ideas the Welch way. *Business Week*, p. 20.

Welch, J. (2005). *Winning*. New York: HarperCollins.

CHAPTER 6

STRATEGIC ORGANIZATION DEVELOPMENT

An Invitation to the Table

Philip T. Anderson

Organization development (OD) is a field deeply rooted in personal values. Values are the scaffolding on which all OD interventions are built. From the beginning, humanistic values have been the driving force in OD and the very reason many practitioners embark upon an OD career. However, if values are the scaffolding, then the building itself is the mission and performance of the organizations we serve.

Somewhere in OD's history, the organization seems to have gotten lost. Here, I will outline why OD practitioners must become business partners and suggest ways they can be invited to the strategic table. I will discuss the ambiguity associated with business strategy and what it means to be strategic. I will tie the proud traditions of OD with the current realities and complex environment in which companies must survive today. Lastly, I will propose a process to develop a sound OD strategy that is linked to strategic outcomes of the business.

Strategic Organization Development: Managing Change for Success
pp. 97–113

Most will agree that OD must become more strategic in the way we facilitate change. However, we must also begin a dialogue about how OD practitioners can become strategic partners. One cannot happen without the other.

WHAT DOES IT MEAN TO BE STRATEGIC?

Organization Development has always been a field guided by strong humanistic values. In our mid-century infancy, we advocated openness, trust, honest feedback and personal growth. Practitioners espoused teamwork, organizational change and a productive work environment based on sound organizational values. It wasn't until the 1980s, some 30 years later, that we began a serious dialogue about strategic organization development. It is an issue we still struggle with today.

There is no argument that a humanistic orientation must continue to be the core of OD (Church, Burke, & Van Eynde, 1994). However, OD practitioners must also provide value to organizations by aligning their work with the business. They must examine issues that leaders believe are important, not just the values that OD advocates. Practitioners must partner with leaders to help them go where they want to go and not just where practitioners want to take them. This is the foundation of strategic organization development.

Strategy is one of those terms that, through its ubiquitous usage, has become ambiguous. It is often used out of context. Many confuse it with tactics and others believe it is synonymous with long range planning. Like organization development, strategy has a number of definitions, one not necessarily better than another. Generally most in the field agree that OD must become more strategic, yet the definition of strategy is very inconsistent. Without consistency in definition, unconscious disagreement has resulted.

Strategy has deep roots in the military. Sun Tzu, the ancient Chinese warrior often quoted by contemporary leaders, operationalizes his definition of strategy in his treatise, *The Art of War*. Tzu espoused, "The skillful leader subdues the enemy's troops without any fighting; he captures their cities without laying siege to them; he overthrows their kingdom without lengthy operations in the field. With his forces intact he will dispute the mastery of the Empire, and thus, without losing a man, his triumph will be complete. This is the method of attacking by strategy" (p. 35). To Tzu, strategy meant effective planning and the ability to adapt to external forces. It was winning without ever engaging the enemy.

Sun Tzu's philosophies, written over two thousand years ago, have been adapted to fit modern day business practices. The *Art of War* has become required reading for many young entrepreneurs. In business terms, Sun Tzu's enemy equates to competition and the marketplace is the new battlefield. Tzu believed that in order to win, one must first look outside the boundaries of their organization. Leaders must be able to understand their competitors before they can develop an effective strategy.

More modern definitions of strategy echo Sun Tzu. Mary Jo Hatch (2000) defines strategy as "management's planned efforts to influence organizational outcomes by managing the organization's relationship with the environment" (p. 101). Ireland, Hoskinsson, and Hitt (2006), describe strategy as the analysis of the internal and external environments to create value for customers and stakeholders. Harrison and St. John (2004) talk of "environmental determinism"—determining the appropriate strategy that best fits the environment. Although contexts may vary, the common theme in all these definitions is the belief that a company's ability to fit with its external environment is vital to its survival. So, if OD is to be strategic, we must help the organization look beyond its boundaries. In addition to our concern for internal alignment (i.e., teambuilding, group process, and communication), we must also concern ourselves with how our efforts align with the external environment to improve organizational performance.

THE VALUE DRIVEN APPROACH TO OD

The field of OD has stalwartly embraced traditional values that most practitioners continue to believe (Church, Hurley, & Burke, 1992). Central to those values is the notion that organizations should provide members with opportunities to influence decisions about their work (Margulies & Raia, 1990); that OD should focus on work life improvements (Greiner, 1980; Marguilies & Raia, 1990; Sashkin & Burke, 1990); and bring to the surface, address, and resolve conflict. Others advocate decision-making based on valid information and not position (Burke, 1982); provide for individual and organizational learning (Beckhard, 1969); and include organizational members affected by the change in the planning and implementation of change (Greiner, 1980).

It is important for us to continue to conduct the business of OD according to these principles; however, we must also be keenly aware of organizational survival issues. Internal consultants, because they are permanent members of the organization, must also be responsible for producing results that are sustainable and impact the company's strategy. Interventions that look inward may all be embedded with OD values, but may not impact strategic fit. To become strategic, interventions must be linked to the mission and long-range plans of the organization and aligned with external business drivers.

THE STRATEGY DRIVEN APPROACH

The business world is in a constant state of change. Much shorter time frames must be embraced to bring about substantive results. Issues of globalization, information technology, consumer activism, and increasingly larger and more complex mergers threaten the very survival of many organizations. The bottom line is that companies are under considerable pressures to produce results in a more fluid and competitive marketplace. An organization that cannot keep up with the demands of this environment is threatened with extinction. Until OD can help organizations solve these basic issues of survival, issues of collaboration and values will always take a back seat.

This rapid rate of change has brought about a new order. In this new order, the implications for organization development are clear. We must proactively approach leaders and help them understand the value OD can provide. Internal as well as external consultants must understand the business at a strategic level to give context to interpersonal and group process interventions. By giving context we can show how OD might impact corporate as well as business strategies. Today OD is seen as an enabler. That perception has to change so that practitioners are viewed as business partners. OD must be seen as integral to organizational success. If we don't embrace this new role, the consequences are dire. According to Jelinek and Litterer (1988), "without substantive change, organizational development may emulate the dinosaur, failing to adapt as the world changes around it" (p. 136).

Although it is important for OD practitioners to be seen as strategic partners, it is also important to be effective at a tactical level. Together, strategic and tactical interventions are practiced at three distinct levels in an organization.

First, OD is practiced at the organizational level. This is the primary level that strategically links OD to the business. At this level, interventions are linked with the strategies and long range plans of the organization. They are systematic and in many instances very complex since they usually involve the whole system.

Below the organizational level, OD is practiced at the group level. Depending on the size of the organization, this could be as small as a department or as large as a division/business unit. At this level, OD activities can be either strategic or tactical. They could be seen as strategic if they link to a larger more systematic intervention that involves the whole system. They can be tactical if they involve only a part of the system and are not linked to a long term strategy.

However, some large organizations may have a divisional structure, which involves many diverse businesses, each responsible for delivering a unique product or service. Normally in this type of structure, there is a corporate entity that prescribes what products or services divisions should produce while the divisions develop a strategy to deliver the products or services. In this case, each division is subject to having a business strategy that supports the corporate strategy. However, OD interventions at the group level (division) may also be strategic since each business has its own strategy that may require OD support.

Below the group level, OD is practiced with individual clients. These are managers within the organization who may need help resolving issues unique to their department/function. These interventions are usually reactive or tactical in nature and generally not planned.

This is not to say that tactical interventions do not have a place in organizations. Tactical interventions, although not directly linked to strategy, are important enablers. They may serve to resolve interpersonal issues, make decision making more effective, increase communication flow or attract and reward employees. They are still an important part of a good OD strategy and are needed to support more strategic interventions. Because tactical interventions generally have a more inward focus, senior leaders are less likely to recognize their value. They are more important to mid-level and first line managers. Senior leaders are more focused on external issues. Their job is to look outward and help the company understand strategic implications of the business environment. Therefore, it is more likely for them to focus on OD interventions that do the same. At lower management levels, the focus is on tactical and process driven issues and tactical OD interventions are more likely to be appreciated.

All three levels of interventions must work in concert in order to be effective (Figure 6.1). Organizational level interventions must be aligned with group and client level interventions that support them. Conversely, group and client interventions must be enabled by interventions at the organizational level.

Although these levels are distinct, the action research process is applied at each level. Action research is the process of linking research closely with action in order to produce change (Cummings & Worley, 2005). It begins with the identification of an organizational issue. Then, data is collected and reviewed by organizational members for action planning, implementation, and evaluations (Figure 6.2). Whether it is an intervention that involved the whole system or just one client, the process itself remains the same.

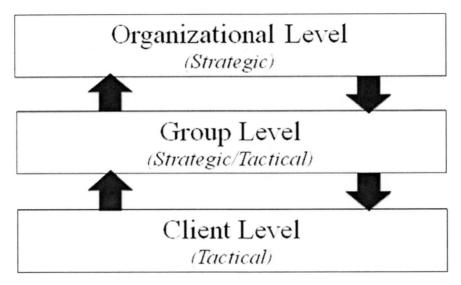

Figure 6.1.   Levels or organization development interventions.

Since the process of OD remains the same at every level, it could be repeated a number of times during a single intervention. Rather than a one dimensional model, it becomes multidimensional aligning itself with the structure of the organization. For instance, if the action research model is applied in a divisional structure (a structure with multiple business units, each with their own resources), the action research model is repeated in each business unit. Likewise, in global organizations, the model is repeated for every country—taking into account the organizational and national culture of each country. In these complex organizations, another role of OD is to bring these various and sometimes disparate business units and global processes together into one targeted intervention at the organizational level.

The example below (Figure 6.3) is taken from an organizational intervention sponsored by a large global pharmaceutical company operating in over 125 countries around the world. It depicts the action research process as it relates to interventions identified through their employee survey. The shapes represent the various roles involved in each step of the process—another dimension of the model which will be discussed later. The oval-shaped steps represent the company's OD staff, the rectangular-shaped steps represent line management, and dotted outline shapes indicate human resource (HR) business partners (generalists) are involved. In this instance, each group, OD, line management, and HR play a distinct

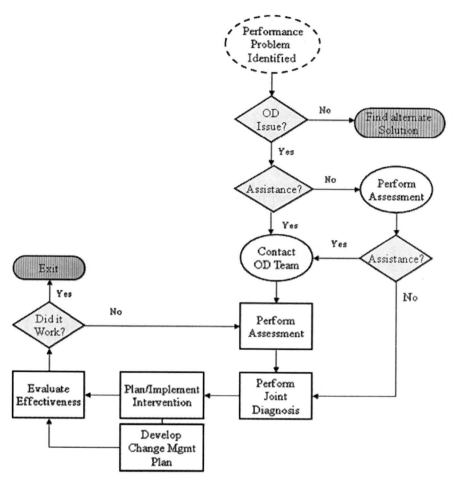

Figure 6.2. Organization development process.

role in executing action research. Each role complements the other to bring about organizational change.

The action research model shown in Figure 6.3 is still largely one dimensional. It takes into account action research applied at the organizational or corporate level. However, when the same process is expanded to include the company's business units and international affiliates, it becomes much more dynamic.

The figure below depicts the multidimensional affects of applying action research at the business unit and international levels of the firm.

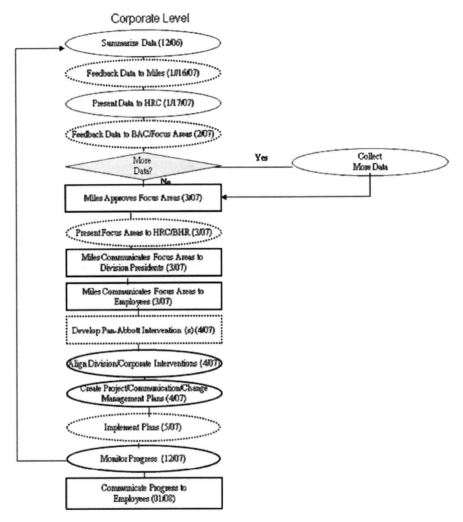

Figure 6.3.   Action research model.

Additionally, roles are expanded to include experts in training and development (depicted in pentagon-shaped steps). These additional resources are needed to expand the reach of the OD intervention. Also, notice that an additional process is added between the business level (group) process and the country process. This addition is necessary to ensure continuity and alignment between the business units and the country affiliates. This process is lead by members of the OD staff and training who act as con-

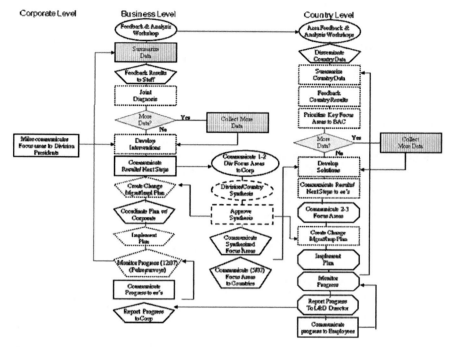

Figure 6.4.   Global action research model.

duits between the business units in the United States and each country outside of the United States

Note how the action research process becomes much more complex as it mirrors the complexity of the organization. Additionally, as it becomes more complex, more functions tangential to the OD function, that is, training and HR are needed to implement the process. These other functions, especially HR play a very important role in strategic organizational development—especially in light of the current wave of HR transformation efforts.

OD AND THE HUMAN RESOURCES FUNCTION

It becomes doubly important to understand the levels of organization development and its relationship to the action research model in light of the transformational change taking place in human resource management (HRM). Human resource management is undergoing somewhat of a metamorphosis. Like OD, in an effort to become more strategic, the field of HR has begun a transformation to make transactional HR activities, i.e., benefits selection, pay administration, and maintenance of employee data more efficient. Technology has made it easier for employees to manage these services themselves, allowing HR to focus on more strategic matters—those activities that help the organization align with its external environment.

As this movement gains steam, both OD and HR managers are asking the same questions about long-term effectiveness when it comes to people and processes. As they do, they are finding many commonalities. In many organizations, the worlds of HR and OD practitioners are quickly converging causing conflict and role ambiguity. To clarify the role of HRM and OD, we must first understand the HR transformation taking place and the implication of the three levels of the OD process.

AN ERA OF HR TRANSFORMATION

In the past, it was relatively easy to distinguish OD interventions from other more traditional HR approaches. HR managers were often involved in employment policies and practices, benefits administration, payroll activity, and many other tasks that can be categorized as transactional in nature. Activities, although important to the business had little to do with external survival issues that occupied the time of senior leaders.

However, in the late 1990s, Dave Ulrich's (1997) book, *Human Resource Champions* began somewhat of a renaissance on the field of human resource management. It sparked HR managers throughout the United States, in organizations large and small, to rethink the business of human resources. Transactional activities, long the staple of HR generalists is becoming automated in favor of work more conducive to consulting and long-term project management. This shift in thinking not only calls for a shift in the role of the HR generalist, but also required new processes and a new HR structure.

Although a new structure is needed, it must still align with the larger organization structure. Specifically, it must:

- centralize those activities that are core to the HR business while allowing local action and decision making;
- like other support services, work seamlessly between functions, that is, staffing, employee relations, compensation, and so on, to deliver value;
- be able to quickly form tasks forces and teams to tackle complex issues and interventions;

- be responsive to the ever-changing needs of the business;
- decrease waste in the form of excessive costs; and
- enable employees.

The structure most commonly adopted to deliver HR value is the shared services model. The shared services model relies on HR business partners and centers of excellence (COE) to seamlessly deliver both transactional and strategic services. This model consists of three elements (Kates, 2007) (Figure 6.5).

The *customer facing side of HR* which is normally the role of the HR business partner senses and scopes the HR needs of the business. They focus on diagnostic activities and organization development. In many cases, they have a matrixed relationship between the corporate HR function and the business unit or division that they support.

The *product focused side* is what most organizations refer to as the center of excellence or COE. The COEs are staffed with subject matter experts in areas such as talent acquisition, compensation, training, and organization development. Business partners depend on these experts to supply tools

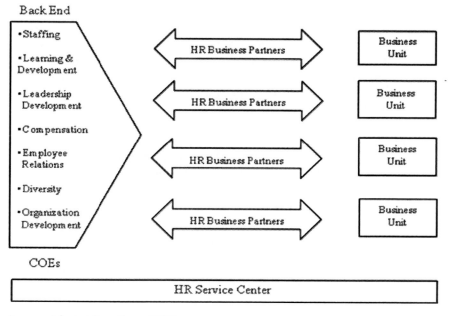

Source: Adapted from Kates (2007).

Figure 6.5.   Human resources shared services model.

and transfer knowledge on complex issues, while the COEs rely on the business partners to roll-out core programs originating from the corporate headquarters. This dual role often creates conflict between members of the COE and business partners over client ownership, especially when it comes to consultative services like organization development.

The *operations or service center* is designed to handle the transactional work traditionally done by the HR generalist. This work includes activities such as payroll administration, generating employee data, and managing employee information. Many organizations have automated this aspect of the new HR structure, which has allowed employees to service themselves on these kinds of transactions.

DETERMINING WHO OWNS OD?

With both the HR business partner and the COE having OD responsibility, conflict over who has responsibility for the OD function of the company arises. Typically, because the HR business partner is client facing, they would conduct the initial diagnosis and determine when the OD COE should get involved. However, in the view of the COE, this is often too late and gives them little flexibility to impact the appropriate intervention. Conversely, when the specialist from the OD COE are brought in too early, business partners often feel overwhelmed—not really knowing who to count on to help solve their problem. Although the hand-off between the business partner and COE should be seamless, this is often not the case. These hand-offs often result in confusion in the eyes of the client and make HR appear unorganized and dysfunctional.

To resolve this problem of ownership, business partners and the COE must resolve decision rights issues related to OD the practice. They must establish who owns each part of the OD process at what level. An efficient way to accomplish this is to assign responsibility based on the OD level involved in the intervention. In other words, OD interventions that have organization-wide impact should be handled by the COE. HR business partners would then be responsible for rolling-out these interventions across the organization. HR business partners would also be responsible for organizationwide interventions; however, they would be mainly concerned with interventions strategic to their assigned business unit. In which case, the OD COE would help support the business partner by providing tools and contracted assistance to HR business partners. At the client level, OD managers would also be responsible for those interventions that are more tactical in nature, such as teambuilding, process facilitation, and human resource interventions, that focus more on internal integra-

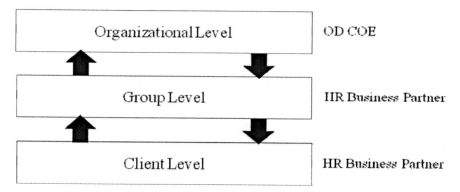

Figure 6.6. Organizational development decision rights.

tion issues rather than external alignment. Figure 6.6 depicts decision rights at each OD level.

AN INVITATION TO THE TABLE

There are a number of ways to get invited to the strategic table. The most obvious is to understand and help leaders align the internal culture with the external environment. Culture change has long been a core competency of OD. However, we've traditionally advocated such changes in order to make the organization more collaborative or humanistic according to ODs core values. However, culture change should not be undertaken just for the sake of embedding values. Values are a means of achieving an end, not the end itself. Culture change, like any other OD intervention, should be undertaken in order to bring the internal environment in congruence with external business drivers.

Although strategic planning processes may differ from company to company, most use the rational model (Figure 6.7). The rational model begins with a scan of the external environment (competition, industry conditions, political and regulatory guidelines, etc.). Once the organization has a good understanding of the environment they must operate in, the next step is to scan the internal environment to assess cultural alignment. This can be accomplished by performing a cultural assessment to uncover dimensions, (i.e., leadership, collaboration, and decision-making) that may be at odds with the strategic orientation of the firm. Rather than embedding values solely for the sake of creating a more humanistic

Strategy Shaping External Factors

(Opportunities and Threats)

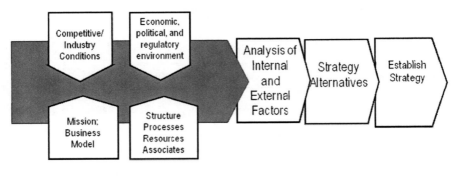

Figure 6.7.   Rational strategic planning model.

corporation, values along with other cultural drivers are aligned with the strategy. A culture assessment gives leaders quantifiable characteristics of the culture that is directly linked with organizational success. Once those characteristics are identified, the culture can be analyzed comparatively with the strategy and strategic culture change alternatives can be agreed upon.

Understanding culture and how it works is an important strategic competency for OD. It is important because strategic decisions can have unintended consequences if leaders do not understand the company's culture. Decisions are products of the culture in which they are made. No matter how well intentioned, decisions can be corrupted by a dysfunctional culture. Additionally, with companies becoming ever larger, culture change is a key part of the merger/acquisition process. It allows leaders of both organizations to make strategic decisions to separate, dominate, or blend the two cultures involved.

Culture is also important when managing a company's lifecycle (Table 6.1). In start-up companies, the culture reflects the company's founder (Schein, 1999). Companies like Disney, HP, and Apple are classic examples. However, in an organization's mid-life, cultural dynamics begin to change. The company's leaders must now maintain elements of the culture that continue to be successful, while eliminating those that do not. They must align various subcultures around a corporate strategy and

Table 6.1. Organizational Life-Cycle

Start-Ups	Mid-Life	Mature Companies
• Culture reflects the founder's beliefs	• Maintain those cultural elements that have been successful • Align subcultures • Change dysfunctional elements	• Cultural transformation

Source: Adapted from Schein (1999).

Table 6.2. How Leaders Shape Culture

Tactics Leaders Use to Shape Culture	OD Competency
• What they pay attention to, measure, and control	• Mission, vision, values development/goals
• How they react to critical incidents	• Collaboration/communication
• Role modeling, teaching, coaching	• Process consultation
• How people are recruited, selected, rewarded, and retired	• Succession planning •
• Organization design and structure	• Restructuring

change dysfunctional characteristics. This is clearly where OD can play a key strategic role.

It is also important to note that many of the tactics leaders use to embed culture are traditional OD competencies (Table 6.2). However, in order to become strategic, we must be mindful of the context. These competencies must be leveraged to drive strategy and not solely to create a utopian-like environment.

DEVELOPING AN OD STRATEGY

Just as organizational leaders develop the business strategy, practitioners must proactively develop a parallel OD strategy that supports the business. For instance, if the organization employs the rational model for strategic planning, organization development practitioners should use a similar model to develop a comprehensive OD strategy (Figure 6.8).

The OD strategy begins with an external scan, just like the business strategy. However, since the OD function is embedded within the busi-

Strategic OD Drivers

(Opportunities/Threats)

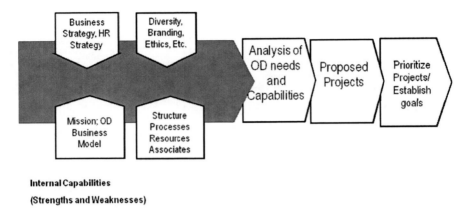

Business
Strategy, HR
Strategy

Diversity,
Branding,
Ethics, Etc.

Analysis of
OD needs
and
Capabilities

Proposed
Projects

Prioritize
Projects/
Establish
goals

Mission; OD
Business
Model

Structure
Processes
Resources
Associates

Internal Capabilities

(Strengths and Weaknesses)

Figure 6.8.   Strategic planning process for organization development.

ness, an external scan would look slightly different. An external scan for OD would involve examining the business (outside of OD) to derive OD implications related to the business. Such implications could involve interventions like diversity and inclusion, corporate identity (branding), launching key product teams, and identifying important links to the human resources strategy.

Strategic OD may also involve teambuilding, conflict resolution, goal setting and other OD interventions that may at first seem tactical. However, if the launch of a major product requires fast and efficient team launches, conflict is interfering with the effective implementation of the strategy, or goals are not aligned with the organizational strategy, these seemingly tactical interventions may be part of a larger strategy and directly impact organizational success. They would be strategic because they are ultimately linked with the success of the company.

In summary, organization development requires a long-term focus and commitment by organizational leaders. Its purpose is to help organizations become more efficient and effective (Cummings & Worley, 2005). By its very nature, it is strategic. However, it is OD practitioners who must become strategic partners. They must link their activities to the very success of the company. They have to help organizations deal with today's complex survival issues; otherwise, OD may have survival issues of its own.

REFERENCES

Beckhard, R. (1969). *Organization development: strategies and models.* Reading, MA: Addison-Wesley.

Burke, W. W. (1982). *Organization development principles and practices.* Glenview, IL: Scott, Foresman and Company.

Cummings, T. G., & Worley, C. G. (2005). *Organization development & change.* Mason, OH: South-Western.

Church, A. H., Burke, W. W., & Van Eynde, D. F. (1994). Values, motives, and interventions of organization development practitioners. *Group & Organization Management, 19*(1), 5-50.

Church, A. H., Hurley, R. F., & Burke, W. W. (1992). Evolution or revolution in the values of organization development: Commentary on the state of the field. *Journal of Organization Change Management, 5*(4), 6-23.

Greiner, L. E. (1980). OD values and the bottom line. In W. W. Burke & L. Goodstein (Eds.), *Trends and issues in OD: Current theory and practice* (pp. 319-332). San Diego, CA: University Associates.

Harrison, J. S., & St. John, C. H. (2004). *Foundations of strategic management.* Mason, OH: Thompson-Southwestern.

Hatch, M. J. (1997). *Organization theory: Modern, symbolic and postmodern perspectives.* Oxford, England: Oxford University Press

Ireland, D. R., Hoskisson, R. E., & Hitt, M. A. (2006). *Understanding business strategy.* Mason, OH: Thompson-Southwestern.

Jelinek, M., & Litterer, J. A. (1988). Why OD must become more strategic. *Research in Organizational Change and Development, 2,* 135-162.

Kates, A., (2007). Redesigning the HR organization. *Human Resource Planning Quarterly, 29*(2), 22-30.

Margulies, N., & Raia, A. (1990). The significance of core values on the theory and practice of organization development. In F. Massarik (Ed.), *Advances in organization development* (Vol. 1, pp. 27-41). Norwood, NJ: Ablex.

Sashkin, M., & Burke, W. W. (1990). Organization development in the 1980s. In F. Massarik (Ed.), *Advances in organization development* (Vol. 1, pp. 393-417). Norwood, NJ: Ablex.

Schein, E.H. (2004). *Organizational culture and leadership.* San Francisco: Jossey-Bass.

Sun Tzu. (2009). *The art of war.* London: Arcturus.

Ulrich, D. (1997). *Human resource champions.* Boston: Harvard Business School Press.

CHAPTER 7

GETTING STRATEGY TO WORK

Achieving Strategic Effectiveness in Practice

Mark Holst-Mikkelsen and Flemming Poulfelt

Faced with intensified competition, turbulence and changes, companies choose various ways to improve their capacity to meet the expectations from different stakeholders. This can take place through changes in the organizational structure, acquisitions and spin-offs where management apparently proves their determination and ability to execute. In many occasions these decisions are combined with a number of initiatives meant to improve the strategic performance of the organization. This can be the introduction of advanced forecasting and market simulation tools, the implementation of a balanced scorecard, or maybe the establishment of a business development department whose purpose will be to support the implementation of the strategic plan and to take the necessary initiatives to ensure a favorable future for the company.

These actions can in many ways be right, but unfortunately they frequently shift focus away from getting a deeper understanding of the organizational dynamics that express the organization's ability to realize its strategic goals fast and effectively. This is supported by a recent survey conducted by McKinsey (Miranda & Thief, 2007) in which 80% of the

Strategic Organization Development: Managing Change for Success
pp. 115–127

respondents did consider their approach to strategy as ineffective and where 44% said that their strategy plans are not being sufficiently implemented.

The question therefore remains if the efforts of working with strategy in practice have the necessary impact on the business and the performance of a company. To be more precise: What are the benefits for a company when management develops and decides upon new strategies but is unable to implement these strategies within the rest of the organization? How to deal with and solve this Gordian knot is the focus for the remaining part of this chapter under the heading "Strategic Effectiveness."

STRATEGIC EFFECTIVENESS?

The effectiveness of an organization can be defined as its ability to create acceptable outcomes and actions. It is important to avoid confusing organizational effectiveness with organizational efficiency, and the difference is well illustrated by an example (Pfeffer & Salancik, 2003, p. 12):

> In the late 60s, Governor Ronald Reagan of California curtailed the amount of money going to the state university system. He was concerned that state university campuses, particularly Berkeley, were indoctrinating students in radical, left-wing ideas. In response to these political pressures and to forestall further budget cuts, the administrators attempted to demonstrate that they were educating students at an ever lower cost per student. Not surprisingly, this argument had little impact on the governor; indeed, it missed the point of his criticism. Producing revolutionaries at lower cost was not what the governor wanted; rather, he questioned whether the universities produced anything that justified giving them state funds.

Organizational efficiency is an internal standard of performance, basically defined as the output per unit of the input (Pfeffer, 2003). In the example with Reagan and Berkeley the internal standard of performance was "cost per student." Normally efficiency is relatively value free in the sense that it asks how much is produced and at what costs, but the nature of the output is not considered in the efficiency equation. However, efficiency is nowadays a valued social ideal, and thereby efficiency can sometimes be defined as a strategic goal in itself and thereby lose its "value free" character.

When people (like Reagan) consider *what* is being measured or produced they are concerned with effectiveness rather than efficiency. Therefore effectiveness is not to be considered value free, since effectiveness is assessed by each evaluator in accordance with his or her own preferences. That makes organizational effectiveness an external standard of how well an organization is meeting the demands of the various groups and organizations that are concerned with its activities.

When people engage in developing a new strategy, they are concerned with the market position, the company's products and services, the customers, the processes, and the competencies. When discussing these issues, decisions are made in relation to what products and services to offer, to which customer segments they should be offered, and how the products and services should be delivered to the customers. These decisions, which we call "strategic decisions," express the core of the organization's strategy, and they are taken with the clear purpose of meeting the demands and expectations of the people involved in the creation of the strategy. Strategic effectiveness can therefore be defined as: *An organization's ability to implement its strategy and translate it into the expected performance.* With this definition in mind we will now look deeper into how strategic effectiveness can be achieved.

HOW TO ACHIEVE STRATEGIC EFFECTIVENESS

The first step toward the strategic effective organization is to create an understanding of the organizational dynamics that express the organization's ability to implement its strategy and translate it into the expected performance. Our research on strategic effectiveness has identified three factors that are in particular critical across industries and size when it comes to companies' ability to increase their strategic effectiveness (Holst-Mikkelsen, 2007):

1. The strategy must *make sense* to the members of the organization. This means that the strategy should be perceived as appropriate, rational and necessary according to the situation the company is facing.
2. There must be *commitment* to the strategy. This means that the members of the organization must have the will and desire to work for realizing the strategy and feel a personal commitment to it. It also implies that the members must be ready to take on new tasks as well as give up others in order to realize the strategy.
3. There must be the necessary energy and *execution ability* in the organization. This means that the members of the organization must have the necessary time and energy to contribute to the realization of the strategy and they must feel themselves capable of doing it. Actually putting the plans into effect is also part of having the ability to execute.

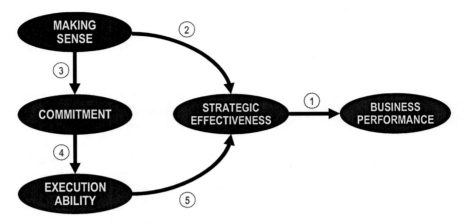

Notes: 1. The figure has been developed by the use of advanced quantitative (multivariate) techniques in a Scandinavian research project involving more than 3,300 people in 60 companies representing sales of about $20 billion and more than 40,000 employees. 2. Business results have been measured as a combination of the development on several criteria: position in market, sales, costs, EBIT, customer results, employee results, and efficiency in internal processes.

Figure 7.1.   A framework for strategic effectiveness.

"Making sense," "commitment," and "execution ability" contribute each in its own way to achieve strategic effectiveness and create business performance. This is illustrated in Figure 7.1.

The figure illustrates that strategic effectiveness has a direct impact on the business performance of a company (1). Furthermore, if a strategy makes sense to the members of an organization, it will have a direct impact on the organization's strategic effectiveness (2) and on the commitment to the strategy (3). Commitment has an impact on the execution ability in the organization (4), but commitment does not have a direct impact on the strategic effectiveness. Furthermore, if a company improves its execution ability it will have a direct impact on its strategic effectiveness (5).

Making Sense

"What are you doing here?" When the employees of a large Scandinavian IT company began working on a sunny day in August 2004, they were met with a sign on their desks with this particular question. The newly appointed chief executive (CEO) had decided to provoke all employees and invite them on a journey over the following three years. He wanted people to participate in the sense making process and along the way make them decide about their own role in the company's future. He did not want people working in the company without the necessary dedication to the company's strategy. That was in fact a risky action in a market with a high demand for people with the skills of his employees. Fortunately for the new CEO and the company, only very few people decided to quit their jobs, and the remaining felt compelled to participate with high enthusiasm.

In a chaotic world the manager plays a central role as "sense maker" (Thayer, 1988) but when it comes to developing a strategy one cannot be sure that a "master code" of a certain nature exists or that the key to the meaningful follows a certain logic (Weick, 2001). When trying to make the world make sense under these conditions people must therefore look for a form of order without being sure that such even exists. They must also decide how to represent this order and they much accept that they never will know if they have found a uniting order (Weick, 2001). There is rarely one true picture that fits to a predefined reality.

Furthermore, people have the need to explain their behavior in a way that makes sense and lies within some acceptable boundaries (Salancik & Pfeffer, 1978). This means that when people do something on a small scale you often do not have to justify it to a very large extent. But as the actions gradually become more important, people automatically seek to justify them in relation to a common purpose or goal. When this need arises in an organization there will often be a need to devote time to a dialogue where new issues get interpreted in relation to the existing mindset. In a strategy process this often takes place in strategy workshops or seminars, where the social interaction between the participants also plays an important role in the sense making process.

The social interactions as well as the interpretation process contributes significantly to making actions meaningful (Weick, 2001) but in practice it is often only management who takes part in the strategic dialogue on strategy workshops and seminars. In return, employees are informed through top management's presentation on a kick-off meeting, through a presentation of their own managers in a department meeting, and through articles on the intranet, handouts, or a DVD movie. The problem is that this is far from sufficient and does not take into account that there are different needs at different levels of the organization.

Commitment

Anyone who has seen Steve Balmer, the CEO at Microsoft, express his dedication for the company can see that he is strongly dedicated the company he is working for.

Our research shows that when people put their hearts and souls into realizing a strategy, it has better chances of becoming a success. More modestly, a personal interest and a will to contribute to realizing the strategy amongst employees is also a valuable asset for managers who aspire for better results. Committed and enthusiastic people are also much more likely to make other people feel the same way. Therefore, it can be a good idea to appoint a number of strategy ambassadors and ask them to communicate the strategy to all the other employees. That is what candidates running for a presidency are doing, and it is also what companies are using actively in order to outmaneuver competitors and achieve success with their new strategies. A typical strategy process therefore places a natural focus on creating commitment among the people involved, not least with the hope that they afterwards are able to pass on their commitment to the rest of the organization.

The concept of commitment can be related to basic motivational theories such as Hertberg's motivation-hygiene theory (Hertberg, 1968). People's commitment to a strategy can grow from "satisfiers" such as greater responsibility, recognition or interesting work assignments. This is under the assumption that "hygiene factors" such as job security, pay-level, relation to colleagues, etc., are satisfied. In addition, participation in the strategic work can contribute to a form of self-realization due to greater personal prestige in the organization, recognition, respect from colleagues, or promotion, and so on.

The importance of commitment is further emphasized by Pascale, who argues that commitment to a vision among people is more important than if a well-thought through strategy plan has been made (Pascale, 1984). This is due to the fact that concentration and passionate dedication is necessary in order to develop specific competencies and success (Miller, 1983).

Execution

When an F-16 pilot flies at the speed of 1,200 miles an hour, it is essential that he feels confident regarding his capabilities towards the mission. He needs to own clarity upon decision making, and he also needs to know that there exists sufficient support and backup throughout his entire flight from takeoff to landing.

The classical approach to execution is expressed by a formal written plan with a clear description of roles, tasks, responsibilities and deadlines. With this in place the next step is on the implementation followed by a continuous monitoring and control of the activities and the results (Johnson, 2004).

Bossidy and Charan focus on how the individual managers can contribute to a more effective organization. According to them, the discipline of execution has to do with how a manager can align people, strategy, and operations, i.e., the three core processes of every business (Bossidy & Charan, 2002). In their quest for execution they focus on these core processes instead of formulating a "vision" and leave the work of carrying it out to others. With the right people in the right jobs, the idea is that a leadership gene pool will conceive and select strategies that can be executed. People will then work together to create a strategy in line with the realities of the marketplace, the economy, and the competition. Once the right people and strategy are in place, they are then linked to an operating process that results in the implementation of specific programs and actions and that assigns accountability.

For Covey, personal effectiveness lies in the balance between a person's ability to produce the desired results and his production capability, i.e., the ability or asset that produces the results. If a person only focuses on the results ("the golden eggs") instead of what produces the results ("the goose"), he will eventually end up without the capability to produce the results (Covey, 1990).

Apart from the role that a manager can play in an organization's ability to execute, there are a number of "organizational dynamics" that can also play a significant role. These dynamics can for instance be the relations between the individuals, the organizational processes, the systems and tools used in the organization, and the organizational structure.

DRIVERS FOR STRATEGIC EFFECTIVENESS

On that basis we have identified a number of potential drivers for strategic effectiveness, illustrated in Figure 7.2.

Our research has shown that there are different drivers for strategic effectiveness according to the different organizational levels, that is, employees, middle managers, and top management. In the following, some of the most important drivers will be mentioned. These drivers have proven to have a significant impact in a Scandinavian context across many companies and industries. The focus will be on the drivers that strategy practitioners in general should not forget to add when designing and facilitating a strategy process. Apart from the drivers mentioned below there will always be some supplementary drivers in the individual company due to its special situation.

Figure 7.2.   Drivers for strategic effectiveness.

Drivers for Strategic Effectiveness Among Employees

In order to get a strategy to make sense to employees, there must be a good *understanding of the strategy.* That includes an understanding of the content of and the background for the strategy, and also its additional choices, rejections etc. According to Norton & Kaplan that is not at all easy, since 95% of all employees are not conscious of or do not understand the company's strategy (Kaplan & Norton, 2005). This is a strong indication that the communication efforts in many companies in relation to the strategy do not have the desired impact.

The most important driver for strategic effectiveness among employees, however, is that every employee understands his or her *personal role in the strategy* and perceives it as important in the big picture. This includes that employees must be able to see how their competencies will be used and utilized while realizing the strategy, and they should experience that their future work situation gets better than the present if the strategy is realized. This driver has a direct impact on making sense, commitment," and execution ability.

Another important driver for strategic effectiveness among employees is to what extent the strategy builds upon the *core competencies* of the company, for example, what the company is already good at and has had success with. If it does, the strategy makes more sense to the employees and it also affects their ability to execute on the strategy. A focus on core competencies as proposed by Prahalad and Hamel is therefore important to the employees (Hamel & Prahalad, 1996). Therefore, a company pursuing a disruptive strategy (Andersen & Poulfelt, 2006) with radical changes should be very carefully articulated and communicated in order to ensure that the strategy makes sense amongst employees.

Drivers for Strategic Effectiveness Among Middle Managers

For middle managers—as well as employees—an *understanding of the strategy* and their *personal role in the strategy* are important elements in relation to making sense of the strategy. In addition, the strategy can be made more meaningful for middle managers if they experience an *alignment in the organization*. The middle managers are in fact the ones, who must work across the organization with other middle managers. Therefore, it appears to be important that the strategic initiatives support the strategy and that the activities are coordinated effectively across the different areas and departments. In reality however, many middle managers are only superficially informed of the many new strategic initiatives and this is far from sufficient to provide a feeling of consistency throughout the activities across the organization.

In general, companies spend a lot of resources trying to make employees as satisfied, loyal and committed as possible. An assumption behind this resource allocation is that employees that are *"company man/woman"* are more likely to feel commitment to the company's strategy. However, the only group we have been able to prove this causal relationship with is middle managers. So the many resources invested in employee satisfaction, loyalty and commitment may not always support the defined strategy.

The research proved that if a strategy makes sense, there is not necessarily commitment to the strategy among middle managers. A possible explanation is that many companies do not include this group seriously in the ongoing dialogue in relation to the strategy. This happens, for example, if middle managers are only briefed about the new strategy or receive a Power Point presentation in the mailbox and instructions to present it to the employees. By not giving this group the opportunity to interact with other managers and especially top management in relation to the strategy, they will not feel the same need for seeking common goals and a way to justify the interaction (Weick, 1979). Based on this, it can be a problem if companies fail to include middle management in the strategic dialogue, since this can lead to lower strategic effectiveness.

In order to increase the execution ability among middle managers, it is very important to make sure that there is the necessary time, money, and work force in the organization to realize the strategy. In relation to this, there must be established an understanding amongst middle management regarding how the resources are to be prioritized with respect to the strategy.

Drivers for Strategic Effectiveness Among Top Managers

Top managers share some of the same drivers for strategic effectiveness as people on lower organizational levels. Thus, top management has a strong need to understand company strategy, and they also need to have a clear understanding of their own personal role in this strategy.

What is special about top management is that they also have a strong need to take part in the decision making process, and it is imperative to be personally involved in the strategy process of the company. This is rarely a problem since top managers typically have the authority to design the strategy process as they wish themselves. The problem, on the other hand, arises when top managers are not conscious of the needs of the remaining groups of employees—and as a consequence does not design a strategy process to match those needs.

Through our research we have observed that many top managers spend a great amount of time and energy on creating coherence in their strategic statements. We have also observed how many top managers take a lot of pride in putting action behind the words as well as taking the necessary consequences if the agreed upon efforts in the strategy are not realized. Therefore, it was expected that these conditions would have an impact on the employees' commitment to the strategy. However, when it comes to creating commitment to realizing the strategy, the perception of top management only plays a significant role for top management itself. In other words: if top management's own perception of their own appearance is positive, top management will feel a stronger commitment to realizing the strategy. But the one-hour speech to the rest of the organization every half-year does not necessarily make any significant difference for the remaining approximately 1,600 work hours of the year.

As it is the case for middle managers, resource allocation is also important for top managers. There has to be the necessary time, money, and work force to realize the strategy in order to create the necessary execution ability.

MANAGERIAL CHALLENGES

Achieving strategy implementation and by this, strengthening value creation still proves to be a major task in the corporate world. Although many companies today have improved their strategic capabilities and enhanced the way strategy is being developed and executed, there is still room for improvement.

From our analysis of strategy work in a Scandinavian context, there is support for this view. The strategic development is being allocated more focus, time and resources. Top management, that is, the board of directors and the CEO and his (or her) management team are giving strategy work more attention, time and commitment. Based upon our research it appears that top management is facing three primary challenges when striving for achieving an improved strategic effectiveness:

Communication

Communication is an important vehicle for disseminating the strategy. This was illustrated by a CEO who did express his managerial recipe in the following way: "It consists of three items: Communication, communication and communication." Our research showed that a good understanding of the strategy is not sufficient. People at all organizational levels need to know their personal role in the strategy and feel it is important. Practice shows that to succeed in strategy communication, organizations have to user other channels of communication than the traditional ones.

Coherence

Many managers are aware that coherence is an important issue in the strategy process. Practice however shows it can be difficult to ensure coherence between the actual activities in a strategy process and the three critical factors for strategic effectiveness: making sense, commitment, and execution ability. For instance, a global Scandinavian production company involved 100 employees (none of them managers) over a three-month period in the strategy development process, and their proposals were more or less approved by top management. However, the managers who were supposed to implement the strategic initiatives did not perceive the strategy as meaningful and did not see the need for it. Half a year after the commitment to the strategy, the 100 employees were reduced to half, and the implementation process had more or less stalled. Millions of dollars had been wasted, and the economic potential related to the strategy was slipping away.

Consistency

Managers are not only being measured for what they achieve. They are also being measured for what they articulate, for what they inform the organization about and for how they behave. In a strategic context this is not different. Therefore, it's extremely important that there is consistency between the strategic messages the managers try to convey to the organization about direction and focus of the company and the actions taken. According to the conceptual framework of Argyris and Schön (1974) the strategy plans can be perceived as the "espoused theories" of the company. However, in the daily life of the organization, managers execute according to their "theories in use." From a strategic effectiveness point of view it is important that there is a fit between the plans and the practice. This means that if the strategy plan is being revised because of an acquisition, a change in the competitive landscape or the replacement of top managers, it is critical to communicate about these changes to the organization in order to ensure that strategy is still making sense. Consistency therefore is critical for companies striving to accelerate strategic effectiveness.

Strategy development has a top priority on the managerial agenda in many companies. We believe that strategy execution and hence achieving an increasing strategic effectiveness will have at least the same attention throughout the coming years. By this, strategy work will also embrace key issues involved in organizational development.

REFERENCES

Andersen, M. M., & Poulfelt, F. (2006). *Discount business strategy. How the new market leaders are redefining business strategy.* New York: Wiley

Argyris, C., & Schön, D. A. (1974). *Theory in practice: Increasing professional effectiveness.* San Francisco: Jossey-Bass.

Bossidy, L., & Charan, R. (2002). Execution: The discipline of getting things done. New York: Crown Business.

Covey, S. R. (1990). *The 7 habits of highly effective people.* New York: Simon & Schuster.

Hamel, G., & Prahalad, C. K. (1996). *Competing for the future.* Boston: Harvard Business School Press.

Herzberg, F. (2003, January). One more time: How do you motivate employees. *Harvard Business Review, 81*(1), 86.

Holst-Mikkelsen, M. (2007, May). *Strategisk effektivitet* [Strategic efficiency]. Paper presented at Danish Academy of Management, Copenhagen.

Johnson, L. K. (2004). Execute your strategy—Without killing it. *Harvard Management Update, 9*(12), 3-5.

Kaplan, R. S., & Norton, D. P. (2005, October). The Office of Strategy Management. *Harvard Business Review, 83*(10), 72-80.

Miranda, G. M. -L. & Thief, K. (2007). Improving organizational speed and agility. *McKinsey Quarterly, 1*, 14.

Pascale, R. (1984). Perspectives on strategy. The real reason behind Honda's success. *California Management Review, 26*(3), 47-72.

Pfeffer, J., & Salancik, G., R. (2003). External control of organizations: A resource dependence perspective. Palo Alto, CA: Stanford University Press.

Salancik, G. R., & Pfeffer, J. (1978). A social information processing approach to job attitudes and test design. *Administrative Science Quarterly, 23*, 224-253.

Thayer, L. (1988). Leadership/communication: A critical review and a modest proposal. In G. M. Goldhaber & G. A. Barnett (Eds.), *Handbook of organizational communication* (pp. 231-263). Norwood, NJ: Ablex.

Weick, K. E. (2001). *Making sense of the organization.* Oxford, England: Blackwell Business.

Weick, K. E. (1979). *The social psychology of organizing.* New York: McGraw-Hill.

PART III

BUILDING AND IMPLEMENTING STRATEGY

CHAPTER 8

STRATEGIC HUMAN RESOURCES AND ORGANIZATION DEVELOPMENT

Managing Change for Success

Jim Dunn

Should we do away with traditional human resources (HR)? In recent years, a number of people who study and write about business—along with many Fortune 500 senior executives—have debated that question. The debate arises out of serious and widespread doubts about the human resource function's contribution to organizational performance. Renowned researcher David Ulrich states "as much as I like HR people, I have been working in the field as a researcher, professor, and consultant for 20 years, but must agree that there is good reason for HR's beleaguered reputation" (Ulrich, 1997, p. 23).

While research over the last 5 years shows that human resources has been at the proverbial crossroads, between demonstrating strategic value and providing traditional HR services, the field of organization develop-

Strategic Organization Development: Managing Change for Success
pp. 131–141
Copyright © 2009 by Information Age Publishing
All rights of reproduction in any form reserved.

ment (OD) shares a similar and not too different story. Some have even argued that the growing frustrations by HR functions will likely consume OD in their quest for being perceived as strategic business partners within organizations. Is all this true? Are both fields experiencing a similar crisis that could potentially impact its long-term existence as we know it?

Some OD historians have argued that OD was created in response to the events following World War II, and it is therefore only fitting that the principles of OD be applied to provide the strategic direction of other fields in current crisis mode, like human resources. This article highlights the current literature around the evolution of the human resources field and the growing imperative of creating strategic HR operations. Specifically, this chapter suggests that the unique skills of OD practitioners in building organizational capability and demonstrating a measurable impact on workforce productivity are emerging as a primary focus of HR organizations. The practical implications of this partnership, as explored through the lens of senior executives in the fields of HR and OD executives, provides relevance for further study in this area.

WHAT'S WRONG WITH TRADITIONAL HR MANAGEMENT?

The evolution of the HR management field, once called "Personnel," has followed the history of business in the United States (Hankin, 2005). As the Industrial Revolution swept the United States in the nineteenth century, rapidly growing organizations forced three major people-related challenges: (1) managing sudden and massive increases in the workforce stemming from industrialization, (2) fighting workforce unionization, and (3) integrating the huge influx of immigrant workers into U.S. workplaces (York, 2005).

From the dawn of the Industrial Revolution in the United States until about 1950, the personnel department's role in most organizations centered around administrative duties. Personnel directors headed up a record-keeping function that included such activities as disciplinary systems, recruitment, safety programs, time and motion studies, and union relations. Senior managers expected that these personnel activities would maintain employee morale and enhance cooperation within their organizations.

From the 1940s into the 1950s, personnel departments emphasized their role in meeting employee needs to achieve economic security. Unions, during this time, were responsible for negotiating wages and such employee benefits as pension plans and health care insurance. Corporate personnel departments were founded in the late 1950s to coordinate across such increasingly specialized functions as benefits, wages, recruitment, and labor relations (Holbeche, 2005). During that time the evolution of functionally specific personnel departments took shape.

The business and social dynamics of the 1960s and 1970s brought increased attention to human relations within the personnel department. Human relations emphasized supervisory training, which often included role playing and sensitivity training, and participative management techniques that included management by objectives and Quality Circles. As one consequence of focusing on human relations, personnel departments were eventually handed responsibility for training and development and for management of reward systems, performance management systems, and succession-planning programs (Rothwell, 1998). At the same time, personnel departments also assumed responsibilities to help their organizations meet new challenges stemming from increasing government laws, rules, and regulations affecting (among other areas) equal employment opportunity, occupational safety and health, and employee benefits.

The transformation of personnel management to HR management was affected by a parallel trend: the emergence of the human resource development (HRD) field from the training and development field. Human resource development, a term coined by Leonard Nadler (York, 2005), prompted a fresh look at the importance of developing people and forced a reconceptualization of how that is done by introducing a conceptual umbrella covering employee training, education, and development (Ulrich, 1997). The shift taking place in HR management, apparent in the early 1980s, may have resulted from the convergence of traditional personnel specialists with HRD practitioners (Bechet, 2002). At this point "personnel" officially became "HR management" to reflect its emphasis on employees as valued organizational resources.

In most organizations today, the HR function provides essential services to such stakeholders as job applicants, employees, supervisors, middle managers, and executives. However, the HR function tends to be positioned at the end of the business chain, on the reactive side, and too often focuses on carrying out activities rather than achieving results (Sullivan, 2004). The role of the HR function is often one of providing people, training, and isolated HR efforts after others have formulated organizational strategy and have initiated operational implementation.

Since the 1990s, HR practitioners have been driven by events in their organizations to direct attention to such issues as downsizing, outplacement, retraining, diversity, employee rights, technological effects on people, and recruitment of skilled talent in a time of labor shortages and record employment (Porras, 1991). Cost-focused management of employee benefits programs such as health insurance, workers' compensation, and pension plans has also figured prominently in an effort to control skyrocketing expenses (Rothwell, 1998). Among other HR issues of interest at present are alternatives to litigation, diversity management, the Employee Retirement Income Security Act (ERISA), family and medial leave issues, employee handbooks, policies and procedures around employee privacy, sexual harassment avoidance, talent acquisition and development, and applicant tracking procedures.

Building organizational capability is emerging as a primary focus of HR organizations (Holbeche, 2005). Organizational capability, defined in simplest terms, is linked to the "things organizations need to do as an entity to act on their strategies" (Ulrich & Brockbank, 2005, p. 473). First those capabilities must be identified, developed, and then measured by comparing current workforce performance to business goals. The key to this performance rests in the hands of people. Never before have HR practitioners been challenged to do so much, Ironically, these demands are being made at a time when many HR functions have lost staff members in recent down or "right-sizing" efforts. The HR function is also required, more than ever before, to align and integrate its efforts with the strategic goals of the enterprise.

WHAT IS STRATEGIC HUMAN RESOURCES?

The term strategy comes from the Greek word *strategos* and is loosely translated to mean *art of the general* (Collis, 2005). Strategy has become so important because "being strategic" means having an impact on the things that are the most important to an organization: the corporate goals and objectives (Sullivan, 2004). Although "strategic" is a commonly used word in HR, there is little agreement about what "being strategic" actually means in practice. That same level of confusion, however, does not exist in other business areas like marketing, product development and supply chain. For example, finance and accounting both deal with numbers and dollars, but finance is considered a strategic function, while accounting generally is not. The primary difference between the two is that accounting focuses on providing reports describing what happened last year, while finance focuses on the future and on increasing profit. Could a potential partnership of HR and OD liken itself to the accounting and finance disciplines with HR as the technical arm (employee relations, benefits administration, recruitment/selection, etc.) and OD providing the strategic impact for building organizational capability? Huselid, Jackson, and Schuler (1997) concluded that technical HR practices, alone, are inadequate as a means of differentiating organizations from their competitors. They also believe that technical HR practices are therefore needed to support effective strategic HR.

WHAT'S WRONG WITH TRADITIONAL OD?

As the field of OD is more than 50 years old, many articles have been written to evaluate its earliest values, philosophy and methods of practice. While not termed OD, elements of OD work began during the 1930s when it was noticed that the productivity of organizations increased due to an increased focus on the "human side of what motivated employees." (Sorensen, 2006). Despite this apparent rise in productivity, post-World War II activities brought about a decrease in such productivity due to an increase in technology. From that point, we witnessed a growing number of "cohesive groups" that rose in protest against the new increase in American technology. OD principles became an often sought approach to addressing the challenges of increased worker productivity and increased technology.

Often termed the human relations movement, the 1940s brought about a focus of research that challenged conventional approaches to management in the United States. Perhaps the best way to indicate why the conventional approaches of management became inadequate is to consider the subject of motivation (McGregor, 1957). Could employees be motivated to provide certain results? Or if left alone, would the very "human side" of individuals produce increased results. These questions and others led to a fundamental research area that explored managerial assumptions and its impact on reactive behaviors of workers.

A host of activities contributed to the field of OD from the 1950s to the 1980s, one of the most significant being the quality movement, whereby the overall quality of U.S. products and services were thought to be significantly behind those of Japan and other countries. The building of effective work teams, often termed work groups or team-building, became critical to the OD profession during this period. A most elaborate spin-off on action research, survey data feedback, was also equally instrumental during this period (Weisbord, 2004).

Because uncertainty threatens organizational survival and reduces its effectiveness, OD as a field has been credited with assisting organizations in developing effective strategies for reducing organizational uncertainty. Two internal strategies of particular concern to the OD practitioner involve assisting organizations with (1) changing the organizational structure as the environment becomes complex and (2) planning and forecasting efforts to create contingency plans aimed at helping organizations adapt to their changing environment.

In more recent years, OD has had many different definitions and conceptualizations (Jamieson & Worley, 2006), yet most share the same commonalities and only seem to differ on the scope of change targets and the ultimate intention of change. Jamieson and Worley (2006) highlight the following common characteristics of most OD efforts:

- A planned process intended to bring about change;
- Through the use of various interventions;
- Using behavioral science knowledge (theory, research, technology);
- Having an organization or systemwide focus; and
- Typically involving a third-party change agent.

One thing OD has brought to the management and change of organizations is a stronger focus on the values that were operating in managing, interviewing and changing organizations (Jamieson & Worley, 2006). Additional research show that OD has had a positive impact on organizations relative to the use of data to guide decisions, involvement and participation of people in decisions that affected them, more effective conflict management, use of teams and team building, and the importance of climate and culture issues. Jamieson and Worley also believe the most important evolution in the practice of OD has been "the integration of strategy and organization design with behavioral science" (p. 32).

Despite recent criticisms, many believe the current state of the OD field to be healthy, in large part, due to the fact that organizations and their environments remain in a constant state of change. According to Burke (2002), "OD has given us a systematic approach to organization change with its emphasis on the total system, clear steps and phases of organization change, and an underlying set of humanistic values to guide the entire process" (p. 88), yet despite the huge accomplishments of OD, to remain effective and relevant, organization development must reinvent itself by developing more comprehensive theories, methods and practices (Katz & Marshak, 1995).

HRD AND ORGANIZATION DEVELOPMENT

Earlier we mentioned the significance of the HRD function in transforming the field from "personnel" to "human resources." This transformation also had an important impact on the practice and ownership of OD skills in organizations.

Grieves and Redman (1999) have described human resource development as "searching for identity while living in the shadow of OD" (p. 92). In their view, HRD became the organization strategy for aligning the organizational objectives of knowledge-centered companies with the competencies and capabilities of their employees. Accomplishing this alignment, of course, required using methods pioneered in OD practice such as team building, survey feedback, and structural design. Many HR and OD practitioners alike believe this to be the cross-point of HR and OD. But were there any distinct differences in approaches between the two worlds of HRD and OD? Let's look at how York (2005) examines the functions of HRD and OD:

> The social system is the entry point for discussions about interventions for the OD professional; for the HRD professional the entry point is often the learning and development needs of individuals. These two different entry points reflect the historical differences between the two disciplines. OD has its roots in the applied behavioral and social sciences; HRD, in the practice of training and development. The paradigmatic values of OD have been humanistic psychology; HRD's paradigmatic values rest in behaviorism, human capital theory, and performance engineering. (p. 101)

HR AND OD PARTNERSHIP: IS IT NEEDED?

Stuart (1992) writes that "the changing business environment is redefining the role of human resources (HR) professionals. HR executives are increasingly being called upon to team up with business managers and to take a more active role in strategy development and organizational design" (p. 86). Sullivan (2004) states that "one of the most drastic changes in the requirements of the HR professional, in recent years has been the increasing need for the top person in the function to see the business perspective. This business dimension has grown in importance in the last 10 to 15 years" (p. 118). During a recent lunch meeting with a new vice president of OD and Strategy for a Fortune 100 firm in Atlanta, Georgia, I was told that he was hired by the firm because none of the existing employees, in either the HR or OD departments were perceived to have a handle on the numbers. The firm found his early background in finance and economics, albeit 15 years prior, to be more aligned with their expectations for a leader in this area.

In an effort of providing a balanced perspective, I would be remiss by not acknowledging that the OD field is not without its own set of challenges. Jamieson and Worley (2006) report that in addition to the current challenges of the field of OD, "as the field has expanded in both the scope of targets and the substantive issues it addresses, today's practitioners cannot excel at all aspects of OD" (p. 13). He believes there to be room for some specialization by specific use of one's previous work life and other academic preparation. This lends a strong hand of support for potential partnerships between OD and other disciplines. For example, those with IT and engineering backgrounds could partner with OD practitioners in socio-technical design and process efforts while strong HR professionals could benefit from OD's expertise in becoming stronger business partners to organizational leadership.

Beer and Walton (1987) had this to say about the potential benefit(s) of partnership between the fields of HR and OD:

> As organizations have struggled in an increasingly competitive economy, superior human resources are increasingly seen as a competitive advantage. This has culminated in substantial interest in developing high-commitment work systems that will attract, motivate, and retain superior employees. Indeed the term human resources is coming to represent an integration of personnel administration, labor relations, and organization development, with OD the senior partner. The human resource function and the practice of human resources management (HRM) are absorbing the values and often the practices of OD. (p. 14)

Simpson (2005) stated in his research around the alignment of the HR and OD functions with internal clients:

> to achieve their mission, Human Resource/Organizational Development (HR/OD) professionals need to form an alliance with internal clients, especially at the senior level, because they can elect to use HR/OD services, or not, and demand that HR/OD professionals prove themselves before partnering with them. This expectation makes it important for HR/OD professionals to differentiate types of internal clients, adopt the most appropriate style with each, and align in the best way with each style. (p. 61)

I was very fortunate to be invited and have the opportunity of serving as a presenter during the New York HR Forum, sponsored by Richmond Events, in May, 2007. The titled workshop, What Your CEO Expects and Needs from HR and OD Professionals, was standing room only as many executives embraced the opportunity for collaborative sharing in what could be considered a "safe space" for collaboration. Many shared that they were not only new to their roles but were new to the fields of HR and OD altogether. When asked to share their most pressing challenges at the time, the five most common themes were:

- connecting the goals of the HR/OD functions to the goals of the business;
- identifying the greatest sources of pain for immediate attention and prioritization of longer-term issues;
- creating a plan that will guide their functions and business partners;

- building a case for change within the function and throughout the organization; and
- creating a powerful personal brand as a business leader and change agent first, and a functional expert second.

CONCLUSION

The OD and HR professionals who will succeed in guiding their organizations into the future will be those who understand and use business strategy; understand corporate culture, plans and policies; recognize future problems and work solutions; can deal with all types of people; can communicate well verbally and in writing; and can recognize, recruit and train future executives. According to Beer and Walton (1987), "those human resource managers with an OD orientation have gained power as organizations attempt to change labor relations from adversarial to collaborative" (p. 339).

As organizations continue to move towards collective systems and combined financial resources for managing their human capital, we are likely to see more organizational structures combining both HR and OD. It can be argued that the underlying concepts of HR and OD are partly overlapping constructs. Yet, OD has been described as the missing concept and core competency of many HR executives today.

Libby Sartain, senior vice president, HR for Yahoo, Inc, shared during a SHRM 2005 symposium on the Future of Strategic HR, that "an important part of fostering growth for HR and OD professionals is painting a picture of success." With a growing number of organizations refocusing their efforts around people and talent strategy systems, we must assume that there are those practitioners who are "getting it right" in achieving efficient outcomes relative to strategic HR and OD. The science fiction writer William Gibson once said,

> the future is already with us, it's just unevenly distributed. This is true for HR and OD as well as we learn to balance new demands with more familiar areas of expertise. For example, strong evidence and analytics—rather than relying on gut instinct—are necessary to determine future talent needs and organizational performance drivers. (Gibson, 1996, p. 65)

A future area of study will need to tell the great stories about people who have made successful transitions to the boardrooms and C-suites across organizations, and inspire those of us passionate about making even greater contributions to our chosen profession.

The time has come to quit debating OD's involvement in HR systems and seek the present opportunities of showcasing the skills of OD in building organizational capacity and having a measurable impact on workforce productivity. OD practitioners must show that they are capable of working faster, deeper, wider, smarter, and with larger numbers of constituents, like human resources, now more than ever before. HR, on the other hand, needs the benefits from the strengths brought by OD to have a strategic impact on organizations.

REFERENCES

Bechet, T. (2002). *Strategic staffing: A practical toolkit for workforce planning.* New York: American Management Association.

Beer, M., & Walton, A. (1987). Organization change and development. *Annual Reviews of Psychology, 38,* 339-367.

Burke, W. (2002). *Organization change: Theory and practice.* Thousand Oaks, CA: Sage Publications.

Collis, D. J. (2005). *Strategy: Create and implement the best strategy for your business.* Boston: Harvard Business School Press.

Gibson, W. F. (1999, November 30). NPR interview.

Grieves, J., & Redman, T. (1999). Living in the Shadow of OD: HRD and the Search for identity. *Human Resource Development International,* 2, 81-102.

Hankin, H. (2005). *The new workforce.* New York: American Management Association.

Holbeche, L. (2005). *The high performance organization: Creating dynamic stability and sustainable success.* Burlington, MA: Jordan Hill.

Huselid, M., Jackson, S., & Schuler, R. (1997). Technical and strategic human resource management effectiveness determinants of firm performance. *Academy of Management Journal, 40*(1), 171-188.

Jamieson, D., & Worley, C. (2006). *Pre-Publication Draft for The Handbook of Organization Development.* Thomas Cummings, Editor, SAGE (2007).

Katz, J., & Marshak, R. (1995). Reinventing organization development theory and practice. *Organization Development Journal, 13*(1), 63-81.

McGregor, D. (1957). The human side of enterprise. *The Management Review, 44*(11), 22-28.

Porras, J., & Silvers, R. (1991). Organization development and transformation. *Annual Reviews Psychology, 42,* 51-78

Rothwell, W., & Prescott, R. (1998). *Strategic human resource leader.* Palo Alto, CA. Davies-Black.

Sammut, A. (2001). HR & OD turfwar: Highlighting the need to establish a clear definition of OD. *Organization Development Journal, 19*(2), 9-18.

Sartain, L. (2005, November). SHRM Symposium on the Future State of HR, Washington, DC.

Simpson, M. (2005). Aligning human resources/organizational development with internal clients needs: A transportation metaphor. *Organization Development Journal, 23*(1), 68-73.

Sorensen, P. (2006, May 21). Class lecture discussion at Benedictine University.

Stuart, P. (1992). Getting to the top of HR. *Personnel Journal, 71*(5), 82-89.

Sullivan, J. (2004). *Rethinking strategic HR: HR's role in building a performance culture.* Chicago: CCH Incorporated.

Ulrich, D. (1997). *Human resource champions: The next agenda for adding value and delivering results.* Boston: Harvard Business School Press.

Ulrich, D., & Brockbank, W. (2005). *The HR value proposition.* Boston: Harvard Business School Press.

Weisbord, M. (2004). *Productive workplaces revisited.* San Francisco: Jossey-Bass.

Yorks, L. (2005). *Strategic human resource development.* Mason, OH: Southwestern.

CHAPTER 9

TALENT MANAGEMENT

The Strategic Partnership of Human Resources and Organization Development

Susan Sweem

Most, if not all, organizations have devised a strategy in order to increase profits and performance. Strategies are developed and implemented but often the performance or profits do not increase as planned (Lawler & Worley, 2006). Why does this occur? If organizations could grasp the "holistic" picture which includes not only developing and implementing a strategy utilizing hard data (i.e., financials, market share, etc.) but also includes the soft data (i.e., human resources), perhaps, they would be more successful.

The missing element for successful organization strategies is the combined perspective of human resources (HR) and organization development (OD). How can an organization increase performance without implementing some sort of change initiative which involves maximizing human potential? By infusing strategy with the HR and OD perspectives, organizations can better understand how to make changes in order to successfully implement a strategy that increases firm performance (Worley, Hitchin, & Ross, 1996).

Strategic Organization Development: Managing Change for Success
pp. 143–163

The HR and OD perspectives combined collaborate towards a talent management strategy. Talent management strategy involves a holistic approach to both human resources and business planning which provides a new route to organizational effectiveness (Ashton & Morton, 2005). This approach may be the defining moment for human resources to change the paradigm in order to become the strategic player at the C-suite table.

This paper will define what strategy is and how HR and OD integrate together into the overall organizational goals and strategy. It will define talent management strategy and the role it plays in organizational strategy. The resource-based theory and the built-to-change theory exemplify the need for a partnership between HR and OD in order to move an organization forward in an ever-changing environment. In addition, the decision science of talent will be examined as a paradigm change for HR and OD. Together, HR and OD strategically have the capability to significantly impact organizational performance.

WHAT IS STRATEGY?

History and Development of Strategy

The term strategy derives its meaning from military roots. The Greek word *stratos* means "army" and -*ag* means "to lead" (Grant, 2005). Business strategy and military strategy share common characteristics in that they both strive to establish a favorable position, must use significant resources to accomplish this goal and are not easily reversible (Ashton & Morton, 2005). Grant (2005) asserts that strategy is concerned with the planning of how an organization or an individual will achieve its goal(s). Organizations today continue to use this premise in their strategy sessions but the tactical goals of strategy have changed and emerged over the years.

In the 1950s and 1960s, organizations were struggling with maintaining control in companies due to rapid growth and rising complexity. Corporate planning departments emerged as a way to coordinate long-term investment and financial decisions. These departments were essentially concerned with economic trends and financial forecasting (Grant, 2005). Corporate leaders embraced it as "one best way" to devise and implement strategies that would enhance the competitiveness of the business (Mintzberg, 1994).

By the 1970s, a shift occurred from strategy planning to strategy making which encouraged an increased focus on competition and the environment. International competition caused companies to re-examine their traditional approach of forecasting three to five years ahead. This approach no longer worked as U.S. companies could not predict what international firms were going to do. They had to focus on the markets and competitors worldwide (Grant, 2005). This emphasis then moved strategy development in the 1980s towards finding the sources of profitability in the external environment. Michael Porter of the Harvard Business School developed an application of industrial organization economics to analyze elements of firm profitability (Grant, 2005). The focus was on the firm's external profitability.

Strategy in the 1990s concentrated on sources of profitability within the organization. Organizations looked at their resources and capabilities to enhance their competitive advantage. This approach emphasized the resource-based viewed of the firm and resulted in a shift from strategy thinking to strategy making utilizing internal resources (Grant, 2005). By 2000, strategy development had even moved further by not only incorporating competition but also sustainability in a global world. The focus became continuous improvement. So as organizations began to try to imitate each other's strategies for success, analysts questioned what differentiates one company from another to attain sustainability?

Porter (1996) concludes that the essence of strategy is the ability to have a unique and valuable position rooted in systems of activities that are extremely difficult to match. Organizations have to make trade-offs among the activities that are critical to the sustainability of the strategy. It means managing a fit across all lines and functions of a business which includes HR and OD. This creates the opportunity for HR and OD to sit at the C-suite table and work together to design and implement an organizational strategy.

Design Versus Emergence

Strategy can be divided into two key concepts: corporate strategy and business strategy (Grant, 2005). Corporate strategy is the responsibility of top management and focuses on the question of how the firm can make money. Business strategy is developed and implemented by the functional areas (i.e., finance, human resources, marketing, R&D) and contributes to answering the question of how the business should compete. This involves establishing the competitive edge which is vital for a firm's success. Without a competitive advantage, the organization will not perform and the strategy is useless. Business strategy is not something that should be solely developed by upper level management who are typically far removed from the details of running an organization on a daily basis. This is a fallacy of conventional strategic management and explains why there are many failures in business today (Mintzberg, 1987).

"The world of business is one of constant change, and the role of strategy is to assist the firm to adapt to changing market and competitive conditions" (Grant, 2005, p. 54). The challenge for firms is to devise new strategies and innovations that will allow them to enter markets that they had not even thought of in the past and to utilize new methods or technologies. These strategies are often emergent strategies. They cannot be designed in one day and implemented the next. This process of creating or making strategies is not a one-time event. Mintzberg (1994) describes this process:

> Such strategies often cannot be developed on schedule and immaculately conceived. They must be free to appear at any time and at any place in the organization, typically through messy processes of informal learning that must necessarily be carried out by people at various levels who are deeply involved with the specific issues at hand. (p. 108)

Companies such as Wal-Mart, Nokia and Toyota have had successful strategies in the past and continue to change strategies as the organization has evolved (Grant, 2005). In the past, business needs usually defined personnel needs and human resource planning which clearly delineated a reactive process (Jackson & Schuler, 1990). This reactive response also followed along the short-term orientation. However, as changes in business, economic and social environments are creating more uncertainties, organizations are forced to integrate business planning with human resource planning and adopting a longer term perspective (Jackson & Schuler, 1990). This emerging strategy is convincing corporate business planners that human resources do represent a major competitive edge that can increase profits. HR and OD as change agents must play a role in the continuous talent development strategy if organizations are going to maximize their human capital capabilities. Successful strategic change from an OD perspective should become part of the mainstream of organizational thinking and it makes sense to place these skills in the HR department (Worley et al., 1996).

In the long run, it is important to note that talent management will not succeed without an organizational structure that supports it. This is the view of David Ulrich who believes too much emphasis may be placed on talent at the expense of organizational design (Grossman, 2007b). "Strategy architects are able to recognize business trends and their impact on the business, and to identify potential roadblocks and opportunities" (Grossman, 2007b, p. 59). It's the ability to identify the business differentiator on the people side of contributing to the overall strategy. The OD skills of mapping organizational design immediately transfer into HR.

Integration of HR and OD Strategy

The common elements of a successful strategy include consistent, long-term goals, an understanding of the competitive environment, resource appraisal and an effective implementation (Grant, 2005). These elements include more than just a financial analysis and this is where HR and OD can make a significant contribution. HR and OD can contribute to a strategy development process by developing talent management strategies that can be implemented throughout the organization. This talent management approach must be flexible yet responsive to adapt to an ever-changing environment.

Change is an essential component that needs to be strategically incorporated into any strategy plan. Strategic change is defined as a "type of organization change that realigns an organization's strategy, structure and process to fit within a new competitive context" (Worley et al., 1996, p. xix). Traditional OD produces incremental improvements, addresses one system at time and does not purport to increase company performance. However, as OD has evolved and connected with HR, it has focused on aligning its practices in multiple roles and directly impacting firm performance (Lawler & Worley, 2006). Management must manage both internal and external environments in both short-term and long-term time frames. It might have been acceptable to only be concerned with external environments but not any longer (Worley et al., 1996). OD is internally focused, process oriented, and dynamic (Cummings & Worley, 2005). It focuses on how organizations and organizational behavior changes over time. Strategy focuses on the relationship between the organization and its environment. What has been the missing link is the development of the internal resources (i.e., people) in conjunction with the ability to change the direction of the organization. This key opportunity has directly connected OD and HR together to develop and implement a talent management strategy.

The term talent management has been used and defined in many different ways. Lewis and Heckman (2006) explored the trade and popular literature for talent management and concluded that there are extensive consultant and practitioner articles but there is no definitive definition of the term talent management. Often the terms "talent strategy", "succession management" and "human resource planning" are used interchangeably. However, Lewis and Heckman (2006) did identify three distinct strains of thought:

1. Talent management is a collection of typical human resource department practices, functions, activities or specialist areas. It is

here that "human resources" is replaced by the term "talent management."

2. Talent management focuses on the concept of talent pools. It is the set of processes that are designed to ensure an adequate flow of employees into jobs with in the organization. This approach is close to what is known as succession planning or human resource planning.

3. Talent management involves managing the pools of talent for all groups of employees rather than for succession planning of particular jobs.

It is evident that the term is used in various ways. However, in most cases, it refers to the concept of bringing together the functions of recruitment, selection and assessment, learning and development, performance management, workforce planning and other functions (Oakes, 2006). Lockwood (2006) broadly defines it as "the implementation of integrated strategies or systems designed to increase workplace productivity by developing improved processes for attracting, developing, retaining and utilizing people with the required skills and aptitude to meet current and future business needs" (p. 2). There is some bantering among business leaders and practitioners that talent management is just another name for finding a way to secure the best, qualified people for an organization. After all, "the East India Company, founded in 1600, used competitive examinations to recruit alpha minds" ("Everybody's Doing it", 2006). GE has ranked its employees for decades and promotes the best to higher positions while the weak employees are gradually eased out. The term talent management, however, takes the concept one step further as managing talent and the strategy for organizational sustainability now means making decisions that impact personnel and how people need to work to efficiently to produce service or products. Organizations are ready to embrace talent management as a strategy which recognizes human capital as an investment in the firm's growth (Boudreau & Ramstad, 2005). It is the HR and OD views that are defining the methods and interventions for ensuring talent is ready across all functions in an integrated fashion for the good of the organization.

Many factors have contributed to this change for HR and OD to become strategic partners (Worley et al., 1996). The transition to a global economy and worldwide marketing of products are major factors. No longer can an organization reside in only one location or country. The competition is too intense and now the cultural requirements of multiple countries must be taken into account. Technology and regulatory changes have also altered industries. New processes, information systems and products must now be incorporated and the organization must be coordinated to facilitate these changes. Another factor is the general trend that organizations feel constrained to change when performance is high. Low performance is considered a catalyst to change, but in high performing companies there is no impetus to change. Sustainable organizations cannot think in this manner. Organizations need to be able to adapt at any level of performance and HR/OD must facilitate this environment. And, finally, stakeholders such as stockholders and employers are playing a role in strategy. Participation and high employee involvement programs are vital for success.

OD and HR have integrated their functions in order to become a business partner to implement organizational strategy. They are no longer the "administrators" or the group that is brought in for a one-time team-building project. As Wright, Dunford, and Snell (2001) confirmed:

> In times of plenty, firms easily justify expenditures on training, staffing, reward, and employee involvement systems, but when faced with financial difficulties, such HR systems fall prey to the earliest cutbacks. The advent of the sub field of strategic human resource management (SHRM), devoted to exploring HR's role in supporting business strategy, provided one avenue for demonstrating its value to the firm. (p. 701)

Outsourcing has enabled the HR department to realign their function to become the "strategic business partner" (Kates, 2006). It has shifted the role of HR from a focus on the "customer/employee" to a focus on the management ranks. The lower value-added transactional work has been pushed to the outside which is no different than outsourcing in other areas of the organization. The core of HR has been to turn to the development of its most valuable resources; it employees.

OD emphasizes the roles that people and organization design can contribute as competitive advantages. OD brings to HR the change management and process expertise as well as the intervention specialty (Worley et al., 1996). HR could only become strategic by integrating OD values and development techniques together. But a challenge that is created within the business partner model questions how best to deliver the OD work (Kates, 2006). HR leaders are finding that no matter how much lower-level work is being shifted, there remains a high level of transactional work which could include rolling out a program driven by regulatory change or filling a senior-level position. Should the OD work be integrated with the generalists or should a centralized OD group lead the work? Many organizations have turned to another model called "The Solutions Center" to answer this question (Kates, 2006). It has a similar configuration to the business partner model but has a maxtrixed group of functional specialists that are the delivery engine. The model turns HR into a professional services firm where the OD specialists are integrated into the various functional teams. There is only one HR person dedicated to each line of business but his role is to coordinate the activity of the solutions teams as needed for projects or teams. It breaks the old mindset and provides a strategy for ensuring collaboration between both HR and OD as one integrated team.

HOW DOES HR/OD STRATEGICALLY FIT TOGETHER TO INFLUENCE ORGANIZATIONAL PERFORMANCE?

Strategic Change Theories

Realizing that there are many different strategies that organizations can follow, it is important to identify the strategies and models that include the internal HR/OD perspective so that it can impact not only the effectiveness but the performance of the organization (Worley et al., 1996). Worley et al. (1996) state that the essential challenge is to develop and implement successful business strategies that strengthen the organization and increase the level of motivation and commitment of the people who are responsible for implementation. If employees are not engaged and committed, it will be difficult to implement the change or strategy necessary for the business to flourish (Saks, 2006).

Traditional Theory

In the past organizations have relied heavily on the "SWOT" framework (Grant, 2005). SWOT essentially entails the organization identifying its strengths, weaknesses, opportunities and threats. The first two relate to the internal environment and the last two relate to the external environment. It appears to be a reliable method to classify factors but does not consider the implications and integration of them. Grant (2005) states that for a strategy to be successful, it must align its goals, values, resources, capabilities and structure systems all together. Many times this requires changing some of the factors in the strategy mix and human resources should be prepared with organization development initiatives to make this happen. Therefore, SWOT has been replaced with other potential theories that relate better to the resource role.

Resource-Based Theory

With "traditional" strategies focusing on profit opportunities in relation to the external environment, the resource-based view is concerned with the pool of resources and capabilities

as the primary determinants of strategy and performance (Grant, 2005). Barney (1991) advocates that role of resources in producing firm-wide results should be taken into consideration. Sustained competitive advantage comes from developing resources that are rare and difficult to imitate. Barney includes human capital in his definition of resources but it must be rare and imitable. Managerial resources are not necessarily rare unless there is a specific attribute that is not found in any other firm (Barney, 1991).

The resource-based view emphasizes that the uniqueness of each company is key to profitability and that exploiting these differences will maintain and sustain competitiveness. This also includes human capital. Deregulation in many industries and globalization have played major roles in this change from a pure profitability view to deploying resources and capabilities. Organizations must have capabilities to undertake a particular productive role. Hamel and Prahalad (1994) coined the term *core competencies* to distinguish those capabilities fundamental to a firm's performance and strategy. They define core competencies as those that make a disproportionate contribution to ultimate customer value and provide a basis for entering new markets. This, too, includes the human capital factor.

Grant (2005) distinguishes between the resources and capabilities of a company. The resources are the productive assets owned by the firm and capabilities are what the firm can do. Human resources must work together as opposed to individually in order to create organizational capability. Capability is what creates successful performance. Resources include tangible (financial and physical assets), intangible (technology, reputation and culture) and human (skills, know-how, communication, motivation) segments. The human resources are productive services. They are not owned by organizations but have a contract or agreement with a firm to produce services. Competency modeling has become a preferred model for identifying a set of skills, knowledge and values that will align human resources with the organization's strategy (Grant, 2005). This is an essential factor or else the organization's overall strategy cannot be implemented and carried forward.

Lado and Wilson (1994) purport that "the resource-based view suggests that human resource systems can contribute to sustained competitive advantage through facilitating the developing of competencies that are firm specific, produce complex social relationships, are embedded in a firm's history and culture, and generate tacit organizational knowledge" (p. 699). Companies such as Marriott, Borg-Warner and Merck have attributed their competitive advantage to their unique methods for managing human resources. A *human resource (HR) system* is defined as a set of distinct but interrelated activities, functions and processes that are directed at attracting, developing, and maintaining (or disposing of) a firm's human resources. It is possible that HR systems could destroy or prevent competencies to be fully developed so it is essential to integrate the HR/OD processes into the strategy. OD contributes by developing the methodology for change to ensure the proper human resources are available at the right time. In order to achieve sustainable competitive advantage, continuous monitoring by the firm of competency patterns is vital as patterns continue to change over time (Lado & Wilson, 1994).

Organizational culture is another piece of the resource-based view. Simply hiring individual contributors is typically not acceptable in an organization that has a strategy of integration or requires teamwork. Collaboration is a key component of a successful strategy and often it relates to an intangible asset which is culture. Schein (1990) eloquently defines culture as "(a) a pattern of basic assumptions, (b) invented, discovered, or developed by a given group, (c) as it learns to cope with its problems of external adaptation and internal integration, (d) that has worked well enough to be considered valid and, therefore (e) is to be taught to new members as the (f) correct way to perceive, think and fall in relation to those problems" (p. 111). This relates directly to resource-based strategy for what a group learns over a period of time as it solves its problems of survival in an external environment and its problems of internal integration is that it becomes a complex process to integrate and account for all together. Culture can become ingrained and difficult to change but this is the function of HR/OD to enable the organization to move forward. The change agent is HR/OD. Many organizational programs fail because culture forces are ignored (Schein, 1990).

Barney (1986) confirms that a firm's culture does generate sustained competitive advantages if they have the required attributes. The required attributes include (1) the culture must be valuable, (2) it must be rare, and (3) it must be imperfectly imitable. The firm must be able to do things that enable it to add economic value and it must have a distinct culture that enables it to differentiate itself from competitors. As with general products, the culture can not be imitable if it is going to be sustainable. This research suggests that if firms can modify their cultures to improve financial results but still maintain a culture that is imperfectly imitable, it will sustain superior performance. Here is where HR/OD can play a pivotal role in developing this type of sustainable culture. It is not merely looking at external forces but relating the type of culture that is needed for both financial and sustainable success. Human resource practices or processes are developed to manage the skills and abilities of talent in order to make them more difficult to duplicate for competitors (Lewis & Heckman, 2006).

It is important to acknowledge that there are criteria that can affect strategy and reduce HR/OD effectiveness (Lado & Wilson, 1994). Such factors include governmental legislation and employment regulations. Although such legislation is enacted for the social good, they often serve to limit the ability to "think out of the box." The mindset turns to legalistic views rather than flexibility. Another factor includes culture. If the culture of an organization impedes members from participation, or perceptions of fairness are biased, a full strategy cannot be implemented. But, again, the emphasis should be on HR/OD changing this culture towards one of collaboration and integration of the organization's overall strategy.

Integrated Strategic Change Model

The integrated strategic change (ISC) model encompasses a process that involves learning and adapting over time to ensure long-term competitiveness to business changes (Worley et al., 1996). This model includes not only formulating strategy but also implementing and executing the strategy. And, most importantly from an HR/OD perspective, it focuses on organizational capabilities, human resources and organizational changes required to implement strategies. It provides for active participation by the members of an organization to be involved to create higher levels of shared ownership and commitment and is a continuous process. The essential factor is the alignment of the firm's structure and processes to support its strategy. In this model, strategy is directly built into both HR and OD as opposed to HR/OD providing input to a strategy group (Worley et al., 1996).

There are four key steps: (1) strategic analysis, (2) strategy making, (3) strategic change plan design, and (4) strategic change plan implementation. In the first step, the organization is reviewing its readiness for change. HR/OD should participate at the beginning with this initial step as it plays a key role in this phase. Often, the organization's employees are not ready for change and an HR/OD development preparation and intervention must occur. This occurred at a data systems company as it prepared for major changes in its industry (Worley et al., 1996, pp. 23-24). Before changes could occur, the employees needed to be accepting and ready for them which included having the correct skill sets. The OD prevalence emphasizes the change management skills and HR emphasizes the actual job skills. Without training and preparation by the combined skill sets of HR/OD, the employees would have resisted change. This first stage also includes reviewing the organization's values and assumptions as well as performance. HR/OD supports this process through culture as well as support activities. The HR system is responsible for selecting, developing and rewarding managers and employees. If this initiative is not in alignment with the overall strategy, the process will fail. This occurred in a hospital where the rewards and training opportunities were not aligned with the hospital strategy (Worley et al., 1996, p. 63). Employees did not attend training as it was viewed as unimportant and not supported by managers. With high workloads, getting the daily job done was rewarded instead of learning new skills. Training needed to be encouraged to develop new skill sets and rewards had to be perceived as significant to make an impact and motivate the employees to contribute positively to the performance of the hospital. This resulted in changing the culture to one of a learning environment with appropriate rewards for new knowledge and behaviors.

In the ISC model, strategy making is also a vital step. The firm's strategic vision is created. The vision should be created by participation of the organization members so they may "buy in" to the vision. Determining the strategic direction should be done in conjunction with the vision. HR/OD can play a role by determining the approach to change and how best to evaluate and design it. Depending on the type of change and the environmental factors, it will vary. Again, it is essential that HR/OD lead this change effort to ensure it can happen through the appropriate support activities.

The third step of developing the strategic change plan is ensuring that the first two steps involve employee participation. Without it, it will be a dismal failure (Worley et al., 1996). Describing the future state and developing the action plans must be done carefully in order to be able to implement the plan throughout the organization. The hospital in the above example was able to encourage employee development through training by enacting a culture of allowing training as a priority even when workload was high (Worley et al., 1996, p. 129).

Given the ever-changing environment of today's business world, when strategic change is necessary, the most valuable resource an organization can have is a change process (Worley et al., 1996). GM and Kodak serve as examples of organizations that were unable to sustain performance and did not recognize environmental change in order to carry out strategic change. Worley et al. (1996) iterates the importance of change when they state:

Unfortunately, while most organizations possess skills and knowledge in both strategic management and change management, the former are more prevalent and more valued than the latter. This is also unfortunate because successful strategic change processes may be more dependent on the OD perspective than on strategic management skills and knowledge. (p. 145)

It is an HR/OD function to ensure change is not inhibited.

Built-to-Change Theory

Rapid change is amongst all organizations (Lawler & Worley, 2006). There is not an industry that is not affected. Although most previous strategies consider change and aim to create long-term competitive advantages, Lawler and Worley (2006) advocate that companies should design a strategy that assumes change is normal. This assumes that instead of having to create change efforts, organizational practices would automatically be built to change.

Similar to the resource-based theory, human capital is critical for a competitive advantage in built-to-change organizations. There is a recognition that market value rests with human capital. Research by Huselid (1995) has shown that the impact of a firm's human capital management practices such as training programs, efforts to create a good place to work and reward systems have found that these practices do produce superior results. Other research suggests that one of the key factors is management talent (Lawler & Worley, 2006). Competitive advantage now rests in a company's people and its ability to organize its human capital rather than compete on the basis of tangible resources. This is a critical component of the built-to-change theory and one where HR/OD plays the major role.

The built-to-change model developed by Lawler and Worley (2006) is a continuous change and adaptive method that consists of environmental scenarios and three primary organizational processes—strategizing, creating value and designing—which all revolve around the organization's identity as displayed in Figure 9.1.

The strategizing is a process for enabling a possible scenario for the future through constant change processes. It involves looking for momentary advantages rather than a design for stable advantages. Organizational capabilities must be created so that change is the key to success. And, this can be accomplished through the partnership of HR/OD with the organization towards building the appropriate structure and configuring the appropriate talent management initiatives and rewards (Lawler & Worley, 2006). Talent management includes developing individuals to provide the skills as the organization and jobs change. It may mean hiring

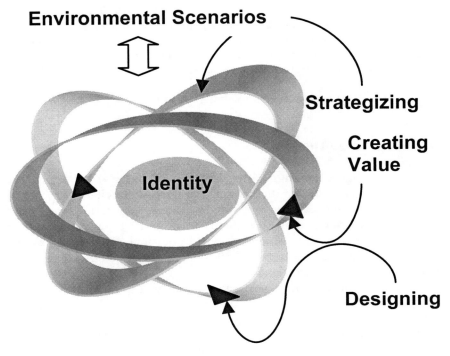

Source: Lawler and Worley (2006).

Figure 9.1.   The built-to-change model.

individuals who already have the desired skill set but who also are willing to change along with the business. In other situations, it could also mean the strategy may be to acquire and discard talent as necessary. This *travel-light* theory, however, may not build a long-term committed workforce. More typically, it is the commitment to develop employees that is part of the employment terms.

The built-to-change model advocates managing human capital and making people responsible for their careers (Lawler & Worley, 2006). An organization needs to keep the right people which mean utilizing appropriate rewards towards satisfaction. Lawler and Worley (2006) point out that one of the great challenges in satisfying employees is achieving alignment between what they value and what the organization can offer. What might not be readily apparent in this model is that culture influences this challenge. "All of the activities that revolve around recruitment, selection, training and socialization, the design of the reward systems, the design and description of jobs, and broader issues of organization design require an understanding of how organizational culture influences present functioning" (Schein, 1990, pp. 117-118). In essence, this is the talent management theory that the HR/OD function can incorporate into the strategy. By measuring the results through attitude surveys and statistics such as turnover figures, the impact can be measured on performance.

IBM is an example of an organization that that has developed HR systems to help employees manage their careers and provide managers with tools to assist in employee recruitment (Lawler & Worley, 2006). By providing tools to the employees, it can retain and develop its human resources for future strategic changes. It is interesting to note that many managers believe that job satisfaction is an important determinant of motivation and performance. Lawler & Worley (2006) advocate that this is false. Job satisfaction does not cause performance but could influence organizational performance. If dissatisfied employees become disgruntled employees, they become disengaged and this could result in activities that deviate from the intended strategy. Hence, it is desirable to create built-to-change organizations that can make strategy adjustments and change easy to accomplish throughout the company.

HAS HR/OD CONVERGED TOWARD ALIGNMENT WITH THE BUILT-TO-CHANGE MODEL OR IS IT STUCK IN TRADITIONAL METHODS?

HR/OD is transforming toward a built-to-change model. A significant step has been the emergence of HR and OD in the same department in models such as "The Solutions Center" where they perform integrated services (Kates, 2006). HR/OD can add more value to corporations by directly improving the performance of the business with effective talent management, helping with the change management, and influencing strategy (Lawler, 2005). As the focus has turned to human capital, HR/OD must be at the table strategizing at the forefront. It cannot sit back and take a wait-to-see approach. Without upfront, initial participation in the strategy development, implementation is doomed to fail. Worley et al. (1996) even suggest that perhaps the strategy function of organizations should be housed in HR. It is true that HR and OD must become credible drivers of the strategic planning by learning to speak and understand the concepts of finance, economics and marketing. This will enable HR and OD professionals to sit at the same table as the CFO and marketing executive.

But are HR/OD professionals really sitting at the table or just in the same room? "People, intellectual capital and talent are ever more critical to organizational strategic success. This observation is so common today that it almost goes without saying" (Boudreau & Ramstad, 2005, p. 18). Yet, when top executives are asked if their decisions about the talents of their people are made with same rigor and strategic connections as their decisions about money, technology, and products, they admit that their talent decisions are not (Boudreau & Ramstad, 2005). This is where HR and OD combined can offer the opportunity to change the view at the table.

Finance, marketing and operations are judged and valued based on their results. How can HR/OD help leaders make better decisions about talent resources to drive organizational effectiveness? Unfortunately, research has shown that two important goals for HR measurement, (1) to enhance decisions about human capital and (2) to connect human resources to strategy, are rarely met (Boudreau & Ramstad, 2005). Today's HR practices still reflect a traditional paradigm of delivering high-quality services in response to client's needs. This is clearly a reactive mode versus a proactive mode. It needs to adopt a more outside-in approach as opposed to an inside-out approach. According to Boudreau and Ramstad (1997), fields such as finance have augmented their service delivery with a "decision science" paradigm that teaches the frameworks to make good choices. HR/OD, like finance and marketing, helps the organization operate within a critical market for talent. It needs a new paradigm of decision science for talent (Boudreau & Ramstad, 2005).

Decision science provides a system to identify and analyze key issues, adapting to the unique information and characteristics of the specific context. According to Boudreau and Ramstad (2005):

> The lessons from marketing and finance tell us that the goal of talent decision Science would be "to increase the success of the organization by improving decisions that impact or depend on talent resources." We have coined the term "talentship" to describe the new decision science, and to reflect the notion of stewardship for the resource of employee talents. Talentship is to HR what finance is to accounting and what marketing is to sales. (p. 20)

Talent decision mistakes are not being made by HR/OD professionals but by leaders who do not have a full understanding of their implications and impact of talent backgrounds of individual employees. The greatest opportunity to improve talent decisions is outside the HR/OD profession.

HR/OD can "control" the decisions or equip those outside the profession to better understand the implications of the decisions they make (Boudreau & Ramstad, 2005). In order for HR and OD to sit at the table with finance and marketing, they must have a perspective for offering a unique talent for improving decisions and not just implementing them.

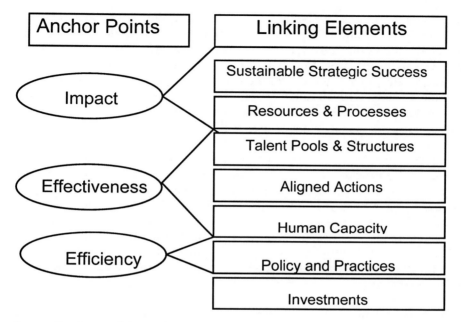

Source: Boudreau and Ramstad (2005).

Figure 9.2.   HC Bridge decision framework model.

The elements of such a talent decision science model include impact, effectiveness and efficiency. Often, business leaders and strategists focus only on business processes and market outcomes while ignoring the human capital factor. Boudreau and Ramstad's (2005) decision framework provide the means to participate in strategy discussions which routinely take into account the connection between talent and strategic success. Their model is shown in Figure 9.2.

Federal Express applied this framework and found that its strategy changed from one on concentrating on pilots and top leaders to one of focusing on the couriers. There is little ability to improve talent success for pilots who simply fly planes as compared to couriers who had much more impact with the customer. This change in paradigm is not just for HR and OD but for the organization as well. Integrating HR and OD functions to improve decisions that matter most toward sustainable strategic success occurs by implementing this decision science strategy within the organization's ongoing processes. It is an opportunity for organizations to achieve success through one their most important resources: the talents of their people.

Talent factories are being built by organizations that have successfully combined OD and HR to face the future together. They don't just manage talent, they build talent factories. Talent factories "marry functionality, rigorous talent processes that support strategic and cultural objectives, and vitality, emotional commitment by management that is reflected in daily actions" which allow organizations to develop and retain key employees to meet evolving business needs (Ready & Conger, 2007, p. 70). However, talent management will fail without commitment from top management. The passion must start at the top and be infused into the culture; otherwise, HR and OD will become bureaucratic processes. The key to this practice is that unlike processes that can be copied by competitors, passion is very difficult to duplicate (Ready & Conger, 2007). Ready and Conger (2007) state that the vitality of a company's talent management process is a product of three defining characteristics: commitment, engagement, and accountability. Fostering commitment begins with the new hire and continues throughout a career. Engagement reflects the degree to which company leaders show their commitment to the talent management. Even down to line management, engagement is vital to ensure strategy is carried out with specific polices and practices oriented towards talent implementation. And, all stakeholders, including the employees themselves, are held accountable for making systems and processes robust. Procter & Gamble has succeeded in creating a talent factory as well as HSBC Group, a financial services group (Ready & Conger, 2007). Both organizations have established systems and processes to deploy and create talent with pipelines of current and future leaders. "To develop local talent while maintaining global standards, HSBC centrally designed its human resources practices and policies but built in some flexibility to accommodate local variations" (Ready & Conger, 2007, p. 71). Procter & Gamble has tied its talent management initiative to its strategy for growth especially in the emerging markets. They are building a global supply-chain of human resources but administering it locally.

Lawler and Worley (2006) proclaim that through their built-to-change theory, it is the virtuous spirals that will set apart the successful and sustainable organizations. Virtuous spirals balance the short and long term goals with the continuous dynamic alignment of business strategy. The organization must have an identity. The identity is the foundation of performance and ability to change. It is reflected in the culture and image (Lawler & Worley, 2006). IBM is an example of an organization that has merged OD and HR into one function and taken that virtuous spiral to the next level. In the 1990s, IBM had to establish a new strategic intent that emphasized services and consulting. It changed its strategy to rely on skills and performance rather than on loyalty (Lawler & Worley, 2006, p. 49). By 2007, the virtuous change has continued and it is once again revising its HR/OD strategy. IBM recognizes that human capital is its most valuable resource and believes it is the deployment of talent that will be the key market differentiator. HR and talent management is the core business of IBM (Grossman, 2007a). The VP of HR, Randy McDonald, has been instrumental with the key strategic and operational decisions of the corporation. He is taking the next step and reorganizing HR so that he will create separate cross-functional HR teams to serve three customer sets: executive and technical resources, managerial talent and rank-and-file employees. Each set will be managed holistically by having talent, learning and compensation and rewards managed in each of the different levels respectively. This will enable IBM to identify what skills will become obsolete and what skills will be needed in the future through segmentation and, hence, a proactive stance.

These organizations have strategically developed HR and OD together to concentrate on the core competencies of the human resources asset in terms of talent development and rewards. Administrative functions are often outsourced (Lawler & Worley, 2006). They place the expertise for administrative duties where it adds the most value. Development and retention of staff, identified as a core competency, remains an internal key strategic function of HR/OD.

There are barriers that may prevent talent management programs from delivering business value. McKinsey & Company asked senior executives to rank the obstacles preventing talent management from delivering value ("Talent Management Barriers," 2007). The top response (54%) was that senior managers don't spend enough time on talent management. The next response (52%) was line managers are not sufficiently committed to people development and, third (51%) was that silos discourage collaboration and resource sharing. The fourth highest concern (50%) was that line managers unwillingly differentiate high, low performers and, fifth, senior leaders (47%) do not align talent management with business strategies. If almost half of senior leaders do not align talent management with business strategies, HR/OD still has a long way to travel to bring HR and OD to the strategy table. However, it could be that the other half are already at the table and are building strategy for sustainable organizations. These firms are the ones likely to succeed with HR and OD as the forefront.

CONCLUSION

Organizations must realize that people are their most valuable asset which must be utilized as a competitive advantage. It is only through maximizing human capital that organizations will be able to achieve growth and sustain success. This is a pivotal key and new paradigm shift for any organizational strategy. Change will continuously occur but developing the people to react to this type of dynamic environment can result in increased organizational performance. Ready and Conger (2007) summarized this concept:

> Leaders have long said that people are their companies' most important assets, but making the most of them has acquired a new urgency. Any company aiming to grow—and, in particular, to grow on the global stage—has little hope of achieving its goals without the ability to put the right people on the ground, and fast. Companies apply focus and drive toward capital, information technology, equipment, and world-class processes, but in the end, it's the people who matter most. (p. 77)

HR and OD must be active partners at the C-suite strategy table representing the talent management component of the organization's overall strategy. Without talented human capital, the success and performance of the firm remains at risk.

REFERENCES

Ashton, C., & Morton, L. (2005). Managing talent for competitive advantage. *Strategic Human Resources Review, 4*(5), 28-31.

Barney, J. (1986). Organizational culture: Can it be a source of sustained competitive advantage? *Academy of Management Review, 11*(3), 656-665.

Barney, J. (1991). Firm resources and sustained competitive advantage. *Journal of Management, 17*(1), 99-120.

Boudreau, J. W., & Ramstad, P. M. (1997). Measuring intellectual capital: Learning from financial history. *Human Resource Management, 36*(3), 343-356.

Boudreau, J. W., & Ramstad, P. M. (2005). Talentship and the new paradigm for Human Resource Management: From professional practices to strategic talent decision science. *Human Resource Planning, 28*(2), 17-26.

Cummings, T. G., & Worley, C. G. (2005). *Organization development & change* (8th ed.). Mason, OH: Thomson-Southwestern.

Everybody's doing it. (2006). *Economist, 381*(8498), 5-8.

Grant, R. M. (2005). *Contemporary strategic analysis* (5th ed.). Malden, MA: Blackwell.

Grossman, R. J. (2007a). IBM's HR takes a risk. *HR Magazine, 52*(4), 54-59.

Grossman, R. J. (2007b). New competencies for HR. *HR Magazine, 52*(6), 58-62.

Hamel, G., & Prahalad, C. K. (1994). Competing for the future. *Harvard Business Review, 72*(4), 122-129.

Huselid, M. A. (1995). The impact of human resource practices on turnover, productivity, and corporate financial performance. *Academy of Management Journal, 38*(3), 635-672.

Jackson, S. E., & Schuler, R. S. (1990). Human resource planning: Challenges for industrial/organizational psychologists. *American Psychologist, 45*(2), 223-239.

Kates, A. (2006). (Re)designing the HR organization. *Human Resource Planning, 29*(2), 22-30.

Lado, A. A., & Wilson, M. C. (1994). Human resource systems and sustained competitive advantage: A competency-based perspective. *Academy of Management Review, 19*(4), 699-727.

Lawler, E. E., III. (2005). From human resource management to organizational effectiveness. *Human Resource Management, 44*(2), 165-169.

Lawler, E. E., III, & Worley, C. D. (2006). *Built to change: How to achieve sustained organizational effectiveness.* San Francisco: Wiley.

Lewis, R. E., & Heckman, R. J. (2006). Talent management: A critical review. *Human Resource Management Review, 16*(2), 139-154.

Lockwood, N. R. (2006). Talent management driver for organizational success. *HR Magazine, 51*(6), 1-11.

Mintzberg, H. (1987). Crafting strategy. *Harvard Business Review, 65*(4), 66-75.

Mintzberg, H. (1994). The fall and rise of strategic planning. *Harvard Business Review, 72*(1), 107-114.

Oakes, K. (2006). The emergence of talent management. *Training and Development, 60*(4), 21-23.

Porter, M. E. (1996). What is strategy? *Harvard Business Review, 74*(6), 61-78.

Ready, D. A., & Conger, J. A. (2007). Make your company a talent factory. *Harvard Business Review, 85*(6), 68-77.

Saks, A. M. (2006). Antecedents and consequences of employee engagement. *Journal of Managerial Psychology, 21*(7), 600-619.

Schein, E. H. (1990). Organizational Culture. *American Psychologist, 45*(2), 109-119.

Talent management barriers. (2007). *Training and Development, 61*(2), 16.

Worley, C. D., Hitchin, D. E., & Ross, W. D. (1996). *Integrated strategic change.* Reading, MA: Addison-Wesley.

Wright, P. M., Dunford, B. B., & Snell, S. A. (2001). Human resources and the resource based view of the firm. *Journal of Management, 27*, 701-721.

CHAPTER 10

NEW APPLICATIONS FOR ORGANIZATION DEVELOPMENT

Jimmy Brown

Organization development (OD) traditionalists believe the field should focus on promoting humanistic values, while organization development pragmatists would rather focus on analytic and rationally based approaches for improving organizations (Worley & Feyerherm, 2003). Increasingly, that pragmatic lens has been applied to areas such as business strategy and senior level decision making, but where else could OD make an impact beyond its traditional boundaries? This chapter explores that question by discussing OD's potential impact on domains that have been identified as common across master's of business administration programs.

There are two predominant views in the OD world: The traditionalists who believe that OD should focus on promoting humanistic values within organizations, and the pragmatists who believe that OD should integrate the field's competencies into analytic and rationally based approaches of efforts, such as strategy formulation (Worley & Feyerherm, 2003). Many pragmatists take the position that properly applied OD has the capability to improve organizational performance dramatically, and that it is incumbent upon OD practitioners to focus on that goal. Unfortunately, many

Strategic Organization Development: Managing Change for Success
pp. 165–174
Copyright © 2009 by Information Age Publishing
All rights of reproduction in any form reserved.

also feel that OD has historically failed to live up to this worthwhile potential (Bradford & Burke, 2004). The perception of this shortcoming has resulted in numerous calls for OD to step out of its traditional behavioral sciences roots, and look for ways to add value in broader contexts (Bradford & Burke, 2004; Greiner & Cummings, 2004; Jelinek & Litterer, 1988; Worley & Feyerherm, 2003; Worley, Hitchin, & Ross, 1996).

Many of the efforts to respond to those calls have focused on how OD can be applied to issues such a strategy formulation and implementation. Greiner and Cumming clearly define how OD is typically absent from critical business decision making processes, even though the field has significant value to add to attempts to make those efforts more successful (2004). Jelinek and Litterer have identified how OD can be leveraged to address how organizations achieve their goals and maintain economic survival (1988). In addition, Worley, Hitchin, and Ross clearly define an OD based process that allows for more effective strategy implementations (Worley et al., 1996). There has even been recent research showing that many top performing organizations use a strategy formulation process consistent with on OD based ontology, even if they do not define it as such (Brown, 2006; Brown, 2007). Based upon these insights, it is not hard to see that OD has significant value to add to the discussion of strategy formulation, but where else could OD add value?

To understand where and how OD can value beyond its traditional domains, appropriate framing of those other domains is required. While there are a variety of opinions for such framing, this discussion will draw from Silbiger's *Ten Day MBA* text (1999). This text was selected because it attempts to summarize the basic concepts that are common across most master's of business administration programs, which is the most prevalent advanced degree among senior level business practitioners. According to Silbiger, there are nine major areas of business study:

- Marketing: Efforts to speak directly to customers through advertising, salespeople, and other promotional activities;
- Ethics: Attempts by management to adhere to socially responsible approaches and decision making processes;
- Accounting: Efforts to audit and report on an organization's assets and liabilities, and clearly communicate that status to appropriate stakeholders;
- Organizational Behavior: Approaches for dealing with human challenges in the workplace;
- Quantitative Analysis: Techniques for operationally defining and assigning numbers to phenomena so that they can be better analyzed and understood;

- Finance: Using analysis techniques, typically quantitative, to understand the monetary behavior of an organization and its environment, and then using those insights to make decisions;
- Operations: Executing activities related to how an organization runs its business (e.g., making products and providing services);
- Economics: Studying how societies allocate resources to the needs and wants of their populations; and
- Strategy: Analyzing a business in relation to its industry, its competitors, and the business environment in both the short-term and long-term so that it can achieve its goals (i.e., be successful) .

Given that the application of OD to the strategy arena has already been explored, and that there is evidence to suggest that applying an OD lens to the discussion of strategy can add significant value (Brown, 2006, 2007; Jelinek & Litterer, 1988; Worley et al., 1996), further discussion of that topic at this point seems redundant. For that reason alone, any additional discussion of OD's application to the study of strategy will be avoided, and the remainder of the discussion will focus on the other eight fields of study. In addition, while this discussion does adhere to the premise that an OD perspective can add some value to any area of study, it recognizes that the additional benefit over and above the current epistemologies is variable. For this reason, the remaining eight fields of study will be categorized into those that could have *limited* additional benefit from the application of the OD perspective, those that could have *moderate* additional benefit from the application of an OD perspective, and those that could have *significant* additional benefit from the application of an OD perspective.

The three areas that would likely receive the most *limited* additional benefit from the application of an OD perspective would be accounting, finance, and quantitative analysis. This determination is based upon the realization that while these areas could receive some moderate to significant benefit from integrating OD's systems thinking perspective, OD's humanistic side would have very little applicability. These three areas are primarily concerned with assigning numbers to some phenomena in the workplace, and then using appropriate analysis to understand what is/did/ could happen relative to the occurrences that those numbers represent. While these approaches could integrate OD's strong research methodological basis, they already have such significantly strong analytical foundations that additional inputs would likely show little additive return.

Another challenge is the disparity of basic perspectives between these areas and OD. OD's basic value propositions have evolved from humanistic and optimistic perspectives which by their very nature recognize and embrace subjectivity (French & Bell, 1999). Areas such as accounting, finance, and quantitative analysis tend to approach issues from a more conservative, objectivist, and logical positivist position. Embracing interpretivist approaches could violate some of those fields' basic assumptions, making the application of the humanistic and optimistic perspectives inappropriate.

Not that there have not been successful efforts to integrate these disparate views before. These efforts, however, have been mostly approached from the perspective of applying the objectivist tools and techniques to the study of people and organizations, rather than the other way around. Three primary examples of this include Fitz-enz *ROI of Human Capital* (2000); Donovan, Tully, and Wortman's *The Value Enterprise* (1998); and Carey and Lloyd *Measuring Quality Improvement in Healthcare* (2001). All three texts included some effort to quantify the value of the intangible aspects of organizations, areas often focused on by OD practitioners, but they do not look explicitly at how to drive and impact that value, as would be the case if an OD perspective were to be applied.

If OD were to look for the one place where it could add additional benefit to these discussions, it would likely find that opportunity in helping the practitioners of these fields understand the integration of the various intangible drivers that impact the outcomes that these fields attempt to measure. Developing that kind of understanding could begin with the application of systems thinking as described by Senge (1994), and also leverage an understanding of organizations as living systems as described by Burke (2002). Both of these approaches address the limitations of reductionisms; which is a key component of the current mindsets of fields such as accounting, finance, and quantitative analysis; and encourage the analysis and understanding of the whole system, not just individual parts. The challenge is that some of the reporting and analysis rules that govern and regulate the approaches relevant to the application of these fields of study are such that efforts must begin with the individual parts. Without modification of these rules, it may prove difficult to make the case for the value of applying a broader perspective. This does not, however, mean that OD practitioners should stop trying. It just means that the field will have to be more creative in how it approaches efforts to impact these other fields of study.

Two fields of study that are somewhat less regulated and more likely to benefit from the application of a systems thinking approach are Marketing and Organizational Behavior. These two fields could receive *moderate* additional benefit from the application of an OD perspective. Marketing is placed into this category because while it may only receive limited to moderate additional benefit from OD's traditionalist humanistic perspectives, there is significant additional value that could be driven from the application of OD's more systemic and holistic perspective. While marketing has historically been about driving outward communications to customers, and seen as a separate function from most of the organization, there is increasing recognition that marketing should be more of a two-way communication process that is integrated with the entire organizational system (Sutton & Klein, 2003). Obviously, whole systems thinking and the metaphor of an organization as a living organism would be useful here as well. Given that OD theorists understand these concepts, and can speak clearly to how to leverage them, there is significant opportunity for integration with this area. To date, however, there has been limited publication on how to apply OD to the study or application of Marketing.

One of the few recent publications that directly addresses this matter is Hatch and Schultz's discussion of the integration of corporate brands with organizational culture (2001). This article clearly demonstrates how the creation of brand equity can be driven by the norms, habits, and behaviors of an organization. Another publication that clearly shows the potential consequences of not considering the impact of culture on how an organization markets itself is Schein's *DEC is Dead, Long Live DEC* (2003), where the organization failed to survive despite better products because its culture prevented the organization from being able to interact in a way that met customers' needs. This new understanding is a significant step forward because while there have been some studies looking at the impact of individual employee's behavior on the customer experience (Hogan, Hogan, & Busch, 1984; Schneider, White, & Paul, 1998), most of those have looked at the phenomena in terms of individual behavior and its impact on customer satisfaction after the purchase transaction, rather than how the organization drives the customer to the transaction. Clearly this is a place where OD has significant value to add.

Organizational behavior (OB) is the study of human behavior in an organizational setting, the human/organization interface, and the organization itself (Moorehead & Griffin, 1992). OD is about applying an understanding of the behavioral sciences to improve the performance of an organization and/or the individuals in that organization (Burke, 2002; Cummings & Worley, 2005; French & Bell, 1999). It is not uncommon for people outside of either field to mistake OB and OD for one another. Both are focused on people issues such as leadership development, talent management, and employee relations. Both are focused on organizational issues such as design and performance. Both also draw from a theoretical basis that grew out of the work of pioneers like of Fredrick Taylor and Abraham Maslow.

Where the two fields appear to differ, however, is that while OB is more focused on organizations as closed systems at a particular point in time, and is further towards the academic side of the scholar-practitioner continuum; OD is more focused on organizations as open systems, looking at how they change and evolve over time, and tends to lean further towards the applied side of the scholar-practitioner continuum. These differences are the primary intersections where OD scholars have an opportunity to positively impact their OB brethren. Just as OD is calling on itself to look for ways to better integrate into other areas of business study, the OD scholars should try to recruit researchers from other behavioral science based fields, such as OB, and Industrial and Organizational Psychology, to follow their lead. Not so much to change what these other fields do or how they do it, but to influence where they look to contribute to the conversations about how organizations become more effective. There are numerous areas; such as economics, operations, and Ethics; where understanding the *people issues* are becoming more and more important, and it is becoming even more important for the scholars who understand those issues to increase their proactivity in attempting to apply their knowledge to other areas. The three fields of study where this application has the most *significant* additional benefit are ethics, operations, and economics.

Given that economic theorists study how societies make decisions about allocating resources, and societies are by definition macro level organizations, it is surprising that OD has not sought to apply both its systems thinking and humanistic perspectives to these efforts. There have been some practitioners of approaches such as appreciative inquiry, whole systems change, and positive organizational scholarship that have touched this topic (Cameron, Dutton, & Quinn, 2003; Cooperrider & Avital, 2005; Weisbord & Janoff, 1995; Whitney, 2005); but these are more efforts by particular individuals or groups than a coherent drive by the field. Evidence for this assertion is based on a review of three leading OD text books which revealed that not a single one of them listed Economics as a topic in either the table of contents or subject index (Burke, 2002; Cummings & Worley, 2005; French & Bell, 1999).

Perhaps one of the reasons for the lack of effort to explicitly apply OD to the study of economics is the field's predominant methodological approaches. While economics purports to seek understanding of the "invisible forces" that underlie the allocation of resources (Silbiger, 1999), a question well aligned to the OD skill-set, the tools and techniques employed in economics to develop those understandings are more in line with the rational and primarily quantitative approaches of other disciplines such as accounting and finance. This may cause some OD scholars to group economics with those other fields as areas where the application of OD could have only limited additional benefit. This, however, is inaccurate as the forces that impact the phenomena that economists study are often much more subjective and open to interpretation than they would like to admit.

Both OD's humanistic and systems thinking perspectives could have a positive impact on the field of economics. One of the more well known of these is Senge's (1994) *Beer Game* simulation that uses systems thinking to teach business managers to consider the up-line and down-line impacts of their decisions and activities. A lesser known but just as important example is Easley, Yaeger, and Sorensen's (2001) description of using Appreciative Inquiry, and its humanistic foundations, to impact troubled youth so that they will be better able to contribute to the future workforce, which can obviously influence the economic drivers of the societies that those youths inhabit. Again, however, these are typically unique efforts by a particular subset of OD theorist and practitioners. Where OD can be best applied to the field of Economics is not so much by doing anything that could be considered particularly new at this point, but by increasing the degree to which it is applied.

Operations is fundamentally concerned with the quality of outputs and the processes that lead to them, and draws from the works of theorists like Edward Deming and Joseph Juran (Carey & Lloyd, 2001; Pande, Neuman, & Cavanaugh, 2000; Silbiger, 1999; Woodall, 2001). It is also a field that OD has tended to shy away from as of late due to operations' focus on the mechanics of an organization's activities and perceived lack of opportunity for creative and cutting edge thought. This is actually quite surprising since operations also draws heavily from the works of people like Elton Mayo and Douglas McGregor who were two of the earliest scholars to recognize human behavior's impact on a process and its outcomes (Silbiger, 1999; Weisbord, 2004). Given OD's ability to fundamentally understand the human-processural system (Burke, 2002), and its ability to implement humanistic values into the organizational entity, OD is in a unique position to make a positive impact on the understanding of these kinds of activities.

There have been efforts to make this impact in the past. The work of Abraham Maslow, the early work at the Tavistock Clinic, and Blake and Mouton's *Grid Organizational Development* approach all demonstrate the potential positive impact of efforts to better understand the humanistic component of the sociotechnical process (French & Bell, 1999; Weisbord, 2004). While there are still some theorist such as Marv Weisbord, Rami Shani, and David Coghlan whose research is related to these questions (Coghlan & Brannick, 2005; van Eijnatten, Shani, & Leary, 2005; Weisbord, 2004), interest in this kind of basic theorizing and understanding has largely waned as the field of OD has become more focused on tools and techniques. If there were to be one call that would come out of this research relative to the application of OD to the field of operations, it would be for OD to refocus itself on developing additional and deeper theoretical understanding of these concepts so as to build upon the foundation of previous work. This and the application of OD to the field of business ethics are the two places where OD could provide the most *significant* additional benefit.

Ethics is a relatively new area of business study (Silbiger, 1999), especially in comparison to topics such as accounting that date back centuries. The goal of this field of study is not so much to mold model corporate citizens, as it is to drive business leaders to consider the ethical implications of their actions (Silbiger, 1999). Conversely, OD has from its earliest days based itself in a value proposition that tends to be humanistic, optimistic, and democratic (French & Bell, 1999). Because of this basis, OD has always been concerned with the ethical implications of its efforts, and seeks to balance the values of humanizing the organizational experience with the need to drive organizational effectiveness (Cummings & Worley, 2005). This is in sharp contrast to some more traditional business disciplines that posit that organizations exist solely to maximize the wealth of the business entities' owners (Silbiger, 1999). Examples of instances where the applications of this philosophy have caused damage to not only the organizations that assume this position, but also the environments in which they operate, are far too numerous to discuss here.

What can be discussed, however, is that OD is far ahead of most other business related disciplines when it comes to studying, understanding, and positively impacting the Ethics related issues that organizations must face. If there were one other place where the application of OD could have the most *significant* additional impact, this would be it. While much of the current OD related writing about ethics is focused on the appropriate application of the OD skill set (Cummings & Worley, 2005; French & Bell, 1999), the fact that the field does have a history of actively discussing these issues means that it is well positioned to take a leadership role in the Ethics dialog. Moreover, many of the OD techniques are tailor made for facilitating these kinds of discussions. As incumbent as it is for the field to become more integrated into issues such as strategy formulation and top business decision making, it is probably even more vital that the field apply its skills, knowledge, and experience to the understanding of how to create organizations that are ethical as well as profitable.

Obviously, there is more work to be done. Not only in terms of how to apply OD to the understanding of the strategy processes, but also in terms of understanding how OD can be applied to other areas of business study. The days of organizational silos that view workers as easily replaceable commodities have long since passed. There is increased recognition of the need for greater integration both within and beyond organizations. There is increased recognition of the value of human capital. There is increased recognition that the ethical treatment of employees, customers, and other stakeholders is no longer optional. There is also increasing recognition that most traditional business disciplines are new to understanding how to make all these different domains work together. Luckily, OD has from its earliest days sought to do just that. Unfortunately, however, much of the debate about how to apply that understanding has been limited to the confines of the OD community. While the confines may be friendly, OD's true value can only be realized by taking that conversation into new arenas. Once that occurs, it is highly likely that the value of including the OD perspective in those conversations will quickly become apparent. That is what this discussion has sought to demonstrate. The hope is that if this discussion did achieve that goal, others will be inspired to seek their own way to make the world a better place through the application of organization development.

REFERENCES

Bradford, D, & Burke, W. W. (2004). Introduction: Is OD in crisis? *Journal of Applied Behavioral Science, 40*, 369-373.

Brown, J. (2006). Application of an OD perspective to develop a new model of the strategy formulation process. *The Business Review, Cambridge, 6*, 26-31.

Brown, J. (2007). *Leveraging an OD perspective to develop a new model of strategy formulation.* Lisle, IL: Benedictine University.

Burke, W. W. (2002). *Organization change, theory and practice.* Thousand Oaks, CA: SAGE.

Cameron, K. S., Dutton, J. E., & Quinn, R. E. (2003). *Positive organizational scholarship.* San Franciso: Berrett-Koehler.

Carey, R. G., & Lloyd, R. C. (2001). *Measuring quality improvement in healthcare.* Milwaukee, WI: Quality Press.

Coghlan, D., & Brannick, T. (2005). *Doing action research in your own organization.* (2nd ed.) Thousand Oaks, CA: SAGE.

Cooperrider, D. L., & Avital, M. (2005). Appreciative inquiry and the changing field of change. In D. L. Cooperrider, P. F. Sorensen, T. F. Yaeger, & D. Whitney (Eds.), *Appreciative inquiry* (pp. 5-8). Champaign, IL: Stipes.

Cummings, T. G., & Worley, C. G. (2005). *Organization development and change* (8th ed.) Mason, OH: Thomas South-Western.

Donovan, J., Tully, R., & Wortman, B. (1998). *The value enterprise.* Toronto, Ontario, Canada: McGraw-Hill Ryerson.

Easley, C. A., Yaeger, T., & Sorensen, P. (2001). Saving tomorrow's workforce. In D. L. Cooperrider, P. F. Sorensen, T. F. Yaeger, & D. Whitney (Eds.), *Appreciative inquiry* (pp. 263-267). Champaign, IL: Stipes.

Fitz-enz, J. (2000). *The ROI of human capital.* New York: American Management Association.

French, W. L., & Bell, C. H. (1999). *Organization development* (6th ed.) Upper Saddle River, NJ: Prentice-Hall.

Greiner, L. E., & Cummings, T. G. (2004). Wanted: OD more alive than dead! *Journal of Applied Behavioral Science, 40,* 374-391.

Hatch, M. J., & Schultz, M. (2001). Are the strategic stars aligned for your corporate brand? *Harvard Business Review, 79,* 128.

Hogan, J., Hogan, R., & Busch, C. M. (1984). How to measure service orientation. *Journal of Applied Psychology, 69,* 167-173.

Jelinek, M., & Litterer, J. A. (1988). Why OD must become more strategic. In R. W. Woodman & W.A. Pasmore (Eds.), *Research in organizational change and development* (pp. 135-162). Greenwich, CT: JAI Press.

Moorehead, G., & Griffin, R. W. (1992). *Organizational behavior* (3rd ed.) Boston: Houghton Mifflin.

Pande, P. S., Neuman, R. P., & Cavanaugh, R. R. (2000). *The six sigma way.* New York: McGraw-Hill.

Schein, E. H. (2003). *DEC is dead, long live DEC.* San Francisco: Berrett-Koehler.

Schneider, B., White, S., & Paul, M. (1998). Linking service climate and customer perceptions of service quality: Test of a causal model. *Journal of Applied Psychology, 83,* 150-163.

Senge, P. M. (1994). *The fifth discipline.* New York: Currency Doubleday.

Silbiger, S. (1999). *The ten day MBA* (Rev. ed.) New York: Quill William Morrow.

Sutton, D., & Klein, T. (2003). *Enterprise marketing management.* Hoboken, NJ: Wiley.

Van Eijnatten, F., Shani, A. B., & Leary, M. (2005). Socio-technical systems: Designing and managing sustainable organizations. In T. G. Cummings (Ed.), *Handbook of organizational development and change* (pp. 277-311). Thousand Oaks, CA: SAGE.

Weisbord, M. R. (2004). *Productive workplaces revisited* (2nd ed.) San Francisco: Jossey-Bass.

Weisbord, M. R., & Janoff, S. (1995). *Future search.* San Francisco: Berrett-Koehler.

Whitney, D. (2005). Postmodern principles and practices for large scale organization change and global cooperation. In D. L. Cooperrider, P. F. Sorensen, T. F. Yaeger, & D. Whitney (Eds.), *Appreciative inquiry, foundations in positive organization development* (pp. 425-440). Champaign, IL: Stipes.

Woodall, T. (2001). Six sigma and service quality: Christian Grönroos revisited. *Journal of Marketing Management, 17,* 595.

Worley, C. G., & Feyerherm, A. E. (2003). Reflections on the future of organization development. *Journal of Applied Behavioral Science, 39,* 97-115.

Worley, C. G., Hitchin, D. E., & Ross, W. R. (1996). *Integrated strategic change.* Reading, MA: Addison-Wesley.

CHAPTER 11

TURNING YOUR ORGANIZATION INSIDE-OUT

Strategic OD's Role in Shifting From a Quest for the Best to a Discovery of Strength

Jason A. Wolf

All too often in business settings, specifically in larger organizations, resources and capital are focused on buying solutions to address organizational challenges. The "best" consultants are engaged, the "best" books are read; all the while the belief is that the organization is focused on doing the "best" thing. It is this quest for the "best" that may actually lead an organization in a different direction than it intended to go—into a place of commonalities versus competitive distinction—and in doing so an organization will all too often overlook the best "best" of all, their own internal strength.

This potential paradox of looking outside to become better inside provides both an interesting challenge and important opportunity for organization development (OD) practitioners and scholars. It also has significant implications for the strategic role OD can play in organizations. How does an OD practitioner stress the importance of looking

Strategic Organization Development: Managing Change for Success
pp. 175–189

inside their organization, to the human capital, know-how and capacity that helps us achieve great things every day? If OD practitioners are to be both valuable contributors and strategic partners in their work, then they must be willing to look in to their own organization, in essence turning their organization inside out, to discover the strength that lies within.

This is the thinking behind an internal study conducted at Healthco, a leading provider of healthcare services focusing on the exploration of high performance hospitals. The premise of the exploration was that in a large organization, with an extensive amount of internal experience and expertise, one could find some of the best within its very walls. This premise carries with it significant implications for the practice of strategic OD.

In fact, in the almost 20 years of increasing dialogue about OD's need to be strategic (Yaeger & Sorensen, 2006), this may be one of the most strategic ways OD can engage with organizations. More than helping to frame strategy through facilitation or developing capacity through direct interventions, or focusing on specific methodologies, processes or functions such as information technology (IT), human resource management (HRM) or positive planned change (Yaeger & Sorensen, 2006), perhaps we need to more distinctly view the role of strategic OD to be that of raising the level of awareness of the strengths an organization already possesses.

The implication here is that strategic OD must be about more than discovering strengths, but also about sharing them as broadly as possible in the system overall. It is important to clarify this is not simply another means for the sharing of best practices and hoping they are applied by others. In fact, it is in fact quite the opposite. Rather it is about rigorous research, clarifying core competence (Prahalad & Hamel, 1990) and capabilities (Ulrich, 1997; Ulrich & Smallwood, 2004) and ensuring these are effectively shared and appropriately implemented throughout the organization. It is about the acknowledgment and recognition of strong performers and creating an internal dialogue of what is truly best. It is about building an intentional program of discovery and development to support others in your organization.

In this chapter, a basic framework for OD and strategy will be constructed, a challenge to best practice provided and a method for rigorous research suggested. An example of this concept in action will be presented in the case of Healthco and implications for strategic OD will be discussed.

FRAMING OD

Woodman's (1993) description of OD best fits the idea of how strategic OD can turn your organization inside out. "Organization development means creating adaptive organizations capable of repeatedly transforming and reinventing themselves as needed to remain effective" (p. 73). The word "description'" is used here rather than "definition" to capture the dynamic nature of OD in its strategic form. Much as Weick and Quinn (1999) suggest "changing" to "change," Woodman's description expresses the nature of OD as active, exploratory and generative. Rather than a static 'OD is' we frame OD in a way that expresses the importance of continual discovery, or transformation and reinvention, not simply the acceptance of one set of practices or one way of being.

This is central to the point, that while a focus of strategic OD is on sharing strengths, this does not mean that an organization will or should rely *only* on those identified strengths. Rather in discovering these strengths, they will find competitive advantage and determine key needs to maintaining strategic significance in the marketplace. This is why supporting the capability to repeatedly transform and reinvent is where OD can have true strategic impact.

DECONSTRUCTING STRATEGY AND THE CHALLENGE OF STRATEGY OUTSOURCING

If one is to make the case of turning strategic OD inside out, it is also important to provide a construct and context for strategy overall. Strategy and OD have not always been the most integrated of organizational processes. In fact, Worley, Hitchin, and Ross (1996) suggest that the strategic management process is entirely missing the "OD perspective," which focuses on the alignment of process, organization design, people, and creating and managing change.

Both Mintzberg (1987) and Porter (1996) provide an even broader critique of strategy. Mintzberg suggests that "strategy is one of those words that people define in one way and often use in another without realizing the difference" (p. 67). He suggests the way in which we talk about strategy has us both looking forward to what is planned, but reflecting backward on what has been accomplished (or more often missed) without true clarity on which we are addressing. Mintzberg believes that strategy often emerges from within our organizations rather than from deliberate formulation, much as a craftsman approaches a project. In fact, Mankins (2006) suggests that the strategic planning process itself has little influence on a company's strategy. Rather, it is identifying a few key themes and critical decision points throughout the year that makes strategy development a continuous, focused and targeted process. This supports our foundational concept of strategic OD's role in discovering what lies within the organization as an active, dynamic process supported by Woodman's description above.

Mintzberg's metaphor of the craftsman supports Mankins' assertion that the process for strategy formulation is one that separates "the work of minds and hands" (p. 69) and therefore breaks the feedback loop that informs both in ensuring the best outcome. Much as one's hands would not move with the support of the mind's intentions, the mind's intentions are not set without the input of the senses such as through the hands. Mintzberg adds:

> The notion that strategy is something that should happen way up there, far removed from the details of running an organization on a daily basis is one of the great fallacies of conventional strategic management. (Mintzberg, 1987, p. 69)

This is where strategic OD can and must play a role. By uncovering the strengths in an organization, the gap between the "up there" and day-to-day detail, can be bridged and the potential for greater outcomes expanded. The challenge that remains is that while strategic management maintains the perspective that change must be continuous and organizations should be adapting as suggested by Woodman, strategy as a concept is rooted in stability and in its creation becomes a means to resist the very changes it seeks to create (Mintzberg, 1987).

Porter (1996) supports Mintzberg's assertions and suggests that the line between strategy and operational effectiveness has become blurred. While operational effectiveness is critical to remaining competitive as an organization, it does not create a strategic distinction. Strategic distinction emerges from what Mintzberg called the hands of the organization. How does an organization's day-to-day performance support its ability to distinguish itself from the competition? This is again a critical touch point for strategic OD. In raising an organization's strengths to the surface you move beyond best practice to competitive uniqueness. It is through the human capital of your organization that you can truly draw strategic distinction.

The challenge for most organizations is that they mistake the uncovering of strengths to equate to the discovery and implementation or best practices. Rather than looking inside the organization to highlight uniqueness and uncover and capitalize on strength, we search for benchmarks and practices that have us move towards "competitive convergence" (Porter, 1996). This process ultimately becomes more of an operational tool than a strategic action and has us appear more and more like our competition, rather than creating a competitive distinction (Nattermann, 2000; Pilkington, 1998; Porter, 1996). In fact, it has been shown in studies across various industries that this herding mentality (Nattermann, 2000; Pilkington, 1998; Porter, 1996) ultimately has a negative impact on the overall marketplace (Nattermann, 2000).

This is seen no more clearly than in a phenomenon I call *strategy outsourcing*. Strategy outsourcing occurs when an organization focuses their resources and capital on buying solutions rather than focusing on the critical components of uncovering strength, supporting emerging strategy, driving successful implementation and consistently focusing on the hard issues of people, process, design and change. In essence, organizations not only outsource execution, but they also outsource ideas, purchasing a prepackaged solution with the hope it will bring a promised or "proven" result.

With the onslaught of management books and publications, popularized concepts reach mass audiences, with the promise of great strategic results. Businesses see a means by which to quickly achieve their objectives, addressing the growing pressures for rapid results, without having to address the hard work that effective execution requires (Bossidy & Charan, 2002). They engage leading consultants, read the top-selling books, and believe they are doing the right thing for the organization.

While done most often with the purest of intention, strategy outsourcing takes on more of a feeling of desperation management (Finkelstein, 2005), which leads companies to jump from one solution to another, in search of a "holy grail" of sorts and never getting it right in the process. This too comes at the expense of working at the fundamentals discussed above—people, process, organization design and change capability. Rather than investing in the core competencies (Prahalad & Hamel, 1990) and capabilities (Ulrich, 1997; Ulrich & Smallwood, 2004) and looking for a systemic and lasting solution for the organization, companies invest in a quick fix (Senge, 2006). Strategy outsourcing, while perhaps an effective short term solution, overlooks organizational strength for purchased expertise (Schein, 1988), potentially leaves an organization drained in energy around core strength as individuals may feel underappreciated for their potential contributions, or creates reduced focus as some might see this as the most recent flavor of the month. This is not to say all strategy outsourcing is bad, but rather that it should be based on expanding organizational strengths rather then providing disconnected solutions.

This discussion of strategy is significant in that it provides an important perspective on the critical elements of strategic OD. Mintzberg and Porter urge organizations to use strategy to strive for competitive uniqueness and align strategy so that ideas match practice. This comes from our ability to uncover organizational strength and temper strategy outsourcing. The impact of best practice was also grounded in these perspectives, but it is important to ensure we clearly distinguish our internal strengths and best practice as we look to applying strategic OD in this framework.

REPLACING THE MODEL OF BEST PRACTICE

While the collection and implementation of best practices (which I will use interchangeably with the term benchmarking) has been identified as a critical operational tool (Brown & Duguid, 2000; Dow, Samson, & Ford, 1999; Marchington & Grugulis, 2000; Nattermann, 2000; Pilkington, 1998; Porter, 1996), it has also been shown to create diminishing competitive distinction and pose greater challenges for an organization.

Nattermann, Porter, and others were fair in expressing the potential positive use of the best practice approach as an operational tool, expressing that best practice benchmarking, the measurement and implementation of successful operational processes or strategy in an industry, can be an effective tool in driving speed, quality, productivity and earnings. They were also quick to point out that the overall goal in business is to uniquely position oneself in a place your competitors are not or do not have the ability to reach, not to move to a position of common strategy at an industry level, based on recycled or widely shared practice.

There have been numerous studies about the application of best practice in the work setting, as it applies to global strategy, applying common methods, and engaging in specific process areas, such as manufacturing or human resource management (Brown & Duguid, 2000; Dow et al., 1999; Marchington & Grugulis, 2000; Pilkington, 1998; Purcell, 1999). Many of these studies offer additional warnings about the application of best practice, speaking directly to the contextual nature of the benchmarking process, and the importance of understanding *where* these ideas will be applied (Cameron, Dutton, Quinn, & Wrzesniewski, 2003; Purcell, 1999). For instance, will all practices that fit in one work environment with a certain type of people, workstyle, etc., easily be transferred and implemented into one where those factors are different? Pilkington (1998) in his examination of the Japanization of the auto industries shows that indeed they are not.

Another significant consideration is *how* they will be applied. In Marchington and Grugulis' (2000) examination of HRM practices they conclude best practices to be at best "problematiclk," presenting at times contradictory messages and missing the mark on universal applicability. This failure to generate results comes back to the early warnings of Mintzberg as he looked at the shortcomings of current strategy processes, that the minds and hands of organizations were not connected. Marchington and Grugulis (2000) found, in fact, that best practice processes tended to leave out active input from employees to the organizations for which they work.

Pilkington (1998) stresses the impact of these concerns in his conclusion stating that "best practice strategy is unlikely ever to provide transformations in organizational performance" (p. 40) and acknowledging that this had been the emerging perspective in the strategy literature for some time In shifting to a new strategic perspective, two prevailing models have emerged, building on one another in expanding the perspective of organizational ability: Prahalad and Hamel's (2001) organizational core competence and Ulrich's (1997; Ulrich & Smallwood, 2004) organizational capability (Rothwell & Lindholm, 1999). It is important to understand these processes as they provide a framework and philosophy for the actions taken by Healthco in determining its own internal strengths.

Prahalad coined the phrase *core competency* as a means to discuss an organization's strategic strength. He stresses this concept is greater than achieving short-run competitiveness of best practices such as performance processes or price/cost management practices and instead focuses on the true core ability that distinguishes an organization. Prahalad equates core competence to the "root system that provides nourishment, sustenance, and stability" (Prahalad & Hamel, 1990, p. 82) stressing that this is where an organization maintains its true inner strength. He also expresses how core competence emerges from the organization itself, from its people, through collective learning, communication and the commitment to work across organizational boundaries. Ultimately, core competence becomes a strategic advantage of an organization as:

1. it provides access to a wide variety of markets;
2. it positively impacts the perceived benefits of the end product by the customer; and
3. it is difficult for competitors to imitate (Prahalad & Hamel, 1990).

Ulrich (1997; Ulrich & Smallwood, 2004) expanded on Prahalad's ideas with the concept of organizational capability. He picks up on Mintzberg's very challenge of strategy, that it looks both backwards and forwards in expressing that an organization's potential emerges in both its past success and perceived future opportunities. He also closely ties the contribution of individual strengths to organizational outcomes in determining organizational capability. Simply stated, he believes "organizational capabilities emerge when a company delivers on the combined competencies and abilities of its individuals." (p. 120).

Ulrich and Smallwood (2004) effectively show the relationship of these central elements. They make clear the connection, yet distinction between the technical foundations of competence and the social framework of ability and capability. In the technical realm, the individual level focuses on functional competence while the organizational level focused on core competencies. Competence in this sense is the passive "having" of a skill or "know-how." It is when we get to the social realm that we begin to move beyond simple competence, to measureable leadership ability and organizational capability. The suggestion here is that while core competence is important to an organization's direction, it is through capability, as a social and strategic element, that an organization can turn its technical know-how in actual results.

These two concepts are introduced here in contrast of best practice strategy as a means to show there are more significant means to focus on an organization's strength and gain strategic advantage. It also helps to frame where it is believed, as presented above, that strategic OD truly has a role to play, in uncovering and supporting the expression of organizational strengths. While best practice methodology has us drive towards commonality in our marketplace, strategic OD through these practices can help us find our unique organizational presence.

Cameron et al. (2003) effectively frame the overall challenge of best practices and move us in the direction of a more systemically driven understanding of organizational competence and capability that pushes us to uncover organizational strengths.

> Highlighting best practices approach to organization behavior avoids system level thinking that explains the processes and dynamics by which organizations become sites for growth and health. Organizations often fail to get results from implementing best practices because these organizations import a set of discrete, unconnected pieces of practice without attending to the underlying philosophy or system in which such practices need to be embedded in order to take root and change the organization. (p. 368)

It is from this perspective that we look to the means by which to identify and capture organizational strength, a central purpose to strategic OD. As strategic OD practitioners, how does one best uncover the strengths that lie within an organization? This is where the fundamental scholar-practitioner model in OD roles finds its place as a true strategic leader. It has been and will continue to be the OD practitioners' role as not only solutions provider, but as researcher and diagnostician (Cummings & Worley, 2004; Schein, 1988; Weisbord, 2004) that supports the role of OD in being truly strategic.

DISCOVERING STRENGTH THROUGH RIGOROUS RESEARCH

One of the core areas supporting the concept of strategic OD is positive change (Yaeger & Sorensen, 2006). The foundation of positive change itself rests on the elevation of inquiry into our strengths (Cooperrider &

Sekerka, 2003). As we review our discussion to this point then, this idea clearly supports the position that a central role of strategic OD is to uncover the strengths within an organization.

It is important to understand that this elevation of inquiry has great implications for an organization and also serves as core means by which strategic OD impacts organizations today. The elevation of inquiry contributes to an expansion of relatedness to others resulting in a fusion of strengths (Cooperrider & Sekerka, 2003), which in itself leads to the strategic role OD can play in organizations. It is through this process of inquiry and an expansion of relatedness that best practice is replaced by the discovery of core competence, organizational capability and the true strategic differentiation that a firm can achieve. It is in this process of inquiry into strengths, the core role of strategic OD, that the whole potential of an organization can be realized and unleashed.

This is not a complicated process or lengthy intervention, but rather a willingness to ask for what is well and good and how it affects the ability of the organization to perform. In fact, by focusing on the strengths an organization brings to bear, you alter the conversation from one of deficit to one of positive social construction (Gergen, 1999) and possibility. But by what means do we achieve these outcomes?

The means in its simplest terms is that of rigorous research. It is not necessarily a logical positivist study of specific sets of performance data, but rather an exploration into the actions that an organization takes in its day-to-day workings. This inquiry into strength is strategic OD at its very essence and is founded on the core principles of cooperative inquiry and ultimately action research (Greenwood & Levin, 2007). The process of looking at your strengths versus choosing strategy outsourcing is not an easy or simple decision, as it does demand a rigor and willingness to solve real-life problems. By adding a positive and constructionist perspective to this process, as exemplified in the action research methodology, appreciative inquiry (Cooperrider & Sekerka, 2003), we can begin to see how the discovery of strengths themselves helps to refocus an organization on its potential versus it problems.

It was with this focus on potential and strength, founded on a framework of rigorous internal inquiry, that Healthco moved beyond the simple identification of best practice, to the discovery of strategic strength. The investigation itself raises an important point shared by Mankins, Pilkington, Prahalad and others. It is in finding common ground and in uncovering shared strengths, through which organizations achieve their greatest outcomes. If we stop creating distinctions in business units, functions and departments and focus on creating cross-boundary solutions, raising core competence and capability, the potential for strategic distinction and organizational success is unparalleled. It is here that the purpose of strategic OD can be no clearer.

STRATEGIC OD AND HEALTHCO

In late 2004, Healthco launched an investigation into the potential drivers of performance in the company. It was believed, that in a company of the size of Healthco ($24 billion in revenue, almost 180 hospital facilities and over 100 other locations) and with the collective expertise and proven performance of our people (over 180,000 employees worldwide), Healthco possessed some of the leading practices in healthcare.

With this premise in mind, a study was initiated to examine the top performing facilities and determine what it is they were doing to generate strong and positive results. Through the research, Healthco looked to develop a model of processes and practices that help frame the characteristics of a high performance facility in healthcare. It was acknowledged from the start of the process that the discoveries made, would most likely not be surprising or earth shattering, but more so, would lead back to the core behaviors believed to drive good organizational health and effectiveness. The outcome of the process was the discovery of seven core characteristics of high performance in the Healthco system and while the actual characteristics are not pertinent to the focus of this chapter, the process of their discovery and sharing certainly is.

This exploration of theory in action frames the premise behind the strategic OD work being conducted at Healthco. The thought process was grounded in the strategic framework of competence and capability versus best practice. This is where the concept of strategic OD played a significant role in the framing and design of this effort and focused Healthco not on searching out external expertise, but on raising the level of awareness of the strengths the organization already possessed, sharing them as broadly as possible in the system overall.

The project was simple in process, but designed to have substantial strategic impact. By identifying high performing facilities across the system, and visiting them to determine core strategy and key characteristics, a common set of strengths could be determined. The project was not designed to uncover best practice with the assumption that these practices could be applied in any healthcare facility across the United States and lead to the same result. This very idea was challenged by Greenwood and Levin (2007) who rejected the notion that generalized knowledge developed in the action research process were transferable between locations. Suggesting that, as we discussed above, transferring knowledge from one location to another relies on understanding the contextual factors where the inquiry occurred, the contextual framework where the knowledge is to be applied and then determining if a link is even possible.

Instead of trying to create generalized knowledge, the intention of the project at Healthco was to identify common shared competencies and capabilities in the organizations studied, share this information with sister facilities in the Healthco systems, and provide the processes and tools for self assessment again, for these findings to determine areas of strengths to expand and potential areas that might require development. The process was designed not to create a one-size-fits-all mentality among facilities, but rather to create a framework of shared capability that would support each facility in recognizing and expanding on its strengths.

The role of strategic OD ultimately played two roles in this project overall. First the framing of the initial research proposition, that one could strategically engage the organization by discovering the strengths that lie within. This role proved the more successful of the two, as the extensive internal inquiry process of interviews, focus groups and surveys led to a clear commonality in competence and capability among the high performing facilities. This discovery also posed a significant challenge to the consultant/researchers in that it is at a point like this in an inquiry where it may be deemed easier to declare these characteristics to be truths (in fact this became the case in sharing these key characteristics with others where they we deemed "simple truths"). This hardening of the inquiry process to form definite practices has the potential to lead us back down the path to the very beginning of our discussion, that best practice more often than not does not lead to *best result*. The trap for the strategic OD practitioner is in settling for the discovery of strengths as definitive versus strengths as emergent and watching from being too prescriptive themselves as the discovery of strengths emerges.

The second key role of strategic OD was one in which some of the pitfalls discussed above could be overcome. This was supported by the creation of processes and tools that allowed other facilities to look at themselves in contrast to the core set of discovered strengths. This was not a means to say that all facilities must possess the discovered characteristics, but at the same time it was shown that these characteristics consistently led to the outcomes the organization was looking to achieve.

In fact, as Healthco analyzed the results associated with the discovered strengths, they were able to see some very tangible strategic implications. Those facilities identified as high performers outperformed a comparison group of lower performers by over five percent in margin, maintained significantly higher employee engagement scores, ran at turnover rates just under ten percent less than the comparison group. The high performers also eclipsed the comparison group on quality measures, showing that there was true substance to these identified strengths.

Seeing these results, tools were created to help individual organizations assess themselves and begin to address the key areas uncovered in the study. The tools and resources were not designed as a requirement that each facility attempt to be exactly the same, but rather were focused on aligning the facilities around the identified strengths, a set of core organizational competencies and capabilities that would support the overall strategy of the organization. Ultimately through both roles, the consultant/researchers played a critical part in framing the strategic pathway facilities to clearly follow to reach the Healthco's strategic goals.

What the consultant/researchers discovered in the process is that the prevailing tendency for an organization is to focus its search for THE answer, the best practice, the way of doing, being, operating that leads to a desired outcome. To move to a process of truly discovering and developing strengths and framing these in a strategic context is a hard concept for most leaders, employees and even OD consultants to follow in trying to achieve these outcomes. It is in understanding the strategic framework of OD, its connections to the core principles of strategy and the rigor of inquiry and action research that shows how strategic OD can be a critical element in generating positive organizational results. The Healthco case helps show that there is energy and value behind the ever present challenge inherent in discovering an organization's strengths, highlighting and celebrating these strengths and having them frame the strategic direction an organization wishes to take.

CONCLUSION

As suggested previously, organizations look to outsource strategy and gain and sustain competitive advantage by buying solutions instead of building the capabilities of their own organizations. If they were to focus on developing and maintaining core strength, organizations would find a new found ability to thrive in today's competitive environment. Rather than outsourcing for the best we need to develop our core strengths and look inward to our own organizations.

In the drive to address effective strategy implementation and execution, in this quest for the best, we overlook all too often the best "best" of all, our own high performers in our very organization. While benchmarking is a critical means of taking one's temperature compared to the external marketplace, it often becomes the only place organizations turn for solutions and ultimately for constructing organizational strategy. Unfortunately, as was discussed above, this more often than not falls far short of the mark (Brown & Duguid, 2000; Dow et al., 1999; Mankins & Steele,

2006; Marchington & Grugulis, 2000; Pilkington, 1998; Porter, 1996; Prahalad & Hamel, 1990). This in particular is an interesting dilemma for OD practitioners and scholars. If OD practitioners are to be both valuable contributors to organizations and maintain a strategic focus in their work, they must be willing to look to their organizations for the value that lies within. Doing this not only supports internal development, but also focuses on expanding competitive strategy. At the heart of strategic OD is building organizations capable of achieving significant results with the very resources they possess.

This may be one of the most strategic ways OD can play a role in organizations. More than helping frame strategy through facilitation or developing capacity through interventions, strategic OD is about raising the level of awareness of the strengths an organization already possesses. Even more than that, it is about discovering those strengths and sharing them as broadly as possible in the system overall. This is beyond simply sharing best practices, it is about rigorous research, clarifying key behaviors and actions and ensuring these are shared and effectively implemented throughout the organization.

This was the framework of Healthco's internal study focused on discovering the best, showing that the best had a true impact on performance results and then integrating them into critical behaviors for the organization. These discoveries have become a critical part of organizational strategy, based on strengths that have come from within. While discovering the best was a critical step, it was linking back to strategy execution and implementation where the greatest value was and can still be added.

IMPICATIONS FOR THE FUTURE OF STRATEGIC OD AND CHANGE

In their new book *Built to Change* (2006), Lawler and Worley suggest that the built to change organization does not search for *the* strategy, but is continuously strategizing and it does not attempt to find *the* organization design, but rather remains in the process of organizing. They stress that "organizations that string together a series of temporary but adequate advantages will outperform organizations that stick with one advantage for a long period of time" (p. 21). It is this dynamic nature of strategic change that calls for us to find our inner strength as organizations. The ideas that we buy are already tried and true, but they are also aging by the moment and at the fingertips of any competitor that has the check with which to pay. The true advantage that we have in driving strategic change in organizations and the ultimate value of strategic OD is to end the outsourcing of strategy by providing a valuable process to follow, by focusing on the discovery of strengths and the effective framing of these strengths as central to strategy. Critical to this point is that discovered strengths are expressed in process, not in prescribed best practice. When all is said and done, the implication for strategic OD may be no simpler than to learn from others, but build from what you know. If we are effective at the process of inquiry into strength and work to create clarity of competence and capability, strategic OD has effectively played its central role in the strategy process itself—to create a unique and valuable position (Porter, 1996) that honors all of what comprises an organization. It is in turning your organization inside out in a search for the strengths that reside within, that you truly establish strategic distinction. It is the role of strategic OD to do nothing more important than that.

REFERENCES

Bossidy, L., & Charan, R. (2002). *Execution: The discipline of getting things done.* New York: Crown Business.

Brown, J. S., & Duguid, P. (2000). Balancing act: How to capture knowledge without killing it. *Harvard Business Review, 78*(3), 73-80.

Cameron, K. S., Dutton, J. E., Quinn, R. E., & Wrzesniewski, A. (2003). Developing a discipline of positive organization scholarship. In K. S. Cameron, J. E. Dutton & R. E. Quinn (Eds.), *Positive organizational scholarship: Foundations of a new discipline* (pp. 361-370). San Francisco: Berrett-Koehler.

Cooperrider, D. L., & Sekerka, L. E. (2003). Toward a theory of positive organization change. In K. S. Cameron, J. E. Dutton, & R. E. Quinn (Eds.), *Positive organizational scholarship: Foundations of a new discipline* (pp. 225-240). San-Francisco: Berrett-Koehler.

Cummings, T., & Worley, C. (2004). *Organization development and change* (8th ed.). Minneapolis, MN: West.

Dow, D., Samson, D., & Ford, S. (1999). Exploding the myth: Do all quality management practices contribute to superior quality performance? *Productions and Operations Management, 8*(1), 1-27.

Finkelstein, S. (2005). When bad things happen to good companies: strategy failure and flawed executives. *Journal of Business Strategy, 26*(2), 19-28.

Gergen, K. J. (1999). *An invitation to social construction.* London: SAGE.

Greenwood, D. J., & Levin, M. (2007). *Introduction to action research: Social research for social change* (2nd ed.). Thousand Oaks, CA: SAGE.

Lawler, E. E., & Worley, C. G. (2006). *Built to change: How to achieve sustained organizational effectiveness.* San Francisco: Jossey-Bass.

Mankins, M. C., & Steele, R. (2006). Stop making plans start making decisions. *Harvard Business Review, 84*(1), 76-84.

Marchington, M., & Grugulis, I. (2000). "Best practice" human resource management: Perfect opportunity or dangerous illusion? *International Journal of Human Resource Management, 11*(6), 1104-1124.

Mintzberg, H. (1987). Crafting strategy. *Harvard Business Review, 65*(4), 66-75.

Nattermann, P. M. (2000). Best practice (does not equal) best strategy. *McKinsey Quarterly, 2*, 22.

Pilkington, A. (1998). Manufacturing strategy regained: Evidence for the demise of best-practice. *California Management Review, 41*(1), 31-42.

Porter, M. E. (1996). What is strategy? *Harvard Business Review, 74*(6), 61-78.

Prahalad, C. K., & Hamel, G. (1990). The core competence of the corporation. *Harvard Business Review, 68*(3), 79-91.

Purcell, J. (1999). The search for best practice and best fit in human resource management: Chimera or cul-de-sac? *Human Resource Management Journal, 9*(9), 26-41.

Rothwell, W. J., & Lindholm, J. E. (1999). Competency identification, modeling and assessment in the USA. *International Journal of Training & Development, 3*(2), 90.

Schein, E. (1988). *Process consultation: Its role in organization development.* Reading, MA: Addison-Wesley.

Senge, P. (2006). *The fifth discipline: The art and practice of the learning organization.* New York: Currency Doubleday.

Ulrich, D. (1997). Organizing around capabilities. In F. Hesselbein, M. Goldsmith & R. Beckhard (Eds.), *The organization of the future* (pp. 189-198). San Francisco: Jossey-Bass.

Ulrich, D., & Smallwood, N. (2004). Capitalizing on capabilities. *Harvard Business Review, 82*(6), 119-127.

Weick, K. E., & Quinn, R. E. (1999). Organizational change and development. *Annual Review of Psychology, 50*(1), 361.

Weisbord, M. R. (2004). *Productive workplaces revisited: Dignity, meaning, community in the 21st century.* San Francisco: Jossey-Bass.

Woodman, R. W. (1993). Observations from the field of organizational change and development from the lunatic fringe. *Organization Development Journal, 11*(2), 71-74.

Worley, C. G., Hitchin, D. E., & Ross, W. L. (1996). *Integrated strategic change: How OD builds competitive advantage.* Reading, MA: Addison-Wesley.

Yaeger, T., & Sorensen, P. (2006). Strategic organization development: Past to present. *Organization Development Journal, 24*(4), 10-16.

CHAPTER 12

STRATEGIC ORGANIZATION DEVELOPMENT

A Change Approach for Health Care Delivery

Barry Halm

The United States health care system is fragmented, costly, severely regulated, and does not provide equal access to affordable health care to all citizens. The American public is calling for radical changes to its health care system which will place many health care organizations in a position of implementing new methods and practices for improving their operating performance and clinical effectiveness. A *strategic change framework* is proposed to assist those health care organizations in responding to a radically different environment.

The strategic change framework will focus on the importance of designing a compelling vision for the future, explore the significance that leadership has facilitating a change process, identify the need for a human performance system, evaluate why restructuring the organization's work processes is important, and emphasizing the implication for new methods of community collaboration.

Strategic Organization Development: Managing Change for Success
pp. 191–211
Copyright © 2009 by Information Age Publishing
All rights of reproduction in any form reserved.

Effective strategic change requires organization development (OD) intervention in the areas of strategy, systems, structure, and process. The specific OD interventions proposed for a health care system's change process will include: strategy (vision development and goal creation), systems (organizational culture and leadership formation), structure (performance systems and organizational design) and process (collaborative approaches and cooperation).

OVERVIEW OF THE HEALTH CARE DELIVERY SYSTEM

Consumers and executives from across corporate America are suggesting that the health care system must deliver a higher quality of care within safer environments, while at the same time being affordable to those seeking health care services. The health care system is confronted with many confounding environmental characteristics such as the aging of society, increasing costs driven by changing patterns of medicine, and a continuing escalation of specialization spurred by new technology. Table 12.1 identifies many of the environmental factors impacting the U.S. health care system. Similar to most industries, the United States health care delivery system operates in a complex social environment faced with increased competition and a changing platform of consumer expectations. This complex technological, political, and social environment in which the health care system operates, has produced a rich opportunity for the implementation of strategic OD.

Presently, the United States spends 16% of the gross domestic product on health care, twice the per capita spending of the typical industrialized nation and yet, almost 47 million Americans do not have health insurance coverage (DeNavas-Walt, Proctor, & Hill, 2006). Borger et al. (2006) enlightened the industry by emphasizing, the cost of U.S. health care is increasing annually at least twice the rate of overall inflation and evidence abounds that there is no end in sight. With health care consuming 16% of gross domestic product, marching inescapably toward 20% in 2015, change will not only be suggested but demanded by consumers, business leaders, and politicians across the country (Borger et al., 2006).

It is anticipated that in the foreseeable future corporate organizations and consumers, faced with dramatic escalation in costs and little to no corresponding increases in quality and accessibility, will place significant pressure upon the political process to introduce revolutionary and transformational change in the way health care is delivered. This change will be manifested through a redesign in the way health care organizations will receive payment/reimbursement for the services they provide. These payment modifications will be advanced by the federal government's attempt

**Table 12.1. Environmental Factors
Affecting the U.S. Healthcare System**

- Constrained reimbursement
- Aging of the population
- Increasing competition
- Burdensome regulations
- Increasing operating costs
- Growth of new technologies
- Aging of facilities
- Increasing demand for capital
- Shortage of professional staff
- Changing consumer expectations
- Governmental demand of quality and patient safety

to balance the federal budget and the need to stabilize the Medicare Trust Fund. Reformation of payment incentives and new social policies will drive system-wide change within this country's health care system. Corporate executives will add their voice to the call for reform. Their message will be "cost containment"; seeking lower benefit costs which will allow their corporations to compete more aggressively within a developing global marketplace.

Many health care reformers are suggesting the creation of "universal coverage" under a single payor system. The concept of universal coverage provides advantages over the current delivery system by increasing accessibility to health care services, reducing the associated costs, establishing standardization of health information technology, and expanding evidence-based medicine to improve safety and efficiency. Universal coverage would radically modify the financing component of the health care system by spreading economic responsibility across society, establishing new payment methodologies, and the introduction of progressive taxes to cover public programs. The impact would be a metamorphosis in both economic incentives (payment methods) and patient care delivery (operating methods) for the health care system and individual provider organizations. These environmental factors coupled with the resulting impact upon the health care industry are suggesting transformational change. Such a change will require strategic OD intervention at multiple levels: the collective health care system and within individual provider organizations.

STRATEGIC CHANGE

The struggle to meet the challenges of a changing health care system will place many health care organizations in a position of implementing new policies and practices for improving their operating performance and clinical effectiveness. Worley and colleagues suggest that organizations which undertake change that realigns their organization's strategy, structure and process required to fit within a new competitive context are implementing a process entitled "strategic change" (Worley, Hitchin, & Ross, 1996). Cummings and Worley (2005) explained in *Organization Development and Change* that strategic change involves improving the alignment among the organization's environment, strategy, and organizational design. Beckhard and Harris (1987) suggest that strategic change interventions include efforts to improve both the organizational relationship to its environment and the connection between the technical, political and cultural systems. Miller and Freisen (1980) identified that strategic change is triggered by some major disruption to the organization such as the lifting of regulatory requirements, change in economic patterns or a technological breakthrough.

Strategic change and the resulting outcomes are not new to the health care delivery system. During the 1950s, rural communities received federal funds through Hill-Burton legislation to build hospitals and clinics in rural America, increasing access for many to needed health care services. The 1960s experienced creation of new entitlement programs such as Medicare and Medicaid, expanding the availability of health services to the aged and uninsured. In the 1970s, legislation was implemented to regulate the rapid expansion of the health care industry through "certificate of need" laws, limiting expenditures for new technology and facility expansion. The 1980s saw new payment approaches introduced such as prospective payment and alternative payment arrangements. These new payment methods forced hospitals to decrease costs and implement innovative operating techniques to increase productivity and reduce slack. The 1990s witnessed the explosion of health maintenance organizations and alternative means of delivering care through outpatient and ambulatory settings. The decade of 2000 has brought increased competition, a focus on cost containment, and greater demand for standardization of quality within an environment of safety. Each decade within the historical past required health care organizations to create a response, a method of adaptation, and some means of modification to continue their existence in the face of change.

This continuous process of environmentally lead change demands the use of specialized "approaches," "methods," and "tools" which may assist health care organizations in responding to the phenomenon of change

(Werr, Stjenberg, & Docherty, 1996). The strategic change process is heavily influenced by OD approaches, theories and methods (Cummings & Worley, 2005). These approaches and methods can assist the collective health care system and individual provider organizations to navigate through a transformational change process. The complexity of the health care system requires a conceptual framework to guide the implementation of a strategic change process. The formulation of a strategic change framework will provide the health care system and individual provider organizations with the underlying principles to transcend the rugged terrain of strategic change.

The health care delivery system within the United States is unique as a result of regulatory factors (legislative regulations and entitlement programs), social forces (demographic and cultural trends), technological factors (new pharmaceuticals and medical diagnostic/treatment methods), economic factors (cost shifting and changing payment methods) and competitive forces (competitiveness of physician practices and group health plans) (Berkowitz, 2006). This uniqueness demands precise intervention techniques which are specific to the health care system.

The new health care system and individual provider organizations will operate in a much different environment than the past. The future will require individual provider organizations to establish new integrated operating methods which will enable them to respond to a more dynamic and changing health care environment. The strategic change framework is proposed as a strategic OD approach that may assist health care organizations as they respond to a changing environment.

The strategic change framework emphasizes the necessity of creating a compelling vision for the future, explores the importance of leadership, identifies the critical need for a human performance system, evaluates why restructuring the organization's work processes is important, and emphasizes the need for new methods of community collaboration. The strategic change framework is illustrated in Figure 12.1. The framework suggests OD intervention takes place in the areas of strategy (vision development and goal creation), systems (organizational culture and leadership formation), structure (performance systems and organizational design) and process (collaborative approaches and cooperation).

ORGANIZATIONAL CHANGE

The health care industry in the United States provides the best "medical care" in the world through specialized health care centers, highly trained professionals and innovative technology. But at the same time, health care delivery has been driven by a constant state of "organizational change"

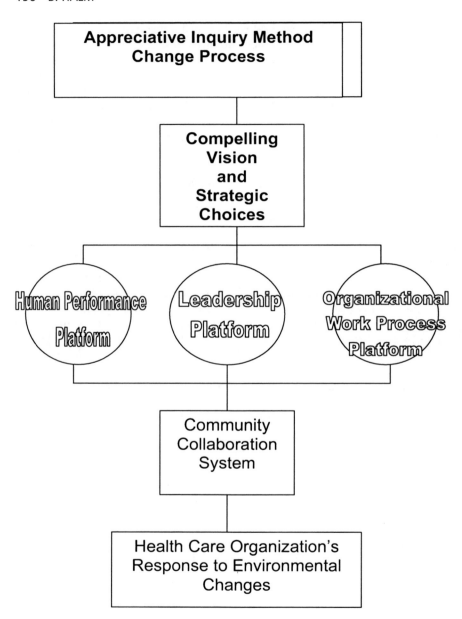

Figure 12.1.   Strategic change model.

resulting in reduced access, increased costs and generating minimal impact on the quality of care being delivered. Previous organizational change efforts has not resulted in any long term benefit for either consumers or the payors (i.e., federal government, private health insurance organizations) of health care services.

Daft (1998) stated in his book, *Organization Theory and Design,* that organizational change as defined by organizational theory is the "adoption of a new idea or behavior by an organization" (p. 14). In organizational behavior change, Wagner and Hollenbeck (1998) defined organizational change as "the act of varying or altering conventional ways of thinking or behaving" (p. 12). Gibson, Ivancevich, and Donnelly (1997) emphasized in their book *Organizations: Behavior, Structure and Processes* that organizational change is described by the description, causes, reactions to, management strategies, and terms which are all integral to the organizational change process. Health care organizations that respond to a mandated call for change, in the way health care services will be financed, will need to create alternative means of adapting new behaviors or designing new methods of altering conventional ways of thinking. New ways of thinking is emphasized in Peter Senge's works on learning organizations.

In *Fifth Discipline* published in 1990, Dr. Senge suggested that five new "component technologies" would be required to develop, what he labeled an innovative learning organization. Each of the components, though separate and distinct, is required to perform together in a combined system which enhances the value of each individual component and collectively generates a higher synergy of organizational benefit. The principles (identified in Table 12.2) for developing a learning organization centered on the five elements of system thinking, personal mastery, mental models, shared vision, and team learning. The concepts of a learning organization (system thinking, team learning, and shared vision) are elements of a strategic change model when properly implemented with the theories and principles of organization development. The OD theory's of group dynamics, organizational change, organizational learning, positive organizational scholarship and strategic change will be required to move health care organizations into the next frontier of service delivery and financing.

Cummings and Worley emphasized in *Organization Development and Change* the growing applications of OD in the service industry. The authors stated that the traditional application of OD may need to be modified if they are to extend beyond the narrow industrial model (Cummings & Worley, 2005). The authors believe that scholar/practitioners in OD can positively influence the process and outcomes of change in the health care environment. The opportunities include creating effective cul-

Table 3. Description of the
Five Components of a Learning Organization

- System thinking: System thinking is constructed by a conceptual frameworks composed by a body of knowledge and tools which creates patterns that help to see how change can be implemented effectively.

- Personal mastery: Personal mastery is the development of a special level of proficiency that deepens one's personal vision, concentrates energy, and develops patience which allows us to see reality objectively.

- Mental models: Mental models is our understanding of the world in which we live, the assumptions, generalizations, and even pictures or images that influence our ability to respond to the world in which we reside.

- Building shared vision: Building shared vision is the practice of unearthing a common "picture of the future" that foster genuine commitment and enrollment to create a new reality.

- Team learning: Team learning is the creation of a practice that brings the discipline of dialogue and the process of group dynamics together in a common framework to facilitate accelerated learning.

Source: Senge (1990).

tures; developing systems and services that cost effectively differentiate and meet needs; job and process redesign to maximize effective use of expertise; and restoring trust in and among stakeholders (Cummings & Worley, 2005).

Creating a planned change process for the health care industry will require a multidisciplinary approach simultaneously addressing numerous operational components to bring about transformational change. Such a comprehensive process is necessary due to the complexities of the financing and delivery components of the health care system.

Cummings and Worley (2005) offered a set of principles and beliefs that describe effective OD interventions in the health care industry. These principles present future challenges to the practice of health care administration and practitioner of OD in health care delivery. In summary, the authors suggest four principles for OD intervention in health care:

1. Organizational intervention must be linked to strategic performance to assist the organization to achieve and sustain competitive advantage;

2. Organizational intervention must to constructed upon a deeper systemic foundation to support sustainable change such as cultures built on trust and learning;

3. Organizational intervention must be built around leadership competences required to respond to the changing discipline of health care delivery such as regulatory and financial policy changes, and restructuring clinical care systems; and

4. Organizational intervention must construct a common vision integrating all components of a community's health care system to effectively deploy limited resources (Cummings & Worley, 2005).

Health care organizations will rely on OD intervention techniques and strategic OD methods as they undertake planned change processes to transcend the chasm between the current "open market" delivery system and the "universal—single payor" delivery arrangement anticipated in the foreseeable future.

Cummings and Worley created a definition of organization development under the assumption that organizations must adapt and change in response to their environment. "The pace of global, economic, and technological development makes change an inevitable feature of organizational life. Organization development is directed at bringing about planned change to increase an organization's effectiveness and capability to change itself" (Cummings & Worley, 2005, p. 22). The authors go on to state that "all approaches to OD rely on some theory about planned change" (Cummings and Worley, 2005). Change is a pervasive aspect of our lives and almost a necessity for economic survival. In the present business environment there are people to whom change happens and people who like to make it happen. Health care leaders will need to positively embrace change and invite OD specialists to participate with them in the change process. It is through this collaborative effort that health care organizations will have access to OD talent and technique required to respond to a shifting health delivery system.

Cummings and Worley (2005) stated, the

> public demand for less government and lowered deficits forced public sector agencies to streamline operations and to deliver more for less. Rapid changes in technologies (as experienced by the health care industry) rendered many organizational practices obsolete, pushing firms to be continually innovative and nimble. (p. 480)

Organization transformation interventions are a major discipline of Organization Developmental practice and will be a critical component in the process of transforming the health care system within the United States.

ORGANIZATIONAL CHANGE PROCESS

Strategic OD process provides methods, approaches and tools for implementing a change process. Successful organizational change initiatives require an ongoing adaptive process that allows for constant adjustments. Weick and Quinn (1999) wrote in *Organizational Change and Development* that organizational change research suggests that organizational change is initiated as a result of failure within structure, technology, environment, and/or strategy. The health care system is currently experiencing failure in structure, environment and strategy.

In their writing, the authors state that there are two primary methods of change—"episodic" (infrequent, discontinuous, intermittent) and "continuous" (evolving, incremental) (Weick & Quinn, 1999). Historically, most health care organizations undertook episodic change. As the environment changed, these organizations often address a single situation or problem, concentrating significant amount of resources with a single focus until a particular situation has been resolved. An example may include, decreasing employee turnover (structure) or enhancement of market share in a particular clinical service (strategy) or responding to a changing reimbursement system (environment). In each case the organization focused on a single concern using an episodic approach.

In fact, most organizations embark on a process of "punctuated equilibrium" as they initiate some form of change in strategy or structure. Punctuated equilibrium is a process by which organizations undertake a change process with deliberate and sequential steps intersperse with intermediate periods of evaluation and assessment. Punctuated equilibrium is a resemblance of Lewin's three stages of change—unfreeze, moving, and refreeze. Given the conservativeness of most health care organizations, they prefer a rhythm of change occurring over long periods of time which supports more diligent monitoring and provide adequate time for adjustments. Health care organizations are, by their community service obligation, conservatively governed and operate with extreme caution. Because of the nature of health care organizations, these organizations have supported an adaptive change process mostly utilizing Lewin's three-stage change model. This method of change—incremental and single purpose will not provide the comprehensiveness needed to respond to the significant program modifications proposed for the health care delivery system.

Burke (2002) discussed organizational change as either discontinuous (revolutionary, or transformational) or continuous (evolutionary, or transactional). Burke suggests that discontinuous change is required to interface the organization with its external environment, focusing on the organization's mission, strategies and culture as targets of change. The health care system and individual health care provider organizations will need to undertake a process of discontinuous change in response to an environment that will be altering the means for allocating economic resources. Health care organizations will need to establish an inclusive discontinuous change process that focuses on mission, culture and driving strategies to redesign how health care can be delivered with less cost, higher quality and equally accessible to all across this country. The fundamental mission of an organization is to survive (Burke, 2002).

CHANGE PROCESS METHOD

Strategic OD requires flexible and adaptive methods to implement successful organizational change. The change process method must incorporate the mechanisms of inclusion, speed, flexibility, and knowledge transformation. The method selected to assist the collective health care system and individual provider organizations through a transformational change process must represent all participants (providers and consumers), respond to changing environmental conditions quickly, and transfer new knowledge across both the collective system and individual provider organizations.

The preferred change method that responds to the unique characteristics of the health care system is a positive organizational approach entitled appreciative inquiry. Appreciative inquiry is associated with the social science called "positive organizational scholarship" and is an engaging positive approach to change. Barrett and Fry (2005) suggests that appreciative inquiry is not about implementing a change to get somewhere; it is about changing ... convening, conversing, and relating with each another in order to tap into the natural capacity for cooperation and change that is in every system. Appreciative inquiry is about the coevolutionary search for the best in people, their organization, and the relevant world around them (Cooperrider, Whitney, & Stavros, 2005). The human attributes of Appreciative inquiry are directly relational to the human values prescribed by most health care organizations. Linking the positiveness of Appreciative inquiry with the human condition that resides within each health care organization can create new opportunities for effectiveness in the way health care is delivered.

The five theories of change, which are embedded in appreciative inquiry, are critical components for creating change within a social system such as health care delivery. Gervase Bushe discussed in *Appreciative Inquiry: Foundations in Positive Organization Development,* the five theories and the relationship to the change process of appreciative inquiry. Bushe's (2001) five theories are the socially constructing reality (language as an active agent in the creation of meaning), the heliotropic hypothesis (social systems evolve toward the most positive images they hold of themselves), organization's inner dialogue (creating awareness from use of metaphor of human consciousness), resolving paradoxical dilemmas (releasing the group and allowing for energy and motivation), and finally appreciative process (creating change by paying attention to what is positive than paying attention to problems). These five theories of change develop the foundation for interactive dialogue which occurs in appreciative inquiry and allows for a new understanding/awareness of the unseen possibilities which are necessary for both the health care system and individual health care organizations.

The appreciative inquiry method is constructed around four phases of the appreciative process. The four stage process starts with *Discovery* (appreciating and valuing), *Dream* (envisioning), *Design* (coconstructing the future), and *Destiny* (learning, empowering, and improvising to sustain the future) (Cooperrider et al., 2005).

STRATEGIC CHANGE FRAMEWORK

A new strategic change framework can provide significant benefit to health care organizations as they implement a change process. The strategic change framework will provide a rich guide as health care organizations respond to a changing environment driven by a shifting reimbursement methodology, payments based on clinical performance outcomes and a push toward cost containment while demanding increases in patient quality and safety. This framework is designed to provide a structured approach to the process of change as undertaken by individual health care organizations.

The change process method utilized within the strategic change framework is appreciative inquiry. Appreciative inquiry change process is a vehicle that assists organizations in their quest for whole-system organizational change. Appreciative inquiry, within the strategic change framework, provides a comprehensive approach that integrates human, financial, and operational resources with organizational strategy to create a response to the environment. The Appreciative inquiry process is a mechanism that brings participants together to select the affirmative topics, conduct appreciative interviews, organize meaning-making sessions, facilitate dream dialogues and activities, craft provocative propositions, and select inspiring actions (Whitney & Trosten Bloom, 2003). The strategic change framework operates within the context of appreciative inquiry.

Other components of the strategic change framework are the compelling vision, leadership platform, human performance platform, organizational work process platform, and community collaboration system. The strategic change model is illustrated in Figure 12.1.

Compelling Vision

The strategic change process begins with visioning. Tom Peters (1987) wrote in *Thriving on Chaos,* effective vision emphasizes the creation of enduring capabilities that will allow the organization to execute its strategy. Visioning is the process of developing a commitment to what the organization should become, a picture of how the organization should look in the future which is a strong emotional reason for contributing to the change (Worley et al., 1996). James Collins and Jerry Porras discussed the major components of a well-conceived vision in their book *Built to Last.* Collins and Porras (1994) suggest that the two components are a core ideology and an envisioned future. Core ideology is defined as the enduring character of an organization—its self-identity that remains consistent through time and transcends product/market life cycles (Collins & Porras, 1994). Core ideology is composed of the unchanging purpose of the organization and the underlining values which are the moral principles emulated within the organization.

Worley (1996) states that a key characteristic of an effective vision is that it create a clear focus on the future and through it there is acknowledgement of the present. The present situation prescribes a picture of today's resources, economic standing and position within a competitive environment. Understanding the organization's present situation is necessary in plotting a path to a new future. Vision (what is to become) is a picture of words defining a new future state of the organization. An effective vision statement is critically important in the successful transition of a health care organization. The purpose of vision is to focus the direction of the organization in response to a changing environment. An enduring vision statement is supported by driving strategies.

The creation of four or five driving strategies serves as foundation goals which delineate a blueprint for carrying forward the organization's mission, vision, and values. The driving strategies will guide future resource allocation, focus management attention, affirm operational priorities, and eliminates ambiguity in response to environmental challenges.

Strategic OD theories and practices provides direction in the process of developing compelling vision capabilities—facilitates mission, vision and value statements, generates driving strategies, provides direction to group planning activities, and recommends alignment of organization's structure, systems and strategy.

Leadership Platform

Leading and managing the strategic change process is necessary to improve organizational effectiveness and performance. This is especially true in an environment of unpronounced change. In the book *Leadership in Organizations,* Gary Yukl (2005, p. 8) described leadership as a "process of influencing others to understand and agree about what needs to be done and how to do it, and the process of facilitating individual and collective efforts to accomplish shared objectives." Leading change is one of the most important and difficult leadership responsibly (Yukl, 2005). Fairholm (2000) discussed that leaders need to become specialist in a variety of new leadership technologies—developing a healthy organization, creating a sense of spirituality and moral rightness, and fostering the intelligent organization.

Armenakis and Burdg stated in their 1988 article *Consultation Research* that an organization's capability to adapt to environmental changes significantly affects its effectiveness. The authors stated that managing change is an important responsibility of organization leadership (Armenakis & Burdg, 1988). They continue to suggest that in managing change, organizations often rely on specialized assistance offered by OD scholar/practitioners. Understanding both the multifarious of health care organizations and the complexity of the change process will be necessary in assisting organizations undertaking a strategic change process. Leadership is an important contributor to dynamic alignment because it is the glue that holds structure, information systems, talent, and reward systems together (Lawler & Worley, 2006).

Burke (2002) stated in *Organization Change*—without leadership, planned organization change will never be realized. Yukl (2005) shares that the role of top management in implementing change is to formulate an integrating vision and general strategy, build a coalition of supporters who endorse the strategy, then guide and coordinate the process by which the strategy will be implemented.

In the book *Good to Great*, Jim Collins discusses "level 5 leadership" which was described as the highest level of hierarchal executive capability identified within their research which moves good organizations to great organizations.

> Level 5 leaders channel their ego needs away from themselves and into the larger goal of building a great company. It's not that Level 5 leaders have no ego or self-interest. Indeed, they are incredibly ambitious—but their ambition is first and foremost for the institution, not themselves. (Collins, 2001, p. 21)

The basic function of leadership is constructed around Henri Fayal's five primary managerial tasks—planning, organizing, staffing, directing, and controlling (Fayol, 1949). These management tasks highlight the fundamental operating principles of effective organizational management. Establishing effective organizational management processes is necessary as an organization undertakes a process of organizational change. Fayal's five management functions are highlighted to assure that management work is organized and executed to cope with the demands of a change process. The basic constructs of Fayol and Luther Gulick's principles is the ability to administer and control daily events occurring within the workplace. It is this need, to manage both the daily activities and the unintended variables that appear in the strategic change process which are relevant to achieving the organization's desired vision and new strategic direction.

Strategic OD theories and practices provides direction in the process of strengthening leadership capabilities—identifying resistance to change activities, conducting organizational diagnosis, facilitating the change process, providing methods for shaping and influencing organizational culture, and providing knowledge and understanding about organizational change processes.

Human Performance Platform

The competitive demands for lower costs, improved workforce productivity and increased quality outcomes will be mandated as a result of change occurring within the health care industry. The success of a major change effort is dependent on an engaged and committed workforce which is dedicated to bring about a new future.

Cummings and Worley (2005) emphasize that empirical studies have found a consistent relationship between employee involvement practices and such measures as productivity, financial performance, customer satisfaction, labor hours, and waste rates. Increasing the quality of work life also has a relationship to improved employee motivation. One of the great challenges in satisfying employees is achieving alignment between what they value and what the organization can offer (Lawler and Worley, 2006). Linking the employee needs to the values of the organization enhances employment stability. Lawler and Worley (2006) conclude by suggesting that effective management of human capital needs to be based on keeping the right people. The right people, doing the right task, at the right time, with the right results is a basic principle of continuous quality improvement management and an underpinning of quality health initiatives endorsed by many health care enterprises.

A major component of strategic OD is its behavioral science foundation which supports the values of human potential, participation, and development in addition to performance and competitive advantage (Cummings & Worley, 2005). The role of most health care provider organizations is to provide direct access to patient care and offer support to those most in need—engaging in life and death decisions. Health care can only be provided by the human dimension (physicians, nurses, technicians, support personnel) with the support of modern facilities and innovative technology. The human resource component is the core of the health system and its most valued asset.

Creating a "quality of work life" enhances the operational effectiveness of the organization. Operational effectiveness is measured by patient and family satisfaction, employee engagement, and organizational financial and clinical outcomes. Health care organizations must create participatory management systems which establishes recruitment and selection methods that are team centered, create reward systems that are based on gain sharing, formulate personnel policies that encourage stability, create job design that enriches each individual, endorse interpersonal skill development, minimize layers of management and encourages individual employee participation. The development of a participatory organizational structure that promotes high levels of involvement and personal accountability will contribute to employee engagement and involvement. High levels of quality of work life enhance the organization's ability to implement change.

Strategic OD theories and practices provides direction in the process of developing human performance capabilities—inspiring employee involvement and engagement, facilitating work redesign, developing goal performance management processes, establishing reward and recognition systems, structuring evaluation and performance appraisal processes, and facilitating group dynamic practices and conflict management techniques.

Organizational Work Process Platform

The strategic change process requires an alignment of the organizations work processes with the strategic direction of the organization. Employee engagement, work performance effectiveness, and adaptation to the environment are relational to achieving positive operating results for the organization. It is important to establish linkages between the operational components (i.e., structure, human resources, finance policy, and operational strategy) of the organization and the environment in which it functions.

Yukl (2005) stated that organizational effectiveness is the long-term prosperity and survival of the organization. Grant (2005) emphasized in

Contemporary Strategy Analysis that great strategy must be linked to successful implementation. Organizational work processes provide the mechanisms of communication, decision making, and control systems that allow health care organizations to respond to environmental change. Four management systems are of primary importance in the ability to implement change: the information system, the strategic planning systems, the financial systems, and the human resource management systems (Grant, 2005).

The organizational work processes of the health care industry are impacted by several critical trends. They include imbalanced supply and demand, severe workforce shortages and the need for increased diversity, growing attention to patient safety and accountability, continued investment in technology and persistent financial pressures (Cummings & Worley, 2005). These forces have had a profound impact upon the daily work process within health care organizations. The hierarchal design, work flow methods, organizational alignment, communication patterns, and methods of delegation have been constant from the beginning of modern medicine. As a result of the highly regulated health care industry and the lack of adaptation, most health care organizations has been slow to adopt new means of work processes and even shy away from organizational transformational efforts.

Worley and colleagues (1996) recommend in *Integrated Strategic Change* that organizations undertaking a change process must focus on the specification of each system and assure the organization design should work to create:

1. a fit between strategy and the organization design;
2. a fit between the four different elements of organization design (structure, human resources, information/control, and core activity systems); and
3. information flows that determine agenda and action priorities that match the organization's situation and the context in which implementation must occur.

Connecting the change process to the capabilities of the organization is necessary to assure a successful change effort. Linking the organizational design to strategy will perpetuate the long-term success of implementing the change process. Creating mutual supporting and interrelating methods will work to sustain organization work processes and strengthen the change process. McKinsey's 7-S Framework may serve as a guide to evaluate the individual elements of organizational work processes to assure reasonable connectivity to the change process, and includes the following elements—structure, systems, strategy, shared values, style, staff, and skills.

Strategic OD theories and practices provide direction in organizational work process—diagnosing planned change models, designing work process and intervention techniques, evaluating organization development interventions, creating competitive and collaborative strategies, and facilitating social change processes.

Community Collaboration System

The strategic change process requires health care organizations to operate within and relate to their local community. Health care organizations like other entities must deliver complex services and products and convert those services and products into economic resources in order to grow and prosper. However, for many health care organizations this conversion process is difficult and filled with regulation and unique payment arrangements which limit their ability to compete in an open market society. Often times, these health care organizations compete against each other for market share, managed care contacts, and high risk patient populations.

The health care industry is structured with unique characteristics and does not respond to the market place the same way as most industries. First, the demand for health care services is relatively elastic—as demand for service increases, so does the cost of those services. Second, the health care environment is severely regulated—fixed payment arrangement under Medicare and Medicaid. Third, the consumers are sheltered from decision making—services are often ordered by a health professional for the good of the patient. Fourth, demand for care is driven by the introduction of new technology or the science of medicine—consumers are uninformed on how to evaluate the quality of services provided by health facilities and practitioners. Health care is essentially different because of the general nature of its goods and services, decisions are often made by clinicians, and the market does not operate in a rational manner.

As a result of these unique health care characteristics, there is a greater need for health care organizations to create collaborative strategies within their market or service area. Cummings and Worley (2005) identify collaborative strategies as alliances, networks, joint ventures, and long-term contracts that create a positive relationship between two organizations. These relationships should be mutually beneficial and have a material benefit to each participatory organization. The underlying intention is to reduce costs, eliminate duplication, and provide a higher level of service to the community's residents. This requires the sharing of goals and strategies and the building and leverage of trust between the collaborative organizations.

When two or more organizations agree to work together it represents a fundamental shift in strategic orientation. This shift in orientation results in the organizations becoming interdependent and supportive of each other's strategies, goals, structures and processes (Cummings & Worley, 2005). The complexities and unique characteristics of the health care system demands that new forms of collaboration and coordination be established to reduce duplication, generate economies of scale, and maximize the usage of human, material, and economic resources for the benefit of each community.

Strategic OD theories and practices provide direction to the process of establishing community collaborative systems—recommending collaborative networks, suggesting organizational design and structures, assessing potential partners, developing operational blueprints, and facilitating culture integration activities for collaborative organizations.

SUMMARY

The United States health care industry has and will continue to respond to an environment of change. The anticipated budgetary interventions will require the formation of new social policy and a reallocation of economic priorities affecting each health care organization in this country. Consumers and corporate executives alike will be calling for reform of the health care system as costs continue to rise.

Strategic OD can play a profound role in assisting health care organizations in the process of strategic change and transformation. Most OD textbooks (Burke, 2002; Cummings & Worley, 2005; Grant, 2005) highlight the different elements of OD practice, specifically strategic OD interventions which can provide proven methods and approaches to support organizations undertaking a change process.

OD was founded on humanistic values and ethical concerns like democracy and social justice, and most practitioners would agree that OD tends to emphasize human development, fairness, openness, choice, and balance of autonomy and constraints (Burke, 1997; Worley & Feyerherm, 2003). These OD attributes fit the humanistic values which are the underpinnings of the U.S. health care system. The blending of the humanistic values of OD with the compassion and caring values of the health care system will provide a strong foundation upon which health care organizations can initiate a process to transition, in a turbulent and changing environment.

Strategic OD processes can provide significant guidance as health care organizations respond to a changing environment. The strategic change framework is created to present a perspective on elements of strategic OD which can provide methods, approaches, and tools, to assist health care organizations in their response to environmental change. The strategic change framework suggests that in order to change, a compelling vision must be created and supported by three platforms—leadership, human performance, and organizational work process. The three platforms combined with a compelling vision and strategic choice need to incorporate a focus on community collaboration, which develops a comprehensive response to a changing environment. A community collaborative effort is designed to minimize duplication of services and maximize the desired cost containment objectives without jeopardizing access and quality objectives. Finally, the strategic change framework is implemented within the strategic OD approach of appreciative inquiry. Appreciative inquiry is a proven process of engagement that brings the best in people to identify innovative approaches in response to a changing environment.

REFERENCES

Armenakis, A., & Burdg, H. B. (1988). Consultation research: Contributions to practice and directions for improvement. *Journal of Management, 14*(2), 339-365.

Barrett, F. J., & Fry, R. E. (2005). *Appreciative inquiry: A positive approach to building cooperative capacity.* Chagrin Falls, OH: Taos Institute Publications.

Beckhard, R., & Harris, R. (1987). *Organizational transitions: Managing complex Change.* Reading, MA: Addison-Wesley.

Berkowitz, E. N. (2006). *Essentials of health care marketing.* Sudbury, MA: Jones and Bartlett.

Borger, C. S., Truffer, C., Keehan, S., Sisko, A., Poisal, J., & Clemens, M. K. (2006). *Health spending projections through 2015: Change on the horizon.* Retrieved March 6, 2007, from http://affairs.org/cgi/reprint/hlthaff.25.w61v1.pdf

Burke, W. W. (2002). *Organization change: Theory and practice.* Thousand Oaks, CA: SAGE.

Bushe, B. R. (2001). Advances in appreciative inquiry as an organization development intervention. *Organization Development Journal, 17,* 14-22.

Collins, J. C. (2001). *Good to great.* New York: Harper Collins.

Collins, J. C., & Porras, J. I. (1994). *Built to last.* New York: Harper Collins.

Cooperrider, D. L., Whitney, D., & Stavros, J. M. (2005). *Appreciative inquiry handbook: The first in a series of AI workbooks for leaders of change.* Brunswick, OH: Crown.

Cummings, T. G., & Worley, C. G. (2005). *Organization development and change.* Mason, OH, Thomson-Southwestern.

Daft, R. I. (1995(. *Organizational theory and design.* St. Paul, MN: West.

DeNavas-Walt, C., Proctor, B. D., & Hill, C. H. (2006). *Income, poverty, and health insurance coverage in the United States 2005.* Washington, DC: U.S. Government Printing Office.

Fairholm, G. W. (2000). *Perspectives on leadership: From the science of management to its spiritual heart*. Westport, CT: Praeger.

Fayol, H. (1949). *General and industrial management*. London, Pitman.

Gibson, J. L., Ivancevich, J. M., & Donnelly, J. H. (1997). *Organizations: Behavior, structure and processes*. Boston: Richard D. Irwin.

Grant, R. M. (2005). *Contemporary strategy analysis*. Malden, MA: Blackwell.

Lawler, E. E., & Worley, C. G. (2006). *Built to change: How to achieve sustained organizational effectiveness*. San Francisco: Jossey-Bass.

Miller, D., & Freisen, P. (1980). Momentum and revolution in organization adaptation. *Academy of Management, 23*, 591-614.

Peters, T. (1987). *Thriving on chaos*. New York: Alfred A. Knopf.

Senge, P. M. (1990). *The fifth discipline: The art & practice of the learning organization*. New York: Doubleday Dell.

Wagner, J. A., & Hollenbeck, J. R. (1998). *Organizational behavior: Securing competitive advantage*. Upper Saddle River, NJ: Prentice Hall.

Weick, K. E., & Quinn, R. E. 1999. Organizational change and development. *Annual Review of Psychology, 50*, 361-386.

Werr, A., Stjenberg, T., & Docherty, P. (1996). The functions of methods of change in the work of management consultants. *Academy of Management Proceedings* (pp. 207-210). Briarcliff Manor, NY: Academy of Management.

Whitney, D., & Trosten-Bloom, A. (2003). *The power of appreciative inquiry*. San Francisco: Berrett-Koehler.

Worley, C. G., Hitchin, D. E., & Ross, W. L. (1996). *Integrated Strategic change: How OD builds competitive advantage*. Reading, MA: Addison-Wesley.

Worley, C. G., & Feyerherm, A. E. (2003). Reflections on the future of organization development. *Journal of Applied Behavioral Science, 39*(1), 97-115.

Yukl, G. A. (2006). *Leadership in organizations*. Upper Saddle River, NJ. Pearson-Prentice Hall.

CHAPTER 13

STRATEGIC LEADERSHIP OF CULTURAL TRANSFORMATION AT ADVOCATE HEALTH PARTNERS

Roxanne Ray and Eric Sanders

All organizations change. There are constant external and internal pressures on any group of human beings that require them to adapt. The key to successful change is strategic leadership. Leadership is defined by Lussier and Achua (2004) as "the process of influencing leaders and followers to achieve organizational objectives through change" (p. 5). Strategic leadership takes that further by defining the change to be made in terms of a strategic objective for the organization. Then the best leaders develop the steps to achieve that objective with their teams, and guide the organization through the change.

This case study will present an example of such leadership at Advocate Health Partners (AHP). The leaders there showed tremendous skill in setting a vision for their organization, modeling the change they needed to effect in others, and involving members at all levels in both designing and

Strategic Organization Development: Managing Change for Success
pp. 213–233

implementing the change. They were flexible throughout the process, and thus smoothed the transition all the organization members had to make. Modeling was the most important part in this process. The leaders changed their own behavior, and led by example to the new desired constructive culture.

We used two change models to facilitate the leaders who guided this cultural transformation. Janet Szumal's (2003) four-phase model from the organizational change challenge details the steps in initiating, planning, implementing and then institutionalizing change, and we present the case using that format. Bridges and Mitchell's (2000) work on transition, "the state that change puts people into," was invaluable in helping the leaders understand how organizational change impacts individuals, and helped them work with their associates throughout the change process.

Strategic leadership is critical in working through this internal transition in the organization members. When done well, as it was at AHP, leaders can guide their organization through dramatic transformations in a very short period of time.

INITIATING CHANGE

AHP is a business unit of Advocate Health Care. It administers full and partial risk contracts for Medicare and commercial products, processing over 1.5 million claims annually for eight physician health organizations. AHP has two main divisions with a total of 163 associates, and serves over 250,000 managed-care patients for over 3,000 participating providers of healthcare.

In 2005, two new vice presidents (VPs) were brought to turn around AHP. The unit had a poor reputation in the market, and the senior leaders of AHP were considering closing it completely. The VPs conducted an initial needs assessment and found the main reasons for AHP's poor reputation were (1) low productivity and service, (2) error-ridden manual production, (3) lack of cooperation between departments and alignment of business lines, (4) high levels of dissatisfaction among clients, and (5) low associate morale.

The culture that led to these results was complacent and bureaucratic, with a large disconnect between leadership and staff. In interviews, associates at all levels of the organization said the work environment was "not safe." People were afraid to make mistakes because individuals were blamed for process problems, which were then aired publicly, with assumptions prevailing over facts. Communication across business lines was difficult and work teams were isolated from one another, creating well-defined silos, "turf wars" and complicated workflows. Leaders had a short-term focus, and protecting the status quo kept them closed to new and different ideas, and "too busy" to set achievement goals.

The VPs realized that they needed to change the culture of the entire organization, starting with the leadership team. They understood that in cultural transformation, associates at all levels take signals from the leaders. In interviews, the AHP VPs said, "If our leaders are modeling different behaviors [than the ones we need], we will not get to our desired state." "We cannot accomplish the goals of the organization without the [leadership] culture being what it needs to be." Changing the organization's culture would require a strong commitment on the VPs' part, provision of clear direction, well-defined goals and the courage to implement the difficult, but needed change. Most important, they had to be role models of the change they wanted in the organization. The challenge would be getting the rest of the leadership team on board with the changes.

ORGANIZATIONAL CULTURE ASSESSMENT

In order to establish a baseline of the organizational culture, and strengthen the motivation for change, especially with the leadership team, we chose a quantitative assessment of organizational culture which could be used to relate culture to performance. Human Synergistics' Organizational Culture Inventory (OCI) (Cooke & Lafferty, 1987) was administered to all members of the AHP leadership team.

The OCI measures the operating cultures of organizations in terms of behavioral norms or "what's expected" of members. It includes 120 statements describing behaviors that might be expected or implicitly required of members of an organization. The results of the assessment are mapped on a circumplex—a circular graph divided into 12 sections like the hours on a clock. The 12 sections represent 12 behavioral styles grouped into three clusters or types of cultures: *Constructive* cultures have norms that promote higher-order satisfaction needs of members, and have a balance between task and people orientations; Constructive styles include achievement, self-actualization, humanistic-encouraging, and affiliative. *Passive/defensive* cultures have norms that promote self-protective behavior in interactions with people; Passive/defensive styles include approval, conventional, dependent and avoidance. *Aggressive/defensive* cultures have norms that promote self-protective behavior with respect to the way that members approach tasks; Aggressive/defensive styles include oppositional, power, competitive and perfectionistic.[1]

AHP DATA

The OCI can be used in two complementary ways. The OCI Current measures the culture at a particular point in time, and OCI Ideal measures what the participants feel culture should be. Both versions of the survey were used at AHP, revealing a current culture with predominant organizational styles in the moderate range of constructive with degrees of oppositional, avoidance, dependent and conventional styles (Figure 13.1). However, the desired culture was strongly constructive, with low levels of both passive/defensive and aggressive/defensive styles.

We analyzed the organizational culture by leadership level to highlight the issues to address at each level (Figure 13.2). The VP/director level demonstrated a moderate passive/defensive style. They wanted to protect their status by using relationships with others in ways that included "going along," and avoiding responsibility for any changes implemented. The managers, on the other hand, were ready for change. They were very constructive, with a healthy amount of opposition, indicating they could constructively criticize new ideas presented to them. The supervisors and

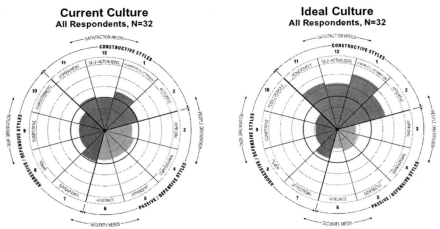

Source: The profiles presented in this and subsequent figures is Copyrighted by Human Synergistics International and used by permission.

Figure 13.1.   Profiles of current vs. ideal culture for AHP leaders in 2005, as measured by the OCI.

Culture by Leadership Level 2005
Organizational Culture Inventory®

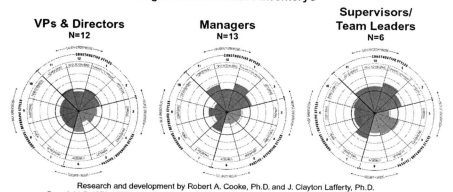

VPs & Directors
N=12

Managers
N=13

**Supervisors/
Team Leaders**
N=6

Figure 13.2.   The 2005 organizational culture profiles by leadership level in AHP, as measured by the OCI.

team leaders were strong on the constructive styles with a slight aggressive tendency, and showing they were ready to develop into even better leaders.

As the VPs recognized, difference between behavioral styles at each organizational level must be addressed early in the cultural change process, or they will lead to greater difficulty in moving the whole organization toward the desired constructive style. Leaders also must model the desired behaviors. Clearly, the directors needed to be convinced that the changes they were implementing were both necessary and desirable. This was the group with whom we focused our greatest efforts.

STRATEGIC PLAN FOR CHANGE

There were two parts to the strategic plan for change. The first part was identifying the desired culture and setting key objectives that would lead to that culture. Based on the OCI results, the interview data and the business results needed, the leadership team agreed to develop a constructive, achievement-oriented culture. They set five key goals to develop that new culture:

- Focus on achievement
- Establish performance standards and expectations
- Address problems and correct processes without blaming individuals

- Find solutions rather than finding mistakes
- Break down barriers between departments

Second, and no less important, was the plan to implement these changes. This may seem like a very straightforward process: establish what needs to change, determine when and by whom, and implement a plan. However, according to Bridges and Mitchell (2000), the details of the intended change are often not the issue, it is the transition itself. Transition—"the state that change puts people into"—occurs in the course of every attempt at change. "Change is external (the different policy, practice, or structure that the leader is trying to bring about), while transition is internal (a psychological reorientation that people have to go through before the change can work)." He goes on, "even when a change is showing signs that it may work, there is an issue of timing, for transition happens much more slowly than change."

Transition takes longer because it requires that people three separate processes, and all of them can be difficult or upsetting: *Saying goodbye, shifting into neutral and moving forward.* Some people struggle to get through transition because they do not let go of the old ways or recognize the need to change, others are fearful and confused and do not give the new process or procedures enough time to see the benefits. For those who make it through the first two phases—they may begin to experience difficulties in the third phase which requires them to begin behaving in a new way—evoking the feeling of incompetence or too much risk. This is especially true for organizations like AHP where the history of punishing mistakes makes the staff want to wait and see how others handle the new processes.

We developed the plan for change recognizing that the AHP associates were at different levels of readiness to make the transition. We worked with the leaders using categories of "Can't, Maybe, and "Let's Go!" to describe both their own readiness for change, and that of the associates they were leading. By understanding the transition process better, and realizing that it takes time to come to terms with the change, the leaders were able to move themselves and their associates through the difficulty of transition.

We created a broad communication strategy to address the transition through increased and sustained two-way communication. Associates at every level were able to express their ideas for the planned changes, as well as voice their concerns and frustrations. This helped the leaders and the associates work together to address the old behaviors that were blocking the change, and helped build the teamwork we needed in the desired future culture. Other stakeholders, including AHP's clients, were educated on changes as they were implemented, and they contributed to the culture transformation as well.

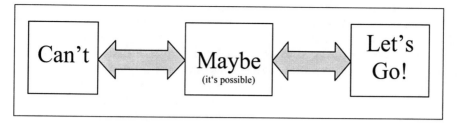

Figure 13.3.   Readiness for change model.

IMPLEMENTING CHANGE

Leadership Development

A key to implementing change is leadership development. At the individual level, leaders need an understanding of their own role in the culture change process. Leadership development focuses on promoting the personal attributes desired in the leader, desired ways of behaving, and ways of thinking or feeling (Day, 2001). Ideally, this is done using objective assessment, coaching and feedback. This combination of inputs allows the individuals to identify potential areas for insight, growth, and self-improvement, and increase their overall effectiveness and performance. At AHP, we implemented a plan to develop the entire leadership team, which included recognition of performance and/or behavioral deficiencies, identification of the causes through assessments, and action planning to address the deficiencies. It was recognized that the development of new skills and behaviors were required to meet the unique needs and circumstances each leader was facing with this cultural transformation.

Life Styles Inventory

The principal assessment of behavioral styles we used was the Life Styles Inventory (LSI) (Lafferty, 1988) from Human Synergistics. This assessment included both a self-evaluation and several descriptions by others to identify both individual leaders' attitudes and their actual behaviors, as perceived by those around them, using the same behavioral styles and circumplex as the OCI. Because of concurrent development programs across AHP as a whole, we also used MBTI and Lominger Voices with some individuals, and had complementary results on those assessments.

The development process included coaching the leaders on how to analyze their LSI results for gaps between their self-perception of their behavioral style compared to how others perceived it. Additionally, the leaders were encouraged to assess how their style enhanced or hindered the effort to move towards a strong constructive organizational culture. The entire leadership team was required to develop individual action plans by choosing one or two specific measurable goals to work on over the year. Examples of the types of goals chosen are shown in Table 13.1.

Individual Action Planning

In the action planning process, the leaders involved their peers and everyone began to support each other in their changes, resulting in increased ability to learn from each other. This was a significant improvement, which helped break down the barriers between the departments.

Simple recognition of the process people go through in change helped logic prevail over emotion as situations arose. Just as steps were taken to automate the processes, steps were taken to help the staff to adjust to the changes as they were implemented. This required a conscious effort and a heightened awareness by all leaders in understanding their impact on others. It required gaining skills in listening, goal setting, giving and receiving feedback, becoming open to new ideas and a willingness to delegate tasks.

Team Leadership

Adopting a constructive cultural style with a focus on achievement required working as teams to set reasonable goals, establish performance and behavioral expectations, seek solutions to general issues, and involve

Table 13.1.   Example Personal Goals set by Members of the AHP Leadership Team

Skill	Action
Listening	Practice attentive and active listening Stop interrupting others
Delegating	Identify routine and important work that can be delegated Share responsibility and accountability
Work life balance	Reduce long work hours, delegate more, go to the fitness center 3 days a week

the right people to correct processes. The directors became involved in weekly meetings seeking feedback from associates on the identified process issues and their potential solutions. They learned to describe the change and why it had to happen, and thus help build support for the transition. Also, by focusing on processes, rather than individuals, the leaders learned just who was going to have to let go of what to make the new system work. Rather then search for someone to blame, they looked for patterns and trends in the data, and used root cause analysis to correct the processes. Thus, they were actually better able to facilitate individuals in making the transition to the new culture and work systems.

One key to our success was the ability to break down the barriers between departments. Joint accountability was established between all directors, and interdependencies within and between departments were identified. In addition, related departments were consolidated physically to facilitate better collaboration on work processes and projects, and move leaders closer to the functional areas that they managed. This required new cooperative attitudes and behaviors—with leaders modeling, providing practice in, and rewarding those behaviors and attitudes. They succeeded and communication and workflow improved markedly.

MEASURING THE CHANGE

Specific performance goals were set for each functional area. The achievement of goals was measured on "dashboards" and reported to the staff regularly (see Figure 13.3). As goals were accomplished, celebrations were held to recognize both team and individual efforts—recognition that did not happen previously. A key operational improvement was installing an automated claim processing system, which required much new learning on the part of most staff members. In addition to regularly held staff meetings, those involved received extensive training on skills required to run the new automated processes. Everyone was given the tools necessary to succeed.

Two Steps Forward, One Step Back

The focus on Achievement required quick changes in all aspects of performance. During the year, staff reductions altered leadership assignments, and added new skill requirements, in addition to the changes in systems and procedures. The speed of the changes in both processes and personnel proved to be too much "movement" for some staff members to handle. Communications became inconsistent, resulting in the right hand

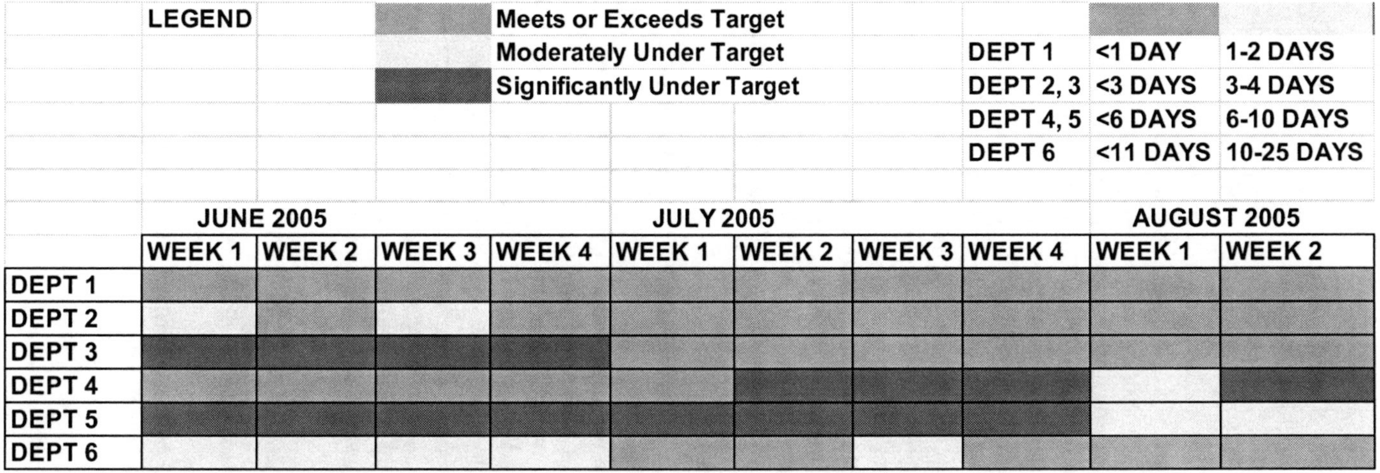

LEGEND

	Meets or Exceeds Target	Moderately Under Target	Significantly Under Target
DEPT 1	<1 DAY	1-2 DAYS	
DEPT 2, 3	<3 DAYS	3-4 DAYS	
DEPT 4, 5	<6 DAYS	6-10 DAYS	
DEPT 6	<11 DAYS	10-25 DAYS	

	JUNE 2005				JULY 2005				AUGUST 2005	
	WEEK 1	WEEK 2	WEEK 3	WEEK 4	WEEK 1	WEEK 2	WEEK 3	WEEK 4	WEEK 1	WEEK 2
DEPT 1										
DEPT 2										
DEPT 3										
DEPT 4										
DEPT 5										
DEPT 6										

Figure 13.4. Example goal achievement dashboard. The goals varied by department in terms of days for processing time.

not knowing what the left was doing. As expected, one response to change was to revert back to familiar old behaviors. As we learned from Bridges and Mitchell (2000),

> The change can continue to move forward on something close to its own schedule while the transition is being attended to, but if the transition is not dealt with, the change may collapse. People cannot do new things that the new situation requires until they come to grips with what is being asked. (p. 3)

Recognizing this, the leadership team as a whole worked hard to overcome the "old" behaviors, and sustain the change effort, addressing the transition issues as they came up for staff members. Goals were adapted to meet reasonable timelines, and adjustments were made in work assignments as necessary to avoid burning out the individuals involved in major process changes. By showing flexibility, while maintaining the direction and momentum for change, the leaders sustained the change to the new culture through the difficult transition period.

Institutionalizing Change

As we have stressed throughout this process, effective leadership plays a vital role in strategic change. The VPs understood from the beginning that the leaders would need to model the change they wanted in the organization before it would be successful. As AHP leaders did this, they gained confidence in the change process, and the transformation gained momentum. The examples below show how the change started with their individual behavioral styles, and then generalized to the organizational culture. This allowed them to sustain and institutionalize the new culture.

Assessment Results

One early advantage to using the OCI and LSI assessments together was that it gave the leaders a common language for culture and the ability to recognize behaviors that were not Constructive. It also assisted leaders in focusing their own development needs. Their individual goals corresponded to the constructive culture they wanted. Their focus on achievement led them to establish performance standards and expectations, and to set reasonable goals toward attaining those expectations. They showed an increased willingness to delegate tasks or ask for assistance, instead of the old perfectionistic behavior of taking on more and more assignments. By addressing problems and correcting processes without blaming individuals, and by finding solutions rather than mistakes, they were more humanistic and encouraging. Last, but not least, by breaking down barriers between departments they greatly increased teamwork, and thus increased their affiliative behavior, another key constructive style.

Life Styles Inventory Results

The leaders at AHP showed very good progress in adapting their own behavior when re-assessed with the LSI one year into the change process.

The leaders shifted their personal styles and moved the culture of the entire organization. Table 13.2 shows the percentage of leaders with primary behavioral styles in each of the LSI style groups. The clock-wise shift around the circumplex, from passive/defensive to aggressive /defensive to Constructive is not uncommon, and we were delighted to see it here.

Since the change in leadership behavior was strategically planned, and critical to the transformation of the organizational culture, we will examine the changes in example leaders at each level, starting with the vice presidents of each of the AHP departments.

The goal of the VP of finance operations was to be the role model for his direct reports (the directors). Faced with numerous required changes, he openly shared his LSI results, and solicited feedback from direct reports on how to improve his behavior. He empowered his direct reports to make decisions on their own instead to pushing the decisions upward. From the start of the change efforts, the VP demonstrated the willingness and ability to make tough decisions. In an effort to breakdown the communication barriers he insisted on teamwork at all levels. Most important, he did not ask the direct reports to do anything he would not do himself.

The 2005 profile for the VP of medical services was taken just 4 months after she assumed the position (see Figure 13.6). She had a high learning curve, because her previous position at AHP was not related to AHP's work, and that shows in her high passive/defensive behavior. In addition, the previous manager was held in very high esteem by the staff, and so

Table 13.2. Percentage of AHP Leaders
Whose Primary LSI Styles Were in Each Cluster

2005		2006	
21%	Constructive	58%	Constructive
34%	Passive defensive	31%	Passive defensive
45%	Aggressive defensive	15%	Aggressive defensive

Leader's Behavioral Styles
Life Styles Inventory™ 2: Description by Others

Finance Operations VP 2005   **Finance Operations VP 2006**

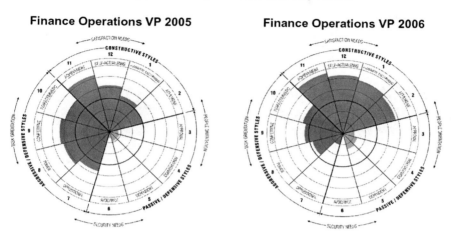

Figure 13.5.   VP of finance operations LSI2 (description by others) comparison from 2005 and 2006.

Leader's Behavioral Styles
Life Styles Inventory™ 2: Description by Others

Medical Services VP 2005   **Medical Services VP 2006**

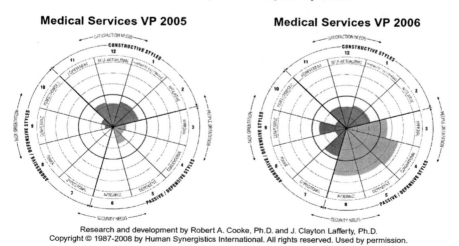

Figure 13.6.   VP of medical services LSI 2 (description by others) comparison from 2005 and 2006.

Leader's Behavioral Styles
Life Styles Inventory™ 2: Description by Others

Example Director 2005   **Example Director 2006**

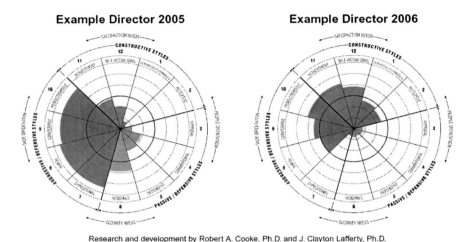

Research and development by Robert A. Cooke, Ph.D. and J. Clayton Lafferty, Ph.D.
Copyright © 1987-2008 by Human Synergistics International. All rights reserved. Used by permission.

Figure 13.7.   Example director's LSI 2 (description by others) comparison from 2005 and 2006.

they initially resisted the transition to her leadership. She worked hard to get up to speed on the unit's operations, and was very supportive of staff during the operational changes (including staff reductions) throughout the year. She actively communicated with her staff, and openly shared information and results.

In 2005, this director's LSI 1 (self assessment) and LSI 2 (description by others) results showed very few gaps confirming the strong orientation to the aggressive/defensive style of leadership (see Figure 13.7). The significant differences in 2006 reflect the acceptance by the director of the need to change her aggressive/defensive style. She understood how in the long term it was not effective—resulting in great levels of dissatisfaction both on a personal level as well as among the staff members. She has worked hard at becoming more cooperative as she willingly shares her knowledge with her team members. She is learning to delegate better, with the desire to reduce her long work hours which she no longer views a "good thing." This increased inclusion of others, better communication and improved work-life balance was found in many of the leaders, and accounts for a large degree of the organizational change made.

One of the managers had a tremendous change in both her self-assessment and in how she was described by others. Realizing how defensive she

Leader's Behavioral Styles
Life Styles Inventory™ 1: Self Description

Example Manager 2005   **Example Manager 2006**

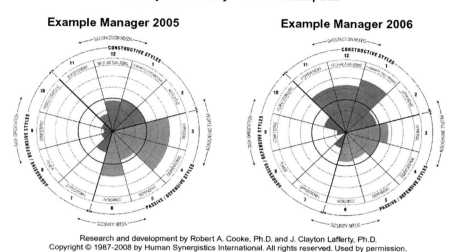

Figure 13.8.   Example Manager's LSI 1 (self description) comparison from 2005 and 2006.

saw her own behavior, this manager used the LSI 1 self-assessment to initiate positive changes in her thinking and behavioral patterns, and increased her personal effectiveness (see Figure 13.8). She set very specific personal and professional goals, to be a better role model for her staff. For example, on a professional level, she began to focus on staff development, and on personal level she made time to go to the fitness center more regularly, so she felt more fulfilled in her life outside of work.

As a result of the personal changes, the LSI 2 descriptions by others reflect much stronger Constructive behavior styles (see Figure 13.9). The spike in the dependent style most likely represents recent organizational changes. The assessment was taken just four weeks after a major reorganization changed her work dramatically.

OCI Results

The strategic goal of the leadership team was to create a more constructive culture, and thus achieve the necessary business results to turn around AHP. The OCI results confirm that their modeling behavior changes was successful in moving the culture of AHP as a whole.

Leader's Behavioral Styles
Life Styles Inventory™ 2: Description by Others

Example Manager 2005   **Example Manager 2006**

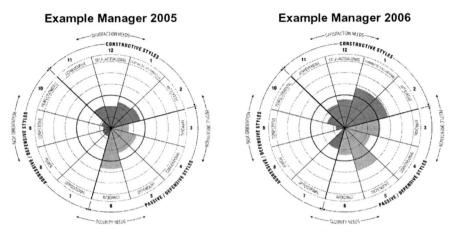

Figure 13.9.   Example Manager's LSI 2 (description by others) comparison from 2005 and 2006.

Culture Change in First Year
Organizational Culture Inventory®

AHP Current Culture 2005   **AHP Current Culture 2006**
All Respondents, N=32   All Respondents, N=29

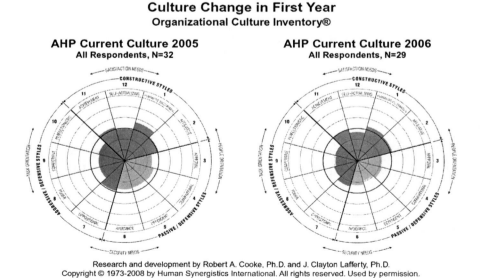

Figure 13.10.   AHP culture profiles from 2005 and 2006, as measured by the OCI.

Culture Change by Leadership Level
Organizational Culture Inventory®

VPs & Directors 2005
N=12

VPs & Directors 2006
N=11

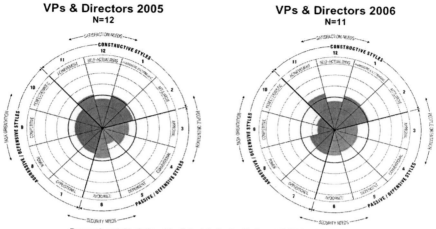

Figure 13.11.   AHP culture profiles according to leaders at the VP and director levels in 2005 and 2006, as measured by the OCI.

There were small but significant reductions in the passive/defensive and aggressive/defensive styles, while maintaining the Constructive styles (Figure 13.5). Note that there was a staff reduction shortly before the 2006 OCI was administered. Achieving these good results so close to such a drastic change demonstrates how well the leaders are moving their teams toward the desired culture. The reduction in defensive behaviors is critical to the success of the organization, and is highlighted when we look at the cultural styles of the different levels of leaders.

In the 2005 OCI survey, the VP/director level showed the lowest strength in constructive styles of any level of leadership (Figures 13.2 & 13.6). The leaders used the LSI results to make significant changes in their own personal behavioral styles. As the VPs began to push decision-making downward, the directors began to feel more empowered in their roles. They moved from primarily passive/defensive styles to primarily Constructive cultural styles. Note that while in 2005 the most prominent style was avoidance; in 2006, the most prominent cultural style was achievement. This is a huge shift in the cultural norms of the organization, and a testament to the leaders "walking the talk."

The team of managers was impacted by the organizational changes that included not only changes in procedures and processes but changes in their roles. Modeling the VPs behavior, the directors have recently

Culture Change by Leadership Level
Organizational Culture Inventory®

Managers 2005
N=13

Managers 2006
N=11

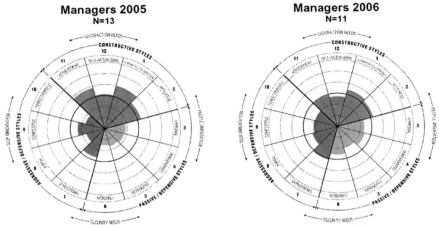

Figure 13.12.   AHP culture profiles according to leaders at the manager level in 2005 and 2006, as measured by the OCI.

identified appropriate decisions to push downward to the managers. One recent example of this empowerment was the delegation of staffing changes. As a team, the managers showed the least movement in their LSI's from 2005 to 2006, even while they experienced the greatest level of staff reductions. Despite these changes, while their perception of the organizational culture is slightly more defensive in 2006 than in 2005, it is still primarily constructive.

The supervisor/team leaders were greatly impacted by the organizational changes, which required them to develop new skills in order to perform the new processes. More authority and responsibility has been delegated to these leaders by their managers, and they have risen to the new challenges. Their avoidance and dependent levels show this, as both contracted nicely. They still have a primarily constructive cultural profile, with the strongest extensions in the humanistic-encouraging and affiliative styles, manifested in a strong team orientation, a friendly atmosphere and increased cooperation among staff members.

Business Results Achieved

None of these leadership behavior and cultural style changes in the business would be important or sustained without complementary

Culture Change by Leadership Level
Organizational Culture Inventory®

Supervisors/Team Leads 2005
N=6

Supervisors/Team Leads 2006
N=6

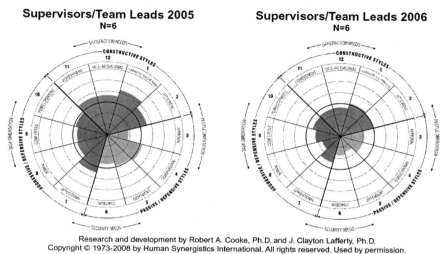

Research and development by Robert A. Cooke, Ph.D. and J. Clayton Lafferty, Ph.D.
Copyright © 1973-2008 by Human Synergistics International. All rights reserved. Used by permission.

Figure 13.13.   AHP culture profiles according to leaders at the supervisor/team lead level in 2005 and 2006, as measured by the OCI.

improvements in the business results of the organization. As expected, those results tracked consistently with the improvement in organizational culture. The key result sought and achieved was reduced processing times for claims, and reduced errors (see Figure 13.14). That resulted in improved cash flows for AHP's clients, and greatly increased customer satisfaction. At AHP directly, the improved cash flow created by the changes reduced interest expenses from 2005 to 2006 by nearly $100,000.

Aligning and automating the claims processes (including over 400 systems corrections) resulted in an increased percentage of claims paid electronically, reduced turn-around time in addressing pending claims, and 98% payment of claims on time, all of which led to significantly reducing client complaints. Streamlining the mechanism for process improvement involved all levels of leadership and staff, and included audits to design skill training for the staff members. The increased skill and knowledge development resulted in a marked increase in the number of internal promotions. Associate satisfaction rose to 98%, which was an all-time high.

CONCLUSION

Strategic leadership of change is critical to the success of any organization, especially one going through a radical cultural transformation as

		1/05 Inventory TAT	1/06 Inventory TAT	Change
1.	First Pass Rates:			
	•EDI filing rate	60%	95%	35%
	•Paid claims adjudication rate	70%	85%	15%
	•Paid claims within 15 days	80%	95%	15%
2.	Pending Claims Volume	17,000	3,000	<14,000>
	•Average TAT	>90 days	<6 days	<84 days>
3.	Pay and Deduct Volume	13,000	4,000	<9,000>
	•Average TAT	21 days	6 days	<15 days>
4.	Fatal Edits Volume	23,000	3,100	<19,900>
	•Average TAT	60 days	2 days	<58 days>
5.	Paper Volume	12,000	<100	<11,900>
	•Average TAT	43 days	1 day	<42 days>
6.	Appeals Volume	11,000	850	<10,150>
	•Average TAT	>95 days	<15 days	<80 days>

Figure 13.14.   Key process indicators for improvement in turn around time (TAT).

AHP did. Starting with the VPs, but involving the entire leadership team, it was important that the leaders set the appropriate vision, modeled the behaviors necessary to attain that vision, involved organization members at all levels in implementing the change, and were flexible during the implementation process.

A critical part of the implementation process was recognizing the difficulty that staff members at all levels would have during the transition period, as they internalized the changes. By maintaining strong, two-way communication with their staff members, the AHP leaders did a tremendous job of working through that transition smoothly. One of the key ways they did that started with the VPs sharing their LSI results with their teams. By being vulnerable to their direct reports, they showed that change is hard for all people, but by working together, we can all successfully navigate the change process.

Last, but not least, the AHP leaders recognized both the business imperative for the change, and the behavioral and social process to implement it. By focusing on improving people processes in order to achieve business results, they were successful on both counts. That is true strategic leadership.

NOTE

1. Cluster descriptions are from the Organizational Culture Inventory, Copyright 1987 by Human Synergistics International. Used by permission.

REFERENCES

Bridges, W., & Mitchell, S. (2000, Spring) Leading transition: A new model for change. Leader to Leader No.16, Spring 2000.

Cooke, R. A., Lafferty, J. C. (1987). *Organizational culture inventory*. Plymouth, MI: Human Synergistics International.

Day, D. V. (2001). Leadership development: A review in context. *The Leadership Quarterly, 11*, 581–614.

Lafferty, J. C. (1988). *Life styles inventory*. Plymouth, MI: Human Synergistics International,

Lussier, R. N., & Achua, C. F. (2004). *Leadership: Theory, application, skill development* (2nd ed.). Mason, OH: Thomson-Southwestern.

Nash, S. (1999). *Turning team performance inside out*. Palo Alto, CA: Davies-Black.

Szumal, J. (2003). *Organizational culture inventory interpretation & development guide*. Arlington Heights, IL: Human Synergistics International.

PART IV

GLOBAL ISSUES

CHAPTER 14

UNDERSTANDING ORGANIZATIONAL CONTEXT

A Key to International and Domestic Strategic Success

Robert C. Kjar

Globalization is often associated with growth achieved by entering new markets, diversification of product lines, efficiency achieved in labor costs, and global mindset development for leaders of the next generation. Much of the taken-for-granted knowledge about globalization originates from the perspective of American or Western multinationals and from an external perspective to the firm, either through an academic or professional services orientation. While such a perspective has added much to the theory and practices associated with successfully negotiating, the turbulent waters of global business, additional insights might be gained by viewing the prismatic diversity of globalization from another angle, exposing another facet to full view.

While some might consider the Western-external view to be the model, an internal view from the perspective of a scholar-practitioner working inside a Japanese multinational firm might shed new light on several key

Strategic Organization Development: Managing Change for Success
pp. 237–246

factors critical for global success broadly. First, viewing a company from within has the advantage of (Coghlan, 2001) gaining access to key stakeholders, informal influence networks, perspective on historical challenges, and company culture from a longitudinal stance. Certainly such benefits could come from the other perspective, given time, but often organizations opt for spending less time on such background information. Second, focusing observation on a non-Western organization might be of worth to Western multinationals who have met with frustration when faced with a high context (Boyacigiller & Adler, 1991) or Confucian (Marshak, 2004) globalization experiment.

Organization development (OD), in the global context, requires a thorough examination of internal systems, and then a thoughtful design that considers the integrated capabilities of the global organization as strategic competitive advantages. Uncovering these global competitive advantages is the first step for OD scholar-practitioners seeking to help their organizations flourish in new markets.

LITERATURE REVIEW

How can a greater understanding of an organization's identity improve its chances of strategic success? This was the question asked by Nag, Corley, and Gioia (2007), claiming that it was "still unclear how organizational identity interrelates with processes critical to strategic formation" (p. 824). Perhaps this arises from the lack of correlation between organizational learning and strategy formulation. The responsibility for organizational learning is often times left up to corporate initiatives that focus too much attention on the employee benefit to be gained rather than strategic benefits to be gained (e.g., employee training that is wrongly applied to improve an employee's sense of well-being or satisfaction with development lacking alignment to an overall corporate purpose or strategy). Rather than focusing solely on the intervention, which can often appear as an externally applied solution, spending time understanding context can help identify the factors that create the internal pull necessary for individual and organizational success. Weick and Quinn (1999) pointed out that leaders who first experience change themselves are more able to use the logics of attraction (my lived experience) rather than a logic of replacement (stop doing x and do y). In other words, the type of learning that arises from a close personal analysis might produce a greater organizational magnetism for alignment rather than pushing another corporate program aimed at increasing global awareness, for example.

Managers who gain deeper insights about the organization can become change agents and critical translators of the context of work and the ground-level tasks to which organizations attempt to align their employees, thus to gain competitive advantage (Gosling & Mintzberg, 2003). Achieving such alignment is part of the ongoing challenge for multinationals to achieve goals in another in ways that are not immediately apparent to its rivals by adopting interdependent strategies that are hard to copy. Harvesting details about organizational context may be one strategy for any corporation that wants to compete skillfully in the global chess game (MacMillan & VanPutten, & McGrath, 2003).

CONTEXTUAL DIAGNOSIS

Viewing the organization from an internal, non-Western perspective, the first principle critical for success is understanding context. High-context countries such as Japan (Hall, 2000) can spawn high-context organizations that require deep contextual understanding of its members, by its affiliate firms, joint venture partners, or suppliers. Such understanding springs from a variety of contextual data sources; for example, such an examination might begin with the country culture of the target organization, and then examining the target industry within the country, and finally, by examining the company's cultural and historical legacy.

Part of understanding and diagnosing the context of an organization comes from other data sources that cannot be overlooked. In interviews conducted with 15 international consultants in 2006, additional sources of gaining contextual data included identifying one or more local guides who might assist in filling in the gaps of what analysis may have been made through study and observation. One consultant with over 10 years international experience called these people "cultural translators" because they were able to point out faulty assumptions or overgeneralizations. While virtually none of the interview subjects relied solely on such guides for data, they provided many examples of how such cultural translators enriched their own observations by providing often a counter perspective, an even deeper internal perspective on the company. Another source of data which was often cited by experienced international consultants, which Western societies may too quickly dismiss, is the informal, after-hours discussion in which casual conversation gives way to details about an organization that can only be learned through such gatherings. A third frequently cited source for rich contextual data was taking time to analyze the informal network of key influencers within the organization.

Armed with these contextual analysis guides, a few questions such as those in Table 14.1 might be prepared and utilized in order to extract knowledge about high context organizations such as in non-Western nations; but arguably similar analyses could be the basis for OD work in other settings as well.

Obtaining information about the country, industry, and company can be relatively simple, devolving from secondary sources such as might be found in libraries and company records, when compared to gathering data from primary sources, which requires first-hand observation and analysis. In the next section, several examples of internal data gathering opportunities are discussed which are derived from global OD strategies.

Table 14.1.   Contextual Analysis Guides for Diagnosis

Country Culture	Target Industry	Company Culture	Additional Sources
• What are the geographical features of the country?	• How long has this industry existed within the country, and how was it established (indigenous or imported)?	• How long has this company existed and how was it founded?	• What local individual(s) can be sought out for advice and direction?
• What historical events have shaped the lives of people in the country—both from its beginning and recent memory?	• What attributes of this industry align with the country culture?	• What has been the company's historical performance?	• What are the customary opportunities for spending informal time together?
• What are the attributes of government and/ or religious authority?	• What is the competitive environment within this industry, and which firms are the leaders?	• What are the most significant challenges faced in the past, and how did that shape the company and its employees?	• Who are the individuals to whom others go for information about the company (information brokers)?
• What are the values exhibited in its legends, myths, and heroes?	• What are the key metrics by which this industry measures success?	• What are the expressed values of the organization, and how are these expressed in lived behaviors of the organization?	• Who are the individuals to whom others go for checking ideas (idea brokers)?
• What is the country's degree of openness to trade and outside influences?		• What does the physical space tell about the company?	• Who are the individuals to whom others go to seek resources (power brokers)?

UTILIZING OD METHODOLOGIES TO
UNDERSTAND CONTEXT AND IMPACT STRATEGIC CHANGE

Viewed from the author's vantage point within a Japanese multinational pharmaceutical firm, this chapter provides several examples of how rich contextual data can be gathered and turned back on the organization in order to create greater organizational learning and strategic impact. Three examples in which the author was an internal participant will be discussed in this section: First, a culturally diverse group of senior leaders who have been assigned to action learning projects by the corporate head office reveals new insights for applying greater contextual understanding to this leadership development practice. Second, a leader sent to work in the Japanese home office as an internal transfer from a Western affiliate provides insights about the challenges and opportunities of expatriate assignments. Third, an American top management team enters strategic planning faced with a need to better understand its Japan-based parent organization.

Example 1: Action Learning Teams

High potential leaders, as key successors in the talent pool, are often considered for projects or assignments as members of international teams, often as the result of a sudden opportunity or crisis. Planning action learning interventions with this group of leaders might provide earlier exposure opportunities to peer-group leaders in other countries, leading to greater consideration of global factors in decision making and having the pragmatic outcome of developing leader networks, which may prove to be a global competitive advantage.

One such program was begun in late 2006 with leaders chosen from across the firm. Leaders came from Japan, the United States, China, Thailand, Indonesia, Italy, France, Germany, and the United Kingdom. The parent company provided the largest number of participants, 15 of the 35 invitees, followed by the United States (10), the United Kingdom (2), and one from each of the remaining countries. An international business school planned the program, and teams were formed to allow the greatest diversity of participants based on country of origin, gender, and internal department affiliation.

Early in 2007, project teams met in a workshop setting and were given instructions regarding their assignments and were told that they had eight months to prepare their plans and recommendations to senior management. The 8-month program consisted of three face-to-face modules in which participants reviewed case studies in leadership topics such as corporate culture, strategy, and globalization. In addition, participants completed a multirater feedback process with peer coaching in small groups and participated in team building events. Action learning teams met as part of these face-to-face workshops in the evenings as desired, many of them choosing to meet several times during the 5-day workshops. Team effectiveness surveys were also given to individual action learning team members, and then a facilitated discussion was conducted by OD professionals to help teams discuss areas of agreement and disagreement. Such network building with multinationals can foster innovation among foreign subsidiaries and may be seen as one competitive source for innovation (Birkinshaw & Hood, 2001).

Example 2: Expatriate Assignment

Expatriate assignments are often used by organizations as a way to expose leaders to international business in general, and to teach them about global operating conditions for the company in particular. Global experience of top leaders has been cited as a key to a firm's international success (Carpenter & Fredrickson, 2001). The total number of expatriate assignments continues to rise, according to the GMAC Report on Global Relocation Trends (*Business Wire*, 2005), which tracks some 125 large organizations. Forty-seven percent of companies reported in the survey indicated an increase in the size of expatriate populations, and 54% anticipated further growth in the coming years.

In 2007, the author was assigned to work in Japan with the parent company's human resources (HR) department on a 1-year exchange. Among the work begun in 2007 was a global employee engagement survey conducted in 19 countries, a global succession planning process conducted locally, then globally, and a project to set global HR guidelines regarding which processes and procedures would be adopted as standard practices across all affiliates and which ones would remain subject to local interpretation.

Prior to the assignment, the author had lived in Japan on two other occasions, and had visited the parent company several times as part of other work, so some of the country and industry challenges were well known. The company had recently restated its corporate values and provided an extensive explanation of each of its operating tenets. However, convinced of the importance of learning more about the informal context, the author set out on an early strategy that included working closely with a local mentor, spending off-hours time with the staff, and a third process, creating a strategic map of the local practices. This third process involved interviewing different members of the staff and creating a one-page summary picture describing the flow of projects and information to achieve the department's goals.

Example 3: Top Management Team

Within the American affiliate of the pharmaceutical firm already mentioned, the top management team struggled to understand more fully the nature of its relationship to the parent firm. Having established a foothold in the United States by recruiting an all-American senior management team and insisting the company would be run according to American management practices, the parent organization was now—according to many senior leaders—beginning to show signs of asserting greater influence on the U.S. business.

Early indicators from the U.S. employee survey and a follow-up study in which 25 senior managers were interviewed regarding key points identified from the survey showed that questions were beginning to arise regarding whether local initiatives were going to be subject to more centralized controls from the Japan-based parent. The OD team called in a local consultant with large-group process facilitation experience and organization design skills, and a cross-functional team of senior leaders, with the company president as its sponsor, to conduct a strategic goal setting process for the top 80 leaders in the U.S. organization comprising all director and vice-president level positions.

Prior to the event, an internal, cross-functional leadership project team was formed to assist in the design and implementation of the strategic goal-setting process. Internal OD specialists, in partnership with the external consultant, conducted several meetings with the top team of vice-presidents to establish a direction for the new fiscal year. In addition, members of the cross-functional project team held discussions within each department to solicit feedback from all employees prior to the event. This information was brought in to the meeting by each respective vice-president and used as the basis for discussion of the company's goals for the new year.

DISCUSSION

Each of the OD initiatives served a dual purpose. While seeking to improve the organization, leaders gained greater contextual understanding of the organization by the methods employed. This learning returned to the organization again as the author became more aware of the context prior to the intervention, but also as the learning folded back on the organization as the author was able to apply that contextual learning to help the organization apply reflective thinking and learning from which to set strategic direction.

First, in the case of the action learning teams, the decision to form the teams and bring them together over an eight-month period, with intervening periods for research and group meetings, was met with some concern early in the implementation about the required time commitment, both from participants and their managers. However, feedback gathered from participants during and after the process indicated that among those design elements considered the most useful were the duration of the program that allowed for groups to go into greater depth regarding the research and recommendations as well as greater in-depth knowledge of team members and their capabilities. Incidental to this was the decision to delay any significant discussion of team theory and team building tools until nearly four months after the teams were assigned. This conscious decision allowed teams to learn more about each other, experience challenges together, and determine acceptable rules of order prior to learning about team theory and tools for diagnosing team success. In addition, the analysis provided in the action learning team proposals was deepened by the requirement to not only propose new business solutions, but also to summarize team development and any roadblocks the team faced during the project. This data was often as pertinent to the company's top leadership team as it revealed greater insights about redundant efforts across the company, challenges associated with many strategic documents being produced only in Japanese, and the time required to gain a shared understanding of key project goals. The findings in these teams revealed the benefit of allowing time for contextual analysis to occur before intervening with a training program.

Second, in the case of the expatriate assignment, while considerable attention was given to the projects that would be completed during the assignment, the Japan-based head of HR pointed out the importance of learning about the organizational context prior to taking significant action. Meetings, observation, and the strategic map helped to facilitate discussions about the organization that benefited the author's understanding. The map discussions also provided the local organization information gained from one group within the HR department to seek clarification from another group, thus producing greater organizational learning arising from the contextual discovery process.

Top management, in the third example, benefited from the organizational analysis conducted among employee populations from survey and interview data, and from additional grass roots discussions that culminated in a strategic planning event. Primary data gathered in individual department meetings was fed back to top management and proved to be one of the most important pieces of data, revealing specific areas where organizational roadblocks were prevalent. As a result of these efforts, one of the strategic goals was tied to increasing understanding and participation with the parent organization. Early warning indicators such as employee surveys or interviews can often fail to produce organizational change unless brought into the strategic planning process and supplemented by greater contextual analysis gained from primary sources.

IMPLICATIONS

Seeking deeper contextual understanding is a critical step in OD. Schein (1998) pointed out the critical role of understanding organizational context in his works on process consultation and organizational culture. Argyris (1977) identified double-loop learning as the way leaders and organizations can benefit from reflecting on contextual data gained from various interventions. Certainly in any competitive environment, being able to mine the competitive advantages that arise from a more complete understanding of the organization is a key factor for any leader's success. For OD professionals, such analysis should be seen not only as preparation for an intervention, but as the intervention itself as knowledge is gained and reflected back to the organization.

In the international world of OD, practitioners and scholars who fail to gain deep knowledge of their clients and company contexts certainly increase the risks associated with implementing organizational change. The concept of getting closest to the action in attempting to continuously improve organizations is at the heart of Imai's *Gemba Kaizen* (1997), in which the manufacturing quality improvements efforts are applied to the workplace. Just as failure to understand the current conditions on a manufacturing line can lead to system breakdowns, failure to understand the workplace context can rob the organization of valuable reflective learning and insights.

Arguably, internal consultants who have greater access to company data, people, systems, and processes can identify contextual markers in ways that can pose to be difficult or costly for external experts. Conversely, scholar-practitioners who reside in rich contexts and fail to observe, reflect, and facilitate organizational learning diminish the significant competitive advantage to be gained by such efforts.

REFERENCES

Argyris, C. (1977). Double-loop learning in organizations. *Harvard Business Review, 55*, 5, 115-125.

Birkinshaw, J., & Hood, N. (2001). Unleash innovation in foreign subsidies. *Harvard Business Review, 79, 3*, 131-137.

Boyacigiller, N. A., & Adler, N. J. (1991). The Parochial Dinosaur: Organizational Science in a Global Context. *The Academy of Management Review, 16, 2*, 262-290.

Carpenter, M. A., & Fredrickson, J. W. (2001). Top management teams, Global Strategic posture, and the moderating role of uncertainty. *The Academy of Management Journal, 44*, 533-545.

Coghlan, D. (2001). Insider action research projects: Implications for practicing managers. *Management Learning, 32*, 49-60.

Gosling, J., & Mintzberg, H. (2003, November). The five minds of a manager. *Harvard Business Review*, 54-63.

GMAC Global Relocation Services launches monthly publication, strategic advisor that provides insights, updates on no major industry trends. (2005, July 25). *Business Wire*, p. 7.

Hall, E. T. (2000). Context and meaning. In L. A. Samovar & R. E. Porter (Eds.), *Intercultural communication: A reader* (9th ed., pp. 34-43), Belmont, CA: Wadsworth.

Imai, M. (1997). *Gemba kaizen: A commonsense, low-cost approach to management*. New York: McGraw-Hill.

MacMillan, I. C., Van Putten, A. B., & McGrath, R. G. (2003). Global gamesmanship. *Harvard Business Review, 81*(5), 62-71.

Marshak, R. J. (2004). Organization development and post-Confucian societies. In P. Sorensen, Jr., P. F., Head, T. C., Yaeger, & D. Cooperrider (Eds.), *Global and international organization development* (4th ed., pp. 295-311). Champaign, IL: Stipes.

Nag. R., Corley, K. G., & Gioia D. A. (2007). The intersection of organizational identity, knowledge, and practice: Attempting strategic change via knowledge grafting. *The Academy of Management Journal, 50*(4), 821-847.

Schein, E. H. (1999). *Process consultation revisited: Building the helping relationship*. Reading, MA: Prentice Hall.

Weick, K. E., & Quinn, R. E. (1999). Organizational change and development. *Annual Review of Psychology, 50*, 361-386.

CHAPTER 15

SUBORDINATING NATIONAL CULTURE TO CORPORATE CULTURE

Implications for Organizational Structure, Leadership, and Operations

Paul H. Eccher and Thomas C. Head

Today's business enterprises are facing unprecedented strategic challenges—due to existing, operating, and growing in a global environment. While foreign direct investment has been around for decades, it really only has been in the last 20 or so years that most organizations have entered into this arena. Unfortunately the transitions, for the most part, have not been very smooth. The newspapers and industry magazines are rife with examples of mistakes, blunders, and missed opportunities.

An earlier version of this paper was presented at the 2001 Academy of Management International Conference on Management Consulting in Lyon, France.

Strategic Organization Development: Managing Change for Success
pp. 247–264

Many of these debacles and near-debacles can be traced back to one common flaw—the lack of preparedness for entering new, and very diverse, human environments. The companies have done their homework with regards to financial, accounting, technological, and government relations, but they have failed to examine their employee related human systems. Given that one, if not the one greatest reason for within U.S. mergers to fail (Gong & Head, 2002) why would we expect anything different at the international level?

There is no question that the failure to incorporate the culture and leadership issues into one's globalization strategy is a mistake. But the questions that beg to be asked before one can build these factors in, is exactly how should they be approached? And, at what levels in the hierarchy?

For several years a debate has raged at the U.S. National Academy of Management concerning the role that national culture plays when operating at the global level One side argues that a good organization development change agent, using well established techniques, will prove effective in any country without having to make significant adaptations to her/his practices. The opposing viewpoint suggests that to be effective consultants must adapt their techniques so that they are compatible with the host country's culture.

This is, of course, not a new debate. The degree of cultural permeability and management approaches can be traced at least as far back as Goodstein (1981) and Hofstede (1980). There is also a growing body of literature supporting both sides of the argument. Regardless of which position one takes, everyone appears to agree that operating internationally dramatically increases the uncertainties organizations face and managing this uncertainty is essential for continued organizational viability. Some organizations have implemented an interesting solution— creating a corporate culture that dominates the various national cultures present in the organization. This paper will illustrate, through a rigorous case study, how one corporation accomplished this feat, while at the same time recognizing that one cannot simply "manage" away national cultural differences.

THE GLOBAL BUSINESS

A clear understanding of the global corporation is found in Harris and Moran (1996) who cite the earlier works of Barnett and Muller (1974):

> The global corporation is the first institution in human history dedicated to centralized planning on a world scale. Because its primary activity is to orga-

nize and to integrate economic activity around the world in such a way as to maximize global profit, it is an organic structure in which each part is expected to serve the whole.... With their world view, the managers of global corporations are seeking to put into practice a theory of human organization that will profoundly alter the nation-state system around which society has been organized for over four hundred years. (p. 11)

Global corporations have realized that the most efficient way to increase growth and profitability is by giving up one nation citizenship and setting up operations throughout the world. Cummings and Worley (1997) view globalization as one of the three most significant trends impacting organizations. They write, "First, globalization is changing the markets and environments in which organizations operate as well as the way they function. New governments, new leadership, new markets, and new countries are emerging and creating a new global economy" (p. 4).

IMPACT OF GLOBALIZATION ON MANAGEMENT

Adler and Jelinek (1986) suggested that from a macro perspective of resource, product, and financial markets, business executives almost have a mandate to "go global." However, they further suggest that from the micro perspective of managing people, "the choice to transcend national boundaries is by no means clear" (p. 73). While a dissenting vote is cast by Levitt (1983), who posits that the cultural differences between employees and leaders can be completely ignored with little risk of negative business consequences, a large contingent of international researchers point to the need to better understand the relationships among national culture, corporate culture, and leadership behaviors (Adler, 1997; Hofstede, 1991; Schneider & Barsoux, 1997; Trompenaars & Hampden-Turner, 1998). In a recent survey of organization development consultants (Kwong & Head, 2007) 82% report that national cultural values play a critical role in the organization development process. All these researchers suggest that the alignment between a leader's behavior and the national culture in which he or she works can have a significant impact on performance and results. Elashmawi and Harris (1998) provide a succinct summary of this perspective stating, "In the growing global marketplace, more and more businesses find themselves confronting new obstacles—obstacles that can endanger the success of global joint ventures" (p. 22). They suggest that the source of these conflicts can often be identified by studying the friction or lack of alignment between organizational leaders and employees who possess different cultural backgrounds.

An opposing view is put forth by Hickson and Pugh (1995) who suggest that leadership, as well as many other organizational components, are going through a process of convergence. That is leaders are becoming much more similar to each other regardless of national culture. This convergence perspective suggests that organizations must actively create cultures, structures, strategies, and managerial practices that transcend any single nation's culture. Harris and Moran (1996) state, "For organizations to flourish, let alone survive in the future, their perspective must be global" (p. 3).

Jaeger (1986) states that "a firm with a strong organization culture tends to have a homogenizing influence on the values of employees" (p. 180). If this is the case, then leaders within an organization that has a strong culture might be expected to share many of the same values, and exhibit many of the same behaviors. Therefore, any leadership theory or practice, if modified slightly, should be transplantable (Goodstein, 1981). Hickson and Pugh (1995) add:

> the non-cultural factors which act in the same direction upon managements of all cultures are getting stronger. As enterprises move more and more towards operating internationally, they are producing a convergence in management functioning which could mean that, in due, course, there will be a common global "management culture." (p. 277)

A few organizations have attempted to manage across multiple national cultures by imposing a convergent solution. These organizations "simply" establish a corporate culture that dominates and subordinates its employees' various national cultures. One early example of this strategy was Citi-Corp when it expanded operations into Asia and Eastern Europe (Sorensen, Head, Johnson, & Gubbins, 1989). For example when CitiCorp entered Japan it realized that no "typical" Japanese individual would desire to work for an "American" bank, so the company did not try to hire "typical" Japanese. Instead, CitiCorp identified those Japanese citizens who didn't fit the "Japanese mold." In other words CitiCorp hired Japanese who, because they were more "Western" in their perspective, were unemployable in Japanese organizations but fit perfectly into Citicorp.

Schein (1985) underscores the critical link between the leaders of organizations and the culture of these organizations. He states that "one of the most decisive functions of leadership is the creation, the management, and sometimes even the destruction of culture" (p. 5). One way that leaders shape the culture of the organization is by articulating a clear vision of the values of the organization, and then institutionalizing and formalizing these cultural attributes through behaviors and reward systems. Specifically, Schein suggests that there are six primary embedding mechanisms that leaders use to shape and transmit culture.

They are: (1) what leaders pay attention to, measure and control on a regular basis; (2) how leaders react to critical incidents and organizational crises; 3) how leaders allocate resources; (4) deliberate role modeling and coaching; (5) how leaders allocate rewards and status, and; (6) the criteria by which individuals are selected, promoted and "excommunicated." These mechanisms have a dual importance for this paper. First, they illustrate why global organizations would desire to establish a corporate culture that dominates all others, and second, they prove the critical importance of imposing the corporate culture upon its executives. Strong corporate cultures remove the greatest source of internal uncertainty for managers—predicting how the employees will act, make, and implement decisions. However, creating a corporate culture strong enough to subordinate the national cultures obviously require executives completely socialized into that same culture.

The remainder of this paper presents a case study of how one large organization was able, through its evaluation and promotion practices, to create a set of executives which subordinated their national cultural values to the organization's cultural values, followed by a discussion of how this concept creates significant alterations at the middle management level.

METHOD

The Director of Leadership Development for a multinational, medical equipment manufacturing company contracted with one of the authors to develop a single leadership-competency model and interview protocol for the company's global executive-band level. The consulting project was divided into two phases. In Phase I, data were gathered to help define a target list of leadership competencies to put into the competency model. Executives from each of the three regions (United States, France, and Japan), were asked to provide input as to the types of leadership competencies they perceived as being important to job performance success in their unique geographic region. Using the importance score of the competencies, Phase I concluded with the development of a provisional competency model and the customization of a structured interview to be used to assess the leadership competencies of a sample of incumbent executives. Phase II involved two primary steps. The first step consisted of the assessment of leadership competencies of 34 incumbent executives. The second step consisted of data analysis to identify the utility of the single leadership competency model across the three geographies, and to assess how effectively the assessment interview was in accurately identifying executives who were highly successful performers.

Study Organization and Subjects

The Fortune 500 corporation is a medical equipment-manufacturing firm headquartered in the United States. Its business is structured around three separate business units according to geographic regions. The three regions are the Americas, Europe, and Asia. The Americas headquarters is located in a Midwestern state. The European headquarters is located in France. The Asian operation is concentrated in Japan. Each business unit is comprised of sales, services, engineering and manufacturing functions. The corporation has annual revenues that exceed $5 billion, and employs well over 20,000 individuals. Over 50% of the corporation's employees are located outside the United States. The organization is considered a market leader in the medical equipment industry.

For the purpose of this study, the population consisted of the 150 executive-band leaders employed by the corporation. In Phase I of the study, each incumbent executive-band leader was given an opportunity to express a viewpoint concerning the types of competencies important in being successful at the executive-band level through either one-on-one, qualitative interviews or the use of a competency-based survey. Overall, nine top executives (CEO and eight direct reports) were interviewed in depth, and 150 surveys were sent to executive-band level managers, 76 of which were completed and mailed back.

In Phase II, 34 of the executives participated. Ninety-one percent of these executives shared the national background of the host-country in which they worked. The 34 participants were selected for participation in the study by the vice president of human resources and the director of leadership development. The criteria for selection into the Phase II assessment were as follows: incumbent at the executive-band level, more than 1 year of experience at this level, and performance evaluation rating data on file within the human resources department. Beyond these criteria, the researchers requested that the Phase II subjects be sampled equally from the three regions. In addition, approximately one-half of the sample was to be drawn from a pool of highly rated, top performers, and the other half of the participants was to be drawn from a pool of average performers.

Instruments

Three data-gathering instruments were utilized in the course of this research project. Two of the instruments were used in Phase I of the study. These two instruments were designed to assist in the development of the provisional competency model. The third instrument is a structured interview utilized to assess the competencies of the sample of 34 executive-band leaders. The first instrument was an 18 question protocol to give the CEO and each of his eight direct reports an opportunity to provide information at the project's onset. For the purpose of the case study, it was imperative that the questions presented the senior executives with a clear opportunity to discuss the following topics: leadership competencies of top performers; competencies desired in newly hired executives; competencies that differentiate average and top performers; differences in competency needs among the three geographic regions; and future leadership competency needs of the organization.

The second instrument was based upon the output gathered from instrument one. All 59 competencies and leadership characteristics mentioned in the senior executive interviews was included in the competency survey. The survey consisted of two sections. In the first section, respondents were asked to read short descriptions of 24 competencies and to select the ones that were most necessary for performance success. The second section listed 35 characteristics and allowed respondents to select the leader characteristics that were believed to be most critical to executive performance success. The third interviewing instrument was a blend of behavioral event interviewing technique and situational based interviewing techniques. The interview questions focused the interviewee on past experience

RESULTS

While the project's purpose was to design a single all-encompassing leadership competency model, the researchers first analyzed the data to establish whether or not unique regional leadership competencies did exist, and if they did, what would be the implication for corporate management.

Table 15.1 displays the 24 leadership competencies identified in Phase I, along with the importance scores, broken out by region: United States, France, and Japan. The numbers in parentheses represent the rank order of the top five important competencies for each region.

While integrity was identified as being the most important across all three regions, a number of interesting findings showed competencies important for some regions as being relatively less important in other regions. The following is a summary of regional importance of competencies:

Table 15.1.   Importance of Competencies by Region/Country

Competency	United States (n = 43)	Japan (n = 14)	France (n = 18)
Integrity	95% (1)	93% (1)	89% (1)
Developing	37%	71% (3)	72% (4)
Discerning	14%	21%	17%
Listening skills	40%	43%	22%
Adaptability	40%	43%	44%
Accountability	56%	21%	33%
Results oriented	72% (2)	57%	83% (2)
Recognizing	37%	36%	39%
Resource allocation	37%	86% (2)	44%
Planning	37%	21%	17%
Inspirational leadership	63% (4)	64% (4)	78% (3)
Decisiveness	58% (5)	64% (5)	61%
Directness	21%	7%	0%
Interpersonal sensitivity	33%	57%	28%
Self-awareness	12%	7%	6%
Motivating	44%	50%	39%
Big picture thinking	44%	43%	44%
Delegating	33%	21%	39%
Quick learning	5%	21%	6%
Selecting	21%	21%	17%
Influential communication	42%	43%	22%
Collaborative	26%	14%	17%
Managing change	67% (3)	43%	50%
Energizer	53%	43%	72% (5)

- Results Oriented was important for the United States (72%) and for France (83%), and less so in Japan (57%)
- Inspirational leadership was important in all three regions
- Managing change was important in the United States (67%) but not for France or Japan.
- Developing was much more important in Japan (71%) and France (72%) than in the US (37%). Resource Allocation was very important in Japan (86%), but fairly low in the United States (37%), and

France (44%). Hickson and Pugh cite that the culture in Japan is focused on planning and efficiency.

- Being an energizer was more important in France (72%) than in Japan (43%) or the United States (53%).
- Interpersonal sensitivity was more important in Japan (57%) than in the United States (33%) or France (28%). The interpersonal sensitivity was consistent with the Japanese culture of collectivism, respect, and close relationships.
- Accountability and directness were more important in the United States (56% and 21%) than in Japan (21% and 7%) and France (33% and 0%).

Based on the review of Table 15.1, there appears to be support for the belief that leadership characteristics are dependent upon national culture, otherwise known as the divergence model. At the same time there are clearly enough similarities so as to establish the possibility of a common core of competencies.

In part two of the survey, executives were asked to refer to a list of 35 characteristics, and consider the following: "If you were chartered with selecting future Corporation X Global Leaders, which characteristics do you believe would be most important for the candidates to possess?"

Table 15.2 presents the 12 most frequently identified characteristics. A review of this list and the corresponding percentages indicates that the

Table 15.2.   Key Characteristics to Hiring Candidates

Characteristic	Percent
Creative	67
Self-confident	64
Enthusiastic	54
Future oriented	51
Focused	51
Passionate	50
Reliable	50
Flexible	46
Respectful	46
Risk-taker	43
Organized	41
Supportive	41

respondents were not consistently drawn to any of the characteristics. The top characteristic chosen, create (67%), was only selected two-thirds of the time. A breakdown of important characteristics by region was then analyzed to determine if regional differences exists and therefore could explain the surprisingly low percentages. This information is located in Table 15.3.

While looking for trends with such small numbers is more of an art then science, it appears to suggest that 10 of the 35 characteristics appear to vary significantly across regions. The characteristics patient and strong willed were fairly dominant in Japan, but had weak support in the United States and France. Charismatic, outgoing, and reliable, were dominant characteristics in France but were relatively unimportant in both Japan and the United States, while emotional stability was strong in these later two nations but not so in France. Flexible and intuitive were dominant characteristics in the United States, but were weak in France. Self-confident was dominant in France, but weak in Japan, and receptive was also weak in Japan, but relatively important in both the United States and France.

While regional differences did exist, the majority of the executive-band leadership characteristics were somewhat stable across regions. That is, regardless of region, candidates for this company should possess characteristics such as self-confidence, enthusiasm, creativity, and focus. Overall the conclusion for Phase I is that there is strong support for the hypothesis that the corporate executives perceived that unique leadership competencies and characteristics were necessary for success dependent on the geographic region in which they worked. Yet, somewhat contradictory, there was also clear evidence that a single, universal, set of executive level selection criteria was possible. In order to develop and validate this protocol, Phase II of the study was implemented.

Phase II

Recall that the project was initiated by the organization's desire to have a single set of universal characteristics with which to identify potential executives. In order to establish this predictor list, profile assessments of current executives were analyzed to first determine if behavioral convergence across regions could be supported, and to secondly determine if a set of competencies could produce an effective model for predicting job performance. Thirty-four (United States $n = 14$; France $n = 12$; Japan $n = 8$) executives were put through the profile assessment that was developed from the competencies. The assessments conducted represented a 23% sampling of the executive population.

Table 15.3.   Most Important for
Candidates to Possess Among Executives

Characteristic	United States (n = 43)	Japan (n = 15)	France (n = 18)
Self-confident	28 (65%)	6 (43%)	14 (78%)
Creative	26 (60%)	11 (79%)	14 (78%)
Enthusiastic	25 (58%)	5 (36%)	10 (56%)
Focused	24 (56%)	5 (36%)	9 (50%)
Flexible	23 (53%)	6 (43%)	5 (28%)
Respectful	22 (51%)	6 (43%)	6 (33%)
Passionate	21 (49%)	7 (50%)	10 (56%)
Future oriented	20 (47%)	6 (43%)	12 (67%)
Organized	19 (44%)	3 (21%)	9 (50%)
Risk taker	19 (44%)	8 (57%)	5 (28%)
Reliable	18 (42%)	6 (43%)	13 (72%)
Competitive	18 (42%)	3 (21%)	6 (33%)
Persuasive	15 (35%)	2 (14%)	5 (28%)
Process minded	15 (35%)	5 (36%)	6 (33%)
Receptive	15 (35%)	0 (0%)	5 (28%)
Supportive	14 (33%)	8 (57%)	8 (44%)
Tenacious	13 (30%)	3 (21%)	7 (39%)
Intuitive	12 (28%)	3 (21%)	1 (6%)
Charismatic	10 (23%)	2 (14%)	14 (78%)
Emotional stability	10 (23%)	4 (29%)	1 (6%)
Compassionate	9 (21%)	2 (14%)	2 (11%)
Data driven	6 (14%)	2 (14%)	3 (17%)
Nurturing	6 (14%)	0 (0%)	1 (6%)
Thick skinned	4 (9%)	0 (0%)	1 (6%)
Conscientious	3 (7%)	1 (7%)	1 (6%)
Patient	2 (5%)	6 (43%)	2 (11%)
Sociable	2 (5%)	1 (7%)	0 (0%)
Outspoken	2 (5%)	1 (7%)	1 (6%)
Humble	2 (5%)	1 (7%)	1 (6%)
Intense	1 (2%)	2 (14%)	1 (6%)
Strong willed	1 (2%)	4 (29%)	1 (6%)
Outgoing	1 (2%)	0 (0%)	2 (11%)
Independent	1 (2%)	0 (0%)	0 (0%)
Politically astute	0 (0%)	1 (7%)	1 (6%)
Cautious	0 (0%)	0 (0%)	1 (6%)

The corporation provided the necessary performance information at this point in the research. The corporation identified each of the 34 executives as either a "top-performer" or a "not top-performer." Twenty-two out of 34 executives were identified as top performers—10 from the United States, 8 from France, and 4 from Japan.

As described previously, the assessment tool yielded 24 behavioral competencies scores. Average scores and measures of distribution were calculated across the 24 competencies for each of the regions. Seven out of the top 10 behavioral competencies were consistent for all 3 regions. Top performers—regardless of region—scored high on the following behavioral competencies: energy/intensity, accountability for results, goal focused, executing priorities, decisiveness, commitment, and assertiveness. This commonality provided the first piece of evidence toward the acceptance of a possible convergence among behavioral competencies of top performers.

A logistic regression analysis was conducted to establish the relationship between job performance and behavioral competencies (using performance as the dependent variable). The stepwise logistic regression procedure developed a model with only two significant predictors: goal focus, and decisiveness. However, this compact model could accurately predict 88% of the executives as top or not-top performers. The model classified 9 out of 12 of the not-top performers correctly, and 21 out of 22 of the top-performers correctly, for accuracy levels of 75% and 95% respectively. The results of this model show that a single set of competencies could be established that accurately and effectively predict the executive's job performance. Most importantly this model also holds up across the regions. Twelve of the 14 United States executives were correctly classified for an 86% accuracy score. Eleven of the 12 executives from France were correctly identified for an accuracy score of 92%. Seven of the eight Japanese executives were correctly classified for an accuracy score of 88%.

The combined results of the two phases, at first, appears to create a paradox. This global organization clearly recognizes that national cultural differences exist within its different operations, and these differences should impact upon what leadership behaviors result in effectiveness. But, at the same time, the organization's effective leaders are those that demonstrate a single set of universalized, convergent competencies.

The explanation to this contradiction can be found in the corporate culture. What was actually "discovered" is that through controlling selection and reward systems this organization was able to create a corporate culture that dominated all others among its executive ranks. While this is clear and understandable, it does lead to another question—how does the organization manage the national cultural differences that its own executives acknowledge actually exist?

DISCUSSION

Perhaps the greatest strategic challenge organizations face in the next several years is establishing exactly how they need to manage the cultural differences that arise between their operations in different countries. We are long past the stage where executives can "learn by their mistakes" on these issues. Clearly the executives must acknowledge that significant differences exist, and these differences create the need to react and implement changes in one direction or the other. Most organizations will find it easiest to change their practices to meet each nation's unique cultural values. Others will try to establish a corporate culture that is so strong that it dominates all national cultures, thereby permitting the company to function with one unique "modus operandi." And still others, like the company in this case, will establish a hybrid system—with the "universal culture" applied at the executive level, but retaining the "fit" to the individual national cultures at the lower levels in the structure.

The case described here illustrates the existence of significant cultural differences that corporations need to manage when operating globally. However, the case also shows how corporations can create an organizational culture that subordinates national cultural differences to that of the corporate culture, at least at the executive level. By subordinating the national cultural value differences, the organization hopes to create a consistency and reliability throughout its global operations, with a side benefit of making the executives completely transplantable. The large Fortune 500 company described here created a corporate culture strong enough that the executives all set aside what they admitted were critical cultural differences and internalized the corporate philosophy. There were no "deep hidden" machinations involved—the organization used the classic cultural change tools of incorporating the corporate values within its performance evaluations, its leadership indoctrination and development, the performance review process and the reward systems.

By utilizing control mechanisms and shaping job roles that led the executives to reflect the culture of the corporation, the senior leadership team created homogeneity among their executives. However, this current research, as well as that of many others, demonstrated that this homogeneity does not tend to be reflected by the rank and file employees of the multi-national corporation. These employees tend to reflect the national culture of the host-country. Therefore a global corporation, such as the one discussed here, must "push" the need to manage national differences down to the middle management ranks.

The dynamics of this situation is presented in the model presented in Figure 15.1. This model posits that the behavior of executives within a multinational, global organization will often display a convergence of

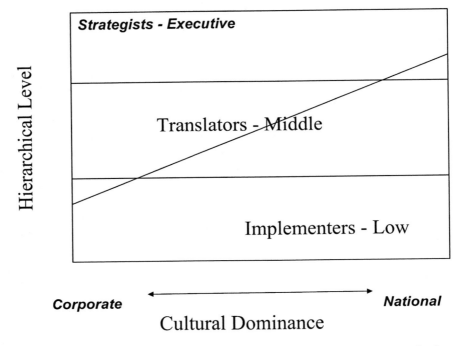

Figure 15.1.   The relationship between hierarchical level and the two sets of cultural values.

leadership competencies, and that these competencies will be reflective of the corporate culture of the organization. However, as one moves through the organization to study the behaviors of midlevel managers and line workers, the national culture will be more clearly reflected within the organization.

Executive level players are referred to as *strategists*; they are the senior leaders within the organization, those who are responsible for the strategic functioning of the organization. They also are accountable for the overall results attained by their charges. These individuals spend a good amount of their time interacting with peers in other parts of the global operation, and with the corporation's global headquarters. They help shape the global strategy and regional strategy for the business, and to ensure that these strategies are aligned with each other. In addition, they carry the key corporate messages to their teams, and they are called upon to enforce the global policies of the organization. As such, these strategists have been fully trained on the "corporate viewpoint" on how to lead and how to conduct business.

Translators represent the next level of management within the organization. These individuals report to the strategists. They are typically responsible for project management and the execution of the strategies of the organization. They take instruction from the strategists and they manage and oversee the work of the implementers. The term "translator" suggests these managers need to be capable of understanding and working with individuals who represent the corporation's culture, as well as working effectively with others whose beliefs, values and behaviors are more aligned with their national culture.

Implementers are the individual contributors within the organization. They may be the workers in a manufacturing plant, frontline supervisors, or individual contributors in any of the functional areas of the organization. These implementers are responsible for producing the output of the organization. If they reach outside the organization, it is simply by interacting with the local customers.

Corporate culture consists of the "pattern of values, beliefs, and expectations shared by organization members" (Cummings & Worley, 1997, p. 2). Specifically, it is the culture of the global headquarters which is being considered. For the purpose of this model, it is assumed that the corporation proactively attempts to shape its global culture.

National culture

> consists of patterns, explicit and implicit, of and for behavior acquired and transmitted by symbols, constituting the distinctive achievement of human groups, including their embodiment in artifacts; the essential core of culture consists of traditional ideas and especially their attached values. (Kroebe & Kluckhohn, 1952, p. 181)

National culture is represented in the beliefs, values, and norms of the implementers in the organization.

The model suggests that the strategists will demonstrate behavioral competencies which reflect the culture and values of the corporation. This will be observed in the convergence of leadership behaviors throughout the organization. This model also suggests that the implementers will demonstrate cultural values and behavioral competencies that most closely align with the national culture. In order to link these two different groups, the middle collective of employees act as "cultural translators" for both the strategists and the implementers. It is suggested that these cultural translators need heightened sensitivity to both the corporate and national cultures that exist within the organization.

Strategists reflect the corporate culture because of the indoctrination process that they are taken through by the corporation. This process serves to homogenize the leadership competencies practiced by the strategists of the organization. This method may be an effective tactic if the organization prescribes to a geocentric, regiocentric, or ethnocentric global strategy. In Moran, Harris, and Stripp's (1993) discussion of types of "global corporations," convergence of leadership competencies seems to be aligned with these three strategies. In a geocentric corporation, the focus on global interdependence and worldwide goals may be more effective if the executives who frequently interact with each other share similar styles and competencies. In a regiocentric corporation, the world headquarters focuses on strategy, global planning, selecting executives, and establishing a corporate culture. This also may lead to a greater likelihood of executive leadership convergence, as the selection and development of leaders is a centralized process. Finally, in the ethnocentric corporation, the bias is clearly toward replicating the world headquarters' culture in all global operations. In this case, the bias is toward leadership convergence and cultural homogeneity.

The implementers do not typically go through the same indoctrination process as the strategists. In addition, the organizational processes for selecting, training and rewarding these individuals are more likely to be controlled at the host-country level. In addition, these individuals are less likely to experience a high degree of interaction with the global headquarters. With these control mechanisms less in effect, and with an increase in the amount of interaction with host-country customers, vendors, and coworkers, it is suggested that the line workers will most closely reflect the culture of the nation in which they live and work.

If, as this study suggests, strategists reflect the corporate culture of the organization, and implementers reflect the national culture of the host-country, how can a multinational corporation function in an effective manner? A focus on the middle managers of the organization holds the answer to this question. The middle managers act as cultural translators between the executives and the line workers. In their job roles they, in effect, interact with both sets of cultures. As direct reports to the strategists, they are involved in team meetings and in touch with worldwide corporate strategy. In addition, they are likely to have been hired and trained by these strategists. As Cascio (1982) discusses, executives often hire in their own image. Clearly, these are significant control mechanisms that would suggest that the middle managers would reflect some of the corporate culture of the organization. However, these translators will also be impacted by the national culture. As managers, they need to lead and motivate teams in order to accomplish tactical goals. In this aspect of their jobs, they interact with and manage implementers. To be effective, in this role, these translators must demonstrate a sensitivity to, and understanding of, the host-nation's culture. Due to their level of interaction with both the corporate and host-country cultures, the translators are impacted by both. In addition, they apply their understanding of the corporate culture to help "translate" corporate strategy and directives to the implementers. Conversely, the "translate" implementers provide issues and concerns to the strategists. Within the proposed model, they become a critical linchpin for organizational communication and strategy implementation. Future studies should focus on this new and developing role within multinational corporations.

IMPLICATIONS FOR
ORGANIZATION DEVELOPMENT CONSULTANTS

With the strategists reflecting the corporate culture and implementers embodying the national culture, the potential for many organizational disconnects, miscommunications, and misunderstandings between these two groups is a certainty. It is critical that the organization development consultant recognizes and understands both the prevailing corporate culture and national cultures impacting the organization. Change strategies and intervention methodologies should be carefully selected and matched to these cultures. This situation also requires the consultant to operate far more closely with the middle managers, the translators, than is typically suggested. In the global organizations, clearly the translator roles overlap those of the consultant far more than the strategist. Further, for organization development consultants, translators can provide keen insight into the "tugs and pulls" occurring throughout the organization. The translators can help the consultant identify the gaps and disconnects between strategy and implementation, and leadership and followership.

Clearly, this proposed model encourages the organization development consultant who is working with multinational corporations to take great care in understanding and appreciating both corporate and national cultures. Therefore, referring back to the original argument, it is not whether the consultant's tools will work across national/cultural boundaries with or without adaptation—clearly adaptation is required—it is at what level does the consultant make these adaptations.

REFERENCES

Adler, N. J., & Jelinek, M. (1986). Is "organization culture" culture bound? *Human Resource Management, 25*(1), 73-90.

Adler, N. S. (1997). *International dimensions of organizational behavior.* Cincinnati, OH: South-Western College.

Barnett, R. J., & Muller, R. E. (1974). *Global reach: The power of the multinational corporation.* New York: Simon & Schuster.

Cascio, W. (1982). *Applied psychology in personnel management.* New York: Prentice Hall.

Cummings, T. G., & Worley, C. G. (1997). *Organization development & change.* Cincinnati, OH: West.

Elashmawi, F., & Harris, P. R. (1998). *Multicultural management 2000: Essential cultural insights for global business success.* Houston, TX: Gulf.

Gong, C., & Head, T. (2002, May). *What lessons have we learned from the merger and acquisition process?* Midwest Academy of Management Conference, Indianapolis, IN.

Goodstein, L. D. (1981). Commentary: Do American theories apply abroad? *Organizational Dynamics, 14*, 49-54.

Harris, P. R., & Moran, R. T. (1996). *Managing cultural differences: Leadership strategies for a new world of business* (4th ed.). Houston, TX: Gulf.

Hickson, D. J., & Pugh, D. S. (1995). *Management worldwide: The impact of societal culture on organizations around the globe.* London, England: Penguin Books.

Hofstede, G. (1980). *Culture's consequences: International differences in work-related values.* Newbury Park, CA: SAGE.

Hofstede, G. (1991). *Cultures and organizations: Software of the mind.* London, England: McGraw-Hill International.

Jaeger, A. M. (1986). Organization development and national culture: Where's the fit? *Academy of Management Review, 11*, 178-190.

Kroeber, A., & Kluchohn, F. (1952) Culture: A critical review of concepts and definition. *Peabody Museum Papers, 47*, 181.

Kwong, F., & Head, T. (2007, May). *Barriers To international consulting: Fact or fiction?* Academy of Management International Conference on Management Consulting, Copenhagen, Denmark.

Levitt, T. (1983, May/June). The globalization of markets. *Harvard Business Review*, 92-102.

Moran, R., Harris, P., & Stripp, W. (1993). *Developing the global organization.* Houston, TX: Gulf

Schein, E.H. (1985). *Organizational culture and leadership.* San Francisco: Jossey-Bass.

Schneider, S. C., & Barsoux, J. (1997). *Managing across cultures.* London, England: Prentice Hall Europe.

Trompenaars, F., & Hampden-Turner, C. (1998). *Riding the waves of culture: Understanding diversity in global business.* New York: McGraw-Hill.

CHAPTER 16

WEAVING DISTINCTIVE MULTINATIONAL OUTCOMES

Embedded Strategic Organization Development

Mary Lou Kotecki

Strategic orientations define the future direction of an organization. They represent an organization's foci for directing and guiding efforts to achieve and sustain superior performance. Multinational initiatives undertaken in response are intended to create positive, time sensitive and cost effective impacts on the organization. Recognition of organization development as a critical and strategic element in the success of multinational efforts is essential. Organization development (OD) knowledge and approaches, if embedded within the organization's culture and work practices, provide a ready means for effectively enabling dialogue, comprehensive, coordinated learning, and collaborative action-taking across the organization. Three case studies offer a view of organization development as a strategic underlying structure.

Strategic orientations are generally formed on the basis of competencies, structures, and resources. They are intended to enable organizations

Strategic Organization Development: Managing Change for Success
pp. 265–278

to compete within targeted market, financial, and technological environments. OD is strategic when its tools and interventions become foundational capabilities for developing and implementing means to attain strategic objectives. As described by Gareth Morgan (2006), metaphors allow "a way of thinking and a way of seeing." They frame our understanding by highlighting insights while ignoring other aspects of the topic under consideration. Although metaphors provide incomplete information, they offer a way of creating images that lead to understanding. To that end, let us consider a simple metaphor to envision strategic OD.

Imagine strategic organization development is reflected in the weaving of a rug. Rug weaving begins with positioning parallel threads that run through the entire length of the carpet. These are known as warp. Weft threads that run across the rug are woven through alternate warp threads. This tight interweaving provides the underlying structure upon which a carpet is built. Because it also provides a distinctive, complex pattern, the weave can produce a kilim or flat surface carpet not unlike a tapestry. For pile rugs it acts as a foundation for knots that loop around the warp. The job of weft threads is to secure the knots to strengthen the rug. Weaving strategies produce different patterns and designs.

Strategic orientations resemble warp threads providing direction and growth and weft threads are symbolic of strategic OD in that they provide interwoven strength. Weft threads carry the visible design just as OD applications provide insights that color learning, decisions and actions. It is upon these insights that initiative solutions, like the knot design in a Persian rug, are derived and solution implementation is enabled.

OD, when strategically interwoven or embedded within the fabric of an initiative, provides early and continuing consideration of organizational, environmental, and cultural conditions. OD contributes to timely and effective outcomes. Multinational initiatives in particular offer unique challenges. In these circumstances OD explorations and interventions offer distinct opportunities to create a positive impact. OD knowledge and approaches potentiate dialogue, comprehensive, coordinated learning, and collaborative action-taking throughout the organization. Such competencies allow work to proceed more speedily and offer surety that all stakeholders' needs and concerns will be valued and receive consideration. In addition, OD tools and techniques open up creative possibilities.

Over the years one Fortune 500 company has gradually embraced OD as a strategic necessity. Three case studies describing multinational strategic initiatives illustrate the inclusion of a variety of OD approaches. The cases reported briefly encapsulate efforts sponsored at the company's highest levels—two by company officers and one by the chairman. Progress on this third initiative receives board level scrutiny. The first case presented provides a more detailed view of organization development as a strategic underlying structure for attainment of targeted deliverables. The following two cases depict brief snapshots of initiatives and the strategic OD approaches employed.

CASE STUDY 1: CAREER DEVELOPMENT INITIATIVE

Business Case

Employee surveys in two successive years indicated that 70% of employees were neutral or answered unfavorably to the question, "How satisfied are you with the opportunity to get a better job with the Company?" In addition, at that time, employee attrition for those with less than 4 years of service was higher than acceptable with some areas experiencing 6% to 9%. New employees made up over 50% of the workforce. Retention efforts were inconsistent. Exit survey data showed that lack of career development was among the top three reasons cited for resignations. These results crossed national boundaries, position responsibilities, and hierarchical levels. The costs associated with turnover were conservatively estimated as 2–3 times an employee's salary. These facts, coupled with projected retirements and associated recruiting costs, built a solid business case for taking multinational action.

Situational Characteristics

This multinational corporation offered no enterprise-wide career development process. Different development elements existed within various levels of the organization, but most employees were unable to access or leverage opportunities beyond the boundaries of their location, function, or division. Languages, divisional priorities, limited systems capabilities, and legal constraints or requirements impacted available information and information access. The company employed approximately 50,000 people who worked in corporate, manufacturing, financial, and leading-edge technology settings.

Objective and Scope

The intent of the career development initiative was to provide career development processes, tools, and a system that encouraged employees to more effectively reach their full potential. The new approach was to be available from hire date throughout an entire career. Specifically, the processes and system targeted for development were to encompass the following:

- an enterprise-wide career development process initially open to all salaried employees on a voluntary participation basis
- processes which place primary responsibility for pursuing development on employees (with supporting tools, guidance, infrastructure)
- Plans to understand and address cultural issues and to overcome low levels of acceptance for change readiness
- Integration with the strategic human resource (HR) Vision as a critical enabler of the company's overarching strategic intent
- Integration with other key strategic HR initiatives such as global job evaluation, performance management, total rewards strategies, leadership development, and talent acquisition and integration and with HR processes such as mentoring, succession planning, staffing, and job posting
- Development and implementation of a career development process and strategic information technology system which provides an infrastructure serving employees worldwide through which the following attributes are delivered:
  o a view to open positions and ability to apply for openings
  o a means to input skills, experiences, competencies, education, and interest
  o support through coaching, mentoring, feedback
  o management engagement in the development process
  o level-setting of employees' expectations with prospective possibilities
- Deliverables targeted to be completed within 18 months also included: terminology definitions and confirmations
  o OD diagnostics, consultations, interventions, and follow up actions
  o process and system design, test, validation
  o communication, training, and implementation plan development and execution
  o redesign of current processes and organizational structures, where necessary

Initiative Participants and Author's Viewpoint

The initiative was championed by the enterprise's HR vice president and sponsored by worldwide HR directors. The team working on the initiative included more than thirty employees representing corporate, equipment and financial divisions, and various functional responsibilities. Team membership evidenced global representation: Argentina, Brazil, Mexico, Finland/Sweden/Russia, United Kingdom, Netherlands, France, South Africa, Australia, China, Canada, United States, Germany, and Italy. As a non-HR business manager, I served as a member of the initiative core team, as a leader for the communication, training, and organization change subteams, as a member of the culture team, and as a reviewer of information system design functionality.

Organization Development Threads

Much of the work encompassed in this initiative followed an action research perspective. An organizational diagnosis on the state of career development was conducted. Development models currently in use were presented. They encompassed a variety approaches from around the world enveloping employee and career development, people and business interfaces, engagement and satisfaction activities, and leadership processes. From those discussions and with knowledge of employee needs, key career development elements were distilled.

The underlying need to understand and appreciate cultural differences manifested itself in the use of a cultural issues check list and cultural exploration methodology. The exploration methodology centered the development and use of a cultural interview protocol. Interviews were conducted worldwide with all HR managers and with targeted executives, line managers, privacy officers, and others. The interviews were led by trained, voluntary interviewers. Data were aggregated for analysis.

Interestingly, not all of the issues uncovered were the result of national differences. Strong cultural differences were found between high technology and traditional manufacturing locations and between large operations and small sites located in areas of regional isolation or strong regional identification. Concerns were expressed about the ability to move employees between large and small units, between divisions, and between countries. These reflected visa and work permit issues as well as the inherent difficulty associated with the inability of small company entities to offer appropriate return positions. This limitation thus positions them to become net talent donors.

The cultural exploration took note of leadership styles and cultures, work hours and time of day differences, terminology and expressions issues, and expanding translation needs. In addition, data privacy and security requirements, current practices, and union representation differed by country.

Other embedded OD techniques included a detailed stakeholder analysis that captured issues, levels of understanding and commitment, influence strategies, key messages, and intervention strategies and assignments. In response to the learning gained through this analysis, comprehensive communication and training plans were developed and executed. These plans included use of a variety of media and deployment methods to satisfy the spectrum of employee expectations and to meet employee needs across the company.

In addition, the organization change subteam assessed numerous OD tools which offered capabilities to identify and prioritize issues. The model chosen for use was the six levers of organization change model. This model is designed to encompass organizational, operational, and strategic issues. Use of that model in concert with a series of mind mapping sessions led to identification of important areas requiring change and to stumbling blocks which would inhibit initiative achievements.

The key stumbling block to the success of career development proved to be management engagement. The team acknowledged that some managers were not skilled in conducting career development discussions, nor were all willing to adopt "new" responsibilities. It was acknowledged that trained and ready-to-step-in facilitators or mediators may be needed. There was also uncertainty about management's support for full project deployment. These management issues were subsequently resolved. With approval of the initiative champion and sponsors, clearly defined career development responsibilities were automatically placed within all supervisory performance goals. Identified organization structural gaps were also resolved through new staffing assignments or responsibilities and through recruitment and training of a broadly dispersed network of voluntary career advisors.

Initiative Outcomes

Clear identification of obstacles and their potential negative influences were uncovered and those most impactive on impeding success were addressed. As designed, the online career site now includes tutorials, self-assessment tools, job and qualifications catalogues, job aids, and links to external resources. An internal resume is established to not only house basic employee information but also to provide an inventory of employee skills, experiences, and interests. The information system design enables employees the opportunity to develop career plans that highlight goals, paths, and action plans for achieving aspirations. Managers' tools are offered to aid with career discussions, coaching, reviews, feedback, and support. The career development process implemented is integrated with other HR processes for staffing needs and requests, succession planning, and employee development.

The initiative team recommended a phased roll-out plan that was very well-received throughout the enterprise. It included a staged implementation progression beginning with North America to build confidence in the approach. In addition to trained career advisors, the plan provided for accessible functional experts, translation resources, systems design, development, and verification, tips and tricks help information, and examples of completed resumes and career paths. Last, the plan included a compliance process designed to systematically check for and remedy cultural and environmental issues which may potentially arise from areas such as language and communication differences, national labor laws, industrial relations, information technology access and deployment, processes and location specific constraints.

Deployment of this initiative's solutions sent a consistent message of career development to all salaried employees. It made additional employee capabilities visible to hiring managers. It created a positive experience for new and existing employees, aided employee retention, and contributed to higher employee satisfaction. Additionally, it supported achievement of the company's overarching strategic intent. And, as a bonus, these processes and system also improved HR efficiency and effectiveness.

CASE STUDY 2: KNOWLEDGE MANAGEMENT INITIATIVE

Business Case

In 1992, Chris Argyris stated that, "The more effective organizations are at learning, the more likely they will be at being innovative." In recent years the emergence of a global knowledge economy and the heightened recognition of knowledge as intangible asset have spurred increased interest in better understanding knowledge and in significantly improving current knowledge management practices and capabilities.

Knowledge management provides a competitive advantage through more efficient and effective use of knowledge resources. Characteristics defining an effective approach include processes that standardize knowledge sharing and technologies that enable the exchange of knowledge and that capture it for future use. Additional attributes include means to develop individual and organizational behaviors that demonstrate commitment to the thoughtful exchange of knowledge and ideas. Successful management of knowledge leads to superior solutions for attainment of business goals through systematic acquisition, organization and distribution of intellectual capital.

Omnipresent challenges are under-use of inherent knowledge, loss of knowledge through retirements or resignations, and ignoring benefits available through leveraging knowledge. These pose a serious threat to the development of individual potential and to future organizational viability and growth. Increasingly, knowledge management is becoming one of the world's most important issues for enabling innovation, globalization, productivity, employee effectiveness, and sustainable competitive advantage.

Situational Characteristics

Over the years, numerous means of managing knowledge have emerged. For example, knowledge is shared through communities of practice and team activities. Tools such as databases and collaborative sharing sites contribute to gathering knowledge and making it available. Mentoring, cross training, and peer-to-peer activities also attempt to transfer knowledge.

Cultural issues present a big hurdle to implementing knowledge management strategies. The organizational environment must encourage sharing, respect for individuals and for individual creativity. Employees must feel reassured and valued and must not be fearful of losing a competitive edge. Challenges to understanding, supporting, and managing knowledge as a priority include leadership commitment, optimization of stored information and knowledge, and determining the best way to gather and transition knowledge to information and information to knowledge.

Objective and Scope

This initiative encompassed development of a business plan to accelerate implementation of a consistent approach for the management of knowledge, while ensuring alignment with and positive impact upon enterprise and division strategic objectives. This work included identification of critical knowledge management needs and integration points. The plan focused on outlining implementation of actions required to meet these needs and on creating a clear understanding of the value and importance of knowledge throughout the company. The plan was to encompass stakeholder analyses and feedback, a communication plan, a plan for addressing cultural changes as well as specific recommendations, anticipated costs, and projected implementation schedules. The plan was also to include development of processes, technologies, and behaviors that support capturing, sharing, and reusing knowledge.

This initiative envisioned knowledge management approaches unfolding and expanding over several years, seeding a rich network of conversations, proposals, pilots, and common practices. The result of this work, which emphasizes key learnings, is intended to provide insights for new generations of leadership and for employee execution of daily work.

Initiative Participants and Author's Viewpoint

Four corporate officers serve as initiative champions, including an individual with direct functional responsibilities. A vice-presidential level steering committee serves as a decision-making body and a cross-company leadership team provides guidance and consultation for the initiative team's efforts. I participated as a member of the leadership team.

Organization Development Threads

The team chose to employ a facilitated change process approach. It included a number of steps. The steps are listed below with a few examples of targeted actions:

- Prepare for Change: charter the project, conduct an organizational assessment, create a stakeholder map
- Connect to Shared Need: conduct appreciative inquiry interviews and an employee survey
- Imagine the Future: complete a stakeholder analysis
- Plan for Change: use tools such as force field analysis to develop strategies for overcoming resistance and to plan for involvement
- Support the Change: design ways to enhance leadership alignment through coaching and training plans
- Engage and Involve: develop and execute communication plans
- Respond to Results: design, develop, test, pilot, implement solutions
- Reward for Change: recognize efforts

Reports on knowledge management from research and practice provided insights, experiences, potential considerations, and challenges. This information surfaced questions on the meaning of the term management and on strategies that should be considered. Information on critical success factors, knowledge importance, definitions, and types, and dependencies provided grounding on current thought.

Team members drafted a strategy map linking strategies to financial, customer, internal processes, employee learning, and growth perspectives. This mapping exercise assisted with a needs analysis and with making a case for change.

A knowledge management needs and culture interview protocol was developed based on appreciative inquiry. It was designed to highlight the importance of knowledge management and to focus interview responses on strengths. These formally designed interviews covered three of the four appreciative inquiry elements:

- Discover—reflecting on what gives life and appreciating the best that is
- Dream—envisioning what might be and what is needed
- Design—co-constructing the ideal

Fifty-six employees representing a diagonal slice of the global organizational community were targeted for interviews. Interviewees were informed that the project team sought, through this inquiry, to uncover an innovative vision for the future of knowledge management. The team sought creative approaches that would inspire new ways for business to access, apply, retain, and benefit from knowledge.

A secondary means of gathering employee perspectives was through administration of a survey sent to approximately 20% of the workforce. The survey instrument was designed to assess the current knowledge management culture and needs. It was based in part on the knowledge management assessment tool authored by the American Productivity & Quality Center and Arthur Anderson in 1995. Analyses of variance were conducted to determine significant differences as were tests for convergent validity using exploratory factor analysis. Discriminant validity was established by correlation and reliabilities were computed.

Initiative Outcomes

This initiative resulted in a clear and simply stated definition of knowledge management. The team provided a plan to be implemented over time that is intended to accomplish the majority of the deliverables sought.

Means of facilitated communication are in place through an extensive grouping of communities of practice, numbering now in the hundreds. These communities are enabled by leading-edge information technologies. The organization's strategic focus on highly aligned teamwork supports these communities and the implementation of recommendations related to networks, teams, channels, idea sharing, feedback sessions, blogs, and so forth. The next step to be taken, again made possible through information technologies, will be a collaborative knowledge center.

CASE STUDY 3: QUALITY INITIATIVE

Business Case

This organization intends to be the industry leader in delivering positive product and service experiences to customers. In today's markets, brand image and customer loyalty can be jeopardized by poor quality. Across the enterprise there is a high degree of variation among factory and field business processes and practices. This variation drives inefficiency in operations, leads to inconsistent and inadequate quality levels and unacceptable costs, and to decreases in customer satisfaction.

Situational Characteristics

There are many compelling reasons to improve product and service quality. Quality is foundational to the brand and to the customer, and high quality levels are necessary to stave off and surpass competition. Quality has always been a major portion of customers' value propositions, and it is one of this organization's core values. In all markets in which the organization competes, customers' quality expectations are increasing. Quality can be a key differentiator with competition. In fact, recent research suggests that product quality and reliability have the highest impact on customer satisfaction and perception of value.

Objective and Scope

To achieve enterprise aspirations for this initiative requires a "whole system" change. This change requires multinational adoption of a common system of metrics, processes, training and tools that will standardize the valuable activities associated with quality planning and execution. This initiative's deliverables include the following:

- an integrated system of business and leadership processes to ensure that product and service quality represents the organization's brand
- identification and tracking of customer-related and financially-based measurements that reflect worldwide customers' and key stakeholders' performance expectations
- a rate of improvement that meets or exceeds customers' expectations and business requirements
- a distinctive customer experience, enhanced brand reputation, and further improved competitive position
- system design which follows strategic orientations and links to key strategies.

Sustainability of the new system is the key to attainment of global aspirations and is to be driven by highly aligned teamwork worldwide.

Initiative Participants and Author's Viewpoint

This initiative is sponsored by the organization's chairman and championed by a cross-divisional group of senior vice presidents. Its steering committee is comprised of vice presidents and directors from across the enterprise. The development team is multinational and comprises all divisions and select corporate areas. The effort is supported by numerous functional groups. Implementation includes working worldwide with factories and marketing entities. I serve on the development team with specific leadership responsibilities for all customer-facing elements of the system.

Organization Development Threads

This initiative involved seeking a solution for a complex and stressful challenge. Resolution required whole system change for processes, practices, and behaviors. The outcome of this work directly impacts the organizations' highest goals. Because of the speed at which this initiative moved, the development team's approach immediately became one of action learning. The team became a learning community, and members became peer consultants for each other. They had to demonstrate system thinking, creativity and flexibility. Over time they evidenced group development, and they integrated development with performance. The effort demonstrated continuous learning, reflection, and action.

Although the development team had two coleaders, the team split into small subteams focused on specific areas of the system. These self-directed groups enacted rotating leadership with individuals taking the lead, as needed, based on knowledge, skills, and time availability. Subteams merged output for review, improvement, and consensus and for steering committee decision. Multinational, multifunctional, cross-divisional collaboration prevailed as development team members served as designers, implementers, consultants, and feedback seekers.

Initiative Outcomes

The system was designed in spite of aggressive deadlines and early changes in guidance. The team which initially evidenced disorder bordering on chaos quickly melded into a unified entity. Members totally relied on and supported each other. The system was piloted. Revisions and multinational training followed prior to initiating worldwide deployment. The development team and a large group of selected functional experts continue with implementation.

The impacts of this initiative are manifested in numerous ways. Efforts are underway to address systemic gaps that cross the enterprise, and divisions and units are working to adopt valuable practices wherever possible. Substantial improvements are evident although full implementation will not be complete for some months. Rigorous methods for capturing and tracking significant common metrics and measures are in place and being executed. Factory and field activities have taken on a heightened level of collaboration.

CONCLUSION

Case studies can accomplish various aims. The purpose here is simply to exemplify the important role organization development can play when it takes on strategic proportions. Strategic OD is more than a toolkit. It is rooted in the understanding that effective change cannot take place without consideration of the current situation, the challenge at hand, organizational culture and context, external environment, and resource availability. It is this understanding that brings forth the most appropriate application of organization development knowledge and skills as a framework upon which solutions or resolutions are built. As noted in the case studies, OD became strategic because it fit the needs of the work at hand. As in the weaving of a rug, weaving strategies produce different patterns and designs and shape different outcomes.

Writing in "Reflections on the Future of OD," Worley and Feyerherm (2003) stressed that OD must reflect more than change management. Rather, they state OD must improve an organization's effectiveness and system capacity. They suggest that an OD definition involves three elements:

- organizational change for one or more systems where action is specifically designed to bring about measurable change;
- interventions that transfer change capability to the organization and embody learning and knowledge transfer regarding change management; and
- interventions deliberately target improved system performance or effectiveness.

Worley and Feyerherm (2003) indicate that OD must demonstrate large system fluency and frank discussions that acknowledge facts. It must be capable of design, working with power and influence, system thinking, broad understanding, and a strong business orientation. OD as enacted within these cases fully meets these descriptions.

OD not only influenced firm performance but rather it created behaviors and actions that helped the organization achieve superior performance. Activities spanned multinational, multidivisional, multifunctional boundaries. Inclusion of OD within the initiatives ensured that work undertaken was rooted in the organization's values and beliefs and in step with strategic orientations. In addition, as noted, OD aids alignment with strategic objectives such as those related to strategic HR, strategic IT (information technology), and enterprise strategic intent. Last, organization development easily integrates with other non-OD analyses and approaches to build robust solutions or to find strength-based opportunities.

The terms warp and weft also describe a generic open source framework for building complex systems with Java code. This framework can easily be used with existing information technology frameworks and systems, and it enables mapping of existing templates to existing code. Another perspective for strategic OD?

REFERENCES

Morgan, G. (2006). *Images from organization*. Thousand Oaks, CA: SAGE.

Worley, C., & Feyerham, A. (2003). Reflections on the future of organization development. *The Journal of Applied Behavioral Science, 39*(1), 97-115.

CHAPTER 17

STRATEGIC VERSUS NONSTRATEGIC ORGANIZATION DEVELOPMENT IN OVERSEAS CHINESE FAMILY FIRMS

A Comparison of Traditional and Progressive Firms

Richard D. Babcock and Bertha Du-Babcock

This paper presents an empirically derived, three stage model of the organizational development (OD) in overseas Chinese family firms and illustrates contrasting OD practices (strategic and nonstrategic) of traditional and progressive small Chinese family firms. The model shows how these firms can use strategic OD to remove the barriers that have resisted their growth and confined them to low technology industries. Using a case study approach, the paper compares nonstrategic OD in a traditional small Chinese family firm and strategic OD in a progressive firm.

Strategic Organization Development: Managing Change for Success
pp. 279–303

279

Overseas Chinese family firms have played a significant part in the economies of the countries surrounding the South China Sea and, in turn, have become involved in international business generally. These owner-manager family enterprises have adopted a distinctive form of organizational behavior (or a "recipe" according to Redding, 1990) that has not only contributed to their success but that also has introduced impediments limiting growth and confining these firms to low technology industries (Weidenbaum, 1996).

OD is especially important in organizations from these Chinese companies as managed and planned OD can guide the transition that firms have to make in their growth from domestic to international and global firms. In this transition, Chinese firms are moved away from relying entirely on contract manufacturing to the introduction of their own brands, from managing a national organization in a single country to managing multicountries and finally international and global organizations, and from having employee staff represented by Chinese only and speaking only Chinese to multicultural and language organizations.

This article examines the durability of this organizational configuration ("recipe") during conditions of rapid change and higher complexity in an increasing global economy, and in the process, develops a model that explains how these firms can engage in strategic OD that unblocks the limits to growth (progressive Chinese family firm) or solidifies the organizational configuration and limits growth (traditional Chinese family firm). Our model is a general description of OD in overseas Chinese family firms and the data we use to develop our model is based on Hong Kong and overseas Chinese family firms in Hong Kong.

Land costs and wage levels in Hong Kong dramatically increased starting in the 1980s while across the border in mainland China, lower cost land, plentiful labor, and governmental incentives have become available. Reacting to these economic imperatives and to the competitive pressures in increasingly globalized industries, the Hong Kong based Chinese family enterprises have relocated their manufacturing facilities to China while retaining their administrative activities in Hong Kong. Economic motives provided the incentives for the first movers. The lagging firms found themselves isolated from upstream suppliers and downstream customers who had already moved their plants to China and consequently followed shortly thereafter. The concurrent wholesale movement resulted in a new concentration of upstream and midstream manufacturing facilities in China. Taken together, these movements created the basis for an altered communication field and necessitated adjustments in the OD process within and between Chinese family firms.

With the commitment and installation of new facilities in China the impetus for examination and change was introduced. The reaction of the

Chinese family enterprises fell into two categories. One set of firms (labeled traditional) stressed continuity and the maintenance of the common characteristics of Chinese family firms, while another set of firms (labeled progressive) saw the possibility for growth and changed the "recipe." The data for the current study and model focuses on two Hong Kong Chinese family firms that represent small Chinese traditional and progressive family firms. A three stage model is developed that traces the OD (both similarities and differences) of traditional and progressive Chinese family firms and also includes examples from the two researched firms to illustrate OD activities.

LOGIC OF STAGE MODELS

Stage models provide the structure to understand and describe the evolving OD of owner-manager Chinese family firms. Our model identifies three distinct stages in the OD of the overseas Chinese family firm where the growth patterns of two contrasting types of overseas Chinese family firms are placed within these three stages where factors that contribute to success at an earlier stage subsequently become dysfunctional at a following stage. As a firm grows and progresses from one stage to the next, a crisis requires or planned OD allows adjustment to a differing set of environmental factors (external adjustment) and to finding the fit among strategies, structure, and systems (internal adjustment). The crisis at the intersection of stages creates the impetus for discarding the organizational system that was characteristic of the previous stage. Higher labor and land costs were the crisis inducing factors that propelled the movement of manufacturing facilities to lower cost areas in China. The physical distance between the administrative and headquarters' facilities (located in Hong Kong) and the manufacturing operations (relocated to China) precipitated and necessitated the introduction of new ways of communicating and coordinating in these overseas Chinese family firms. Lewin's (1946, 1952) three-stage action learning model of unfreezing, moving, and refreezing (stabilization) provides a structure for identifying and tracing events and OD activities in the movement within and between stages. The unfreezing event was the necessity of moving manufacturing operations to remain competitive. The changing activities were the adjustments made to maintain or improve organizational effectiveness and efficiency of the Chinese family firms. The refreezing/stabilization events included integrating new activities into the framework of prior systems and behavior patterns of the firms. The model incorporates Lewin's framework to allow direct comparison of traditional and progressive chinese firms.

Within the stages Galbraith and Kazanjian's (1986) construct of fit is useful; they note that there needs to be a consistency among the elements of the system at each growth stage. The current model identifies environmental variables (labeled enabling factors) and pairs these variables with firm variables in both Traditional and progressive firms. The fit between environmental and firm variables is thereby demonstrated in the OD process. Internal firm variables also are identified; these variables form together to develop a consistent and operational management system (internal fit).

RESEARCH METHODOLOGY

Using a case study research design, data were collected in the two Chinese family firms representing traditional and progressive firms (see Table 17.1 for descriptions). Table 17.2 summarizes the data collection process. The data were collected by using a modified "objectifying interviewing technique" (Redding, 1990; Sjoberg & Nett, 1968). In both firms, data were gathered through interviews, observation, and the collection of company records and documents.

In total, 40 midlevel managers and company CEOs (chief executive officers) were interviewed over a period of 6-to-12 months in 1996. In the progressive firm four research fellows were employed to interview and observe the business operations of the four identified departments in Hong Kong headquarters and Dongguan plant. Two researchers were also involved in the later stage to interview the company CEO and heads of the four departments. The primary information source for the traditional firm was the son of one of the owners who provided information on the

Table 17.1. Descriptions of the Two Researched Companies

Traditional Chinese Family Firm	Progressive Chinese Family Firm
Partnership with ownership and management by two families; active members include two senior managers and the son of a partner	Ownership and management by a single family; founder semiretired and active management by son
Product line of slippers and wall holders	Product is PVC leather cloth and PVC film
Slippers: company's main product sold to hotels in Southern China and Hong Kong	PVC film used for inflatable toys, rainwear, linings, and other industrial products
Wall holders sold to jobbers/ wholesalers	Solid PVC leather cloth used as prime PVC materials for handbags, briefcases, upholders, and assorted items

Table 17.2.   Data Collection Design in the Representative Companies

	Traditional Chinese Family Firm	*Progressive Chinese Family Firm*
No. of researchers	7, including 4 research fellows	2
Data collection period	6 months	6 months
No. of interviewed personnel	32, including CEO, department heads, supervisory staff, operating staff in Hong Kong and Dongguan, PRC	6, including partner's son, Chinese production mangers, supervisors, and operators
Research methodology	Observation of working day by four research fellows Three observations in Hong Kong and one observations in Dongguan, PRC Follow-up interviews by two researchers based on observation data	Observation of Shenzhen plant activities In-depth interviews with partner's son

promise of confidentiality and only because he was a close schoolmate of the research fellow. Observation and interviews were also conducted at the Shenzhen plant.

OVERVIEW OF THE STAGE MODEL OF OD

The three-stage model of OD is progressively presented in Figure 17.1 and Tables 17.3 and 17.4 and Figure 17.2, and explained in the corresponding narrative. The model follows the transition from an equilibrium position in stage 1 where both Traditional and Progressive firms located their administrative and manufacturing functions in Hong Kong (stage 1), through a transitional or a final stage (stage 2) in which plant facilities were moved to mainland China providing either the impetus for change (progressive) or readjustment (traditional) to maintain as much continuity as possible (stage 2), and finally to a mature stage (stage 3) for progressive firms who had unlocked the barriers to growth in the transitional stage (stage 2). In progressive firm strategic OD integrated stage 2 and 3 activities and thereby avoided a transition crisis.

Figure 17.1 provides an overview of the three stages and compares the traditional and progressive firms. traditional firms progress to an equilibrium position in stage 2, whereas progressive firms move on to stage 3. In Table 17.3 the focus is on the pre-move equilibrium position of the Chi-

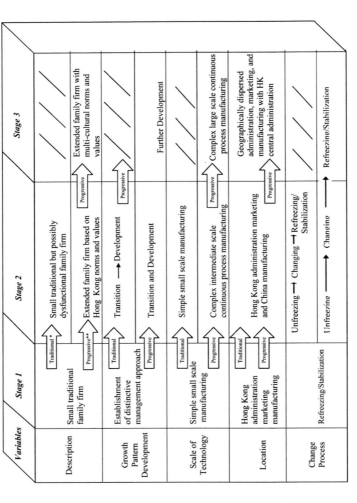

The table shown in the figure:

Variables	Stage 1	Stage 2	Stage 3
Description	Small traditional family firm	Traditional * → Small traditional but possibly dysfunctional family firm	
		Progressive** → Extended family firm based on Hong Kong norms and values	Progressive → Extended family firm with multi-cultural norms and values
Growth Pattern Development	Establishment of distinctive management approach	Traditional → Transition → Development	
		Progressive → Transition and Development	Progressive → Further Development
Scale of Technology	Simple small scale manufacturing	Traditional → Simple small scale manufacturing	
		Progressive → Complex intermediate scale continuous process manufacturing	Progressive → Complex large scale continuous process manufacturing
Location	Hong Kong administration marketing manufacturing	Traditional → Hong Kong administration marketing and China manufacturing	
		Progressive →	Progressive → Geographically dispersed administration, marketing, and manufacturing with HK central administration
Change Process	Refreezing/Stabilization	Unfreezing → Changing → Refreezing/Stabilization	
		Unfreezing → Changing	Refreezing/Stabilization

Key: * Indicates traditional: Tradition Small Chinese family firm. ** Indicates progressive: Progressive small Chinese family firm.

Figure 17.1.   A three-stage model of organizational development: Corporation of traditional and progressive firms

**Table 17.3.   Pre-Move Equilibrium Position
of Overseas Chinese Family Firms in Stage 1**

Factors	*Common Features*
Task environment	• Efficient and hard working work force • Single Chinese cultural and Cantonese language work environment (a small amount of English spoken)
Firm strategies	• Low-cost, no frills strategies • Concentration on simple, standardized products
Managerial tactics	• Personalized management system • Use of didactic tactics

nese family firms (stage 1). Figure 17.2 and Table 17.4 describe stage 2. In Figure 17.2 the adjustments made by both traditional and progressive firms are detailed and related to enabling factors that facilitate the successful transition and implementation of coordination systems into stage 2. Table 17.4 contrasts the differing managerial practices of traditional and progressive firms in stage 2.

The three-stage model (see Figure 17.1) traces the growth of both traditional and progressive firms over two growth stages and projects the progression of progressive firms into a third stage. The model concentrates on the OD (and associated enabling factors) in stage 2. In stage 1 both categories of overseas Chinese family firms exhibited the general characteristics (Redding, 1990). In stage 2 overseas Chinese family firms operated over a broader geographical area by moving production facilities to the adjoining special economic zones (SEZs) and retaining administrative functions in Hong Kong. Within stage 2 traditional firms resemble small but possibly dysfunctional families while progressive firms can be described as extended families based on Hong Kong norms and values. Traditional firms attempted to reestablish organizational equilibrium in stage 2 (completing both transitional and developmental activities) while progressive firms utilized stage 2 to prepare development to international and global operation in stage 3. The change process activities of traditional firms are thus completed within stage 2 while the change process of the progressive firms transcends stage 2 and are continuing into stage 3. Over the three stages progressive firms progressively moved to more complex manufacturing, marketing, and administration while the complexity of these functions remained stable over its two stage adjustment cycle of the traditional firms.

Stage 1

Stage 1 represents a period in which the owner-manager overseas Chinese family firms had stabilized their management and communication systems. A state of equilibrium was achieved and there was convergence toward the general pattern. These Hong Kong family enterprises developed similar managerial systems that fell within what Redding called the recipe of "reasonably standard characteristics of Chinese business" (pp. 205–206). They are small scale, and relatively simple organizational structuring, normally focused on one product or market, centralized decision making with a heavy reliance on one dominant executive, a close overlap of ownership, control, and family; a paternalistic organizational climate, linked to the environment with personalistic networks, normally very sensitive to matters of cost and financial efficiency, commonly linked strongly but informally with related but legally independent organizations handling key functions such as parts, supply, and marketing, relatively weak in terms of creating large-scale market recognition for brands and a high degree of strategic adaptability.

The Chinese owner-manager family firm "recipe" of OD became firmly established in Hong Kong. The strategies and management systems of all Hong Kong firms were similar during this stage. Operating at a small scale and practicing entrepreneurial strategies in a conducive environment, the owner-manager Chinese family firms implemented a predictable strategy. These Hong Kong manufacturers concentrated on mature technologies and were often subcontractors of branded international products, emphasizing low cost-no frills generic strategies.

Both firms in our study adhered to the identified managerial practices to maintain stabilization but the progressive firm initiated unfreezing activities as part of the process of moving production facilities to China toward the end of stage 1. The impetus was a strategic decision to introduce higher quality PVC.

The following is an overview of the management system used by the Chinese family firms in stage 1 of OD. The owner-manager develops the overall strategy for the firm and communicates this strategy through a high-context communication style. Organizational members look for signals of the strategy while performing their jobs. This managerial style means that the organization can operate with only a few formal rules and procedures. Key family members and insiders are stationed throughout the firm to enforce the strategy and provide upward communication to the owner-manager. There is little wasted time in discussions and meetings and increasingly better coordination is achieved as organizational members learn to more accurately pick up signals and communication cues. The owner-manager parcels out information to key individuals who compete with one another for the favor of the owner-manager. The primary purpose of these didactic tactics is to maintain control but the secondary effects are to force the key individuals (insiders) serving as marketing and production managers to work together to adjust the work flow and to create an in-group and an out-group. Irresolvable conflict must be referred to owner-manager thereby keeping him informed and maintaining his control. Direct vertical and horizontal communication channels falling outside the scalar chain but relating to work flow emerge during this process. Jobs are narrowly defined and people are moved temporarily from their jobs as circumstances require cooperating in performing general tasks. These practices make the organization flexible, adaptable, and facilitate the control of the ownership family.

The task environment in stage 1 allowed the firms to place all of their operations (administrative and manufacturing) in a geographically connected space; both the traditional and progressive firms, for example, were located in high-rise industrial buildings. These firms (as was the general pattern) utilized an open office plan for the administrative personnel and supervisor desks were placed directly on the factory floor. Face to face communication and control via observation was facilitated by the geographic spacing and had become the dominant mode of interpersonal communication and control in these Chinese family firms. Cantonese was used as the single mode of intraorganizational communication and this simplified the internal communication process. In the progressive firm, bilingual personnel provided a link to English speaking customers, suppliers, and government, and coincidentally introduced a preparatory learning environment for linking Cantonese-Mandarin speaking personnel when the manufacturing facilitates moved to China in stage 2.

The Chinese family firms perfected low-cost strategies based on production efficiencies. Competitive advantage was also gained through flexibility and adaptability; the firms had the ability, with little notice, to increase or decrease production volumes and to alter product specifications. For example, the traditional firm could sow the labels on slippers and deliver them to a hotel the following day. Likewise, the progressive firm could quickly adjust the production volumes and alter the thickness and texture of PVC sheets. This ability to move quickly to meet changing customer requirements was achieved within the framework of a low cost-no frills strategy.

Although the OD of the traditional and progressive firms could be fitted under the umbrella of the owner-manager Chinese family firm "recipe" there were also major differences. The traditional firm intended to maintain its product strategy whereas progressive firm was investigating the possibility of broadening and upscaling its product strategy. The traditional firm owner-managers deliberately used didactic tactics to maintain control while the use of didactic tactics in the progressive firm was confined to prescribing narrowly defined jobs at lower organizational levels. Gradually seeing that sharing information did not necessarily result in the loss of control and in order to implement a more complex product mix, the progressive firm introduced a computerized information system. Concurrent with and influenced by the widespread availability of information in the management information system (MIS), the CEO of progressive firm reacted by delegating authority to the middle organizational levels. These diverging practices of traditional and progressive firms established the setting for stage 2 in which the challenge of managing geographically separated facilitates speeded up the OD process.

Stage 2

Figure 17.2 lists (a) enabling factors that facilitated the transition to stage 2 and (b) associated common features of overseas Chinese family firms (the characteristics shared by traditional and progressive firms).

Regulatory Relationships

The regulatory environment (stage 2 enabling factor) facilitated the development of smooth, helpful, and time saving interactions with government officials (common stage 2 feature). The Hong Kong Chinese family firms established their manufacturing facilities in the neighboring SEZ, Guangzhou. The Hong Kong owner-managers dealt with newly trained SEZ specialists rather than traditional Chinese Communist Party bureaucrats. Communication was efficiently facilitated for many Hong Kong Chinese firms (as exemplified by the traditional and progressive firms) by being able to communicate directly in a linking language (Mandarin) and sharing common objectives with the SEZ provisional administrators. The tradeoff was that SEZ officials provided access to land, labor, and expedited cross border movement of personnel and goods and the Hong Kong firms provided jobs and housing for Chinese workers. The Hong Kong firms found that regulators were more lax in China than in Hong Kong. A win-win situation was created in which both sides were communicating within the context of complementary objectives.

Physical Distance, Housing, and Infrastructure

Stage 2 enabling factors established conditions that combined to allow continuity in the management systems of the Chinese family firm in stage 2. Within the context of these enabling factors organizational adjustments were made in both firms. First the organizational pattern of a personalized management style and a dominant CEO was maintained through

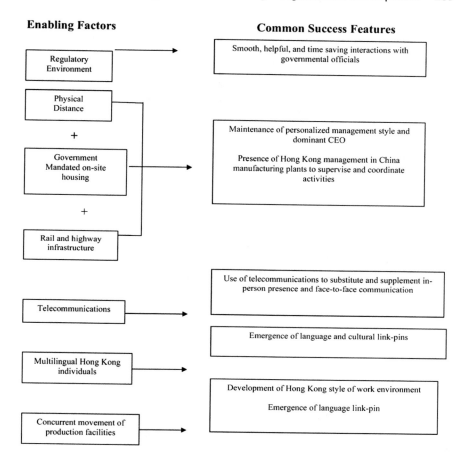

Figure 17.2.   Enabling factors and common success features of traditional and progressive firms in stage 2.

new tactics. Second, Hong Kong personnel were placed in the China manufacturing plants to supervise and coordinate production activities. An enterprise environment was structured in which person-to-person (including face-to-face) communication still could be maintained as the principle coordinating mechanism of the Chinese family firm.

The plants were located within the SEZs of Shenzhen and Dongguan in Guangdong province. The physical distance between headquarters and plant locations of 35 miles (traditional firm) and 70 miles (progressive firm) respectively made day trips possible. An efficient rail, highway, and taxi infrastructure added to the convenience of making these trips. Within Hong Kong a freeway and the Kowloon Canton Railway extend through the new territories to the border. Travel time to the border was 45 minutes to 1 hour. From the border a car trip via side roads to the traditional firm's plant is approximately 45 minutes long in non-rush traffic. Because of the construction new toll road running directly past the firm progressive firm's plant, the travel time to the plant is a predictable and dependable one hour in duration. With a combined travel time of 4 hours to and from Hong Kong sufficient time was still available for constructive work in mainland China in a long and tiring day.

Company apartments (traditional and progressive firms) and dorm rooms (progressive firm) were built on-site in the mainland China manufacturing facilities. The facilities made it feasible and convenient for company personnel to stay over in China. Mandated to establish a minimum of these housing facilities through direct legislation and encouraged to expand the number of rooms through SEZ incentives, both firms had a ready supply of overnight accommodations.

Both the traditional and progressive firms stationed Hong Kong personnel in their Shenzhen and Dongguan plants to supervise and coordinate the production process. To facilitate the efficacy of on-site supervision, both firms made effective use of company housing in China. The influence on OD of having these housing facilities was remarkably different. In the progressive firm, the physical arrangement of the complex was in concert with company policy, and the informal behavior of the Hong Kong managers encouraged and enhanced active employee interaction. There was a common company mess in which management, production supervisors and workers could mix. Led by the CEO who made a practice of sitting with different groups of employees at different meals there was an interactive mixing of the entire work group. In addition, the company sponsored company leagues of badminton, soccer, and basketball. The facilities were kept clean and the article authors observed a sense of pride and "belonging to the big family" in working for this progressive company. The CEO was perceived to be a visible and approachable leader who represented the head of an extended family.

Contrasted to the progressive firm plant complex environment that encouraged interactions among personnel, the physical setting and behavior patterns at traditional firm inhibited communication. In the Traditional firm production plant, there was a strict separation between management and the workforce. On the top floor of the Shenzhen plant there were four apartments: one each for the two partners of the firm, one for the son of one of the partners, and one for the production manager. The workers were located in an adjoining building, six in each small crowded room with no closets and little ventilation. Connected to this building were the kitchen and bathroom facilities. The workers picked up their meals in the kitchen and ate in a courtyard. Needless to say this physical arrangement and the accompanying attitude of the management did not create a feeling of loyalty or pride in working for this company.

In addition to the on-site supervisors, both firms further coordinated their Hong Kong and China operations through day trips or overnight stays lasting up to two to three days. Progressive firm personnel traveled in a company van from the Hong Kong-China border to the Dongguan plant. This 1-hour air-conditioned van ride from the Hong Kong-China border to the manufacturing plant in Dongguan put a changing mix of enterprise personnel in close proximity and this face-to-face contact impacted directly on the organizational culture and on the firms' communication system. To illustrate, on a Friday evening return trip from the plant, the riders included the CEO, a senior production manager, a computer specialist, and a marketing specialist. Also present were the two authors of this article. The focus of the dialogue was a corporate strategy meeting scheduled for the next day. The production manager and the computer specialist were scheduled to make presentations at this meeting. There were three major topics discussed during the 1-hour ride: (a) the production manager went over his overlay presentation and received active input from the CEO and a few comments from the computer specialist; (b) the computer specialist filled the others in on a computer installation in-progress; and (c) the trio discussed aspects of corporate strategy and new product development. Although the marketing specialist did not take part in the discussions and he spoke on-and-off with the article authors, he did overhear the business related conversations. Considering that the 1-hour ride, was taken 2 or more times per week, and that the average number of personnel per trip, the company van rides added an unexpected, but highly efficient, communication environment to the firm's communication system.

The progressive firm gained this unanticipated benefit of acquiring more interactive communication and coordination systems because of the informal communication and coordination occurring in the company van. Organizational members at all levels were put into close contact for an hour as they traveled between the Hong Kong headquarters and the Dongguan plant.

The traditional firm managers traveled to the Shenzhen plant by taxi or private car. The partner's son use of taxi travel minimized travel expense and the private cars of the owner-managers also were used to make customer visits.

The physical arrangement of personnel in the progressive firm created a facilitating condition for decentralization in the Hong Kong office. As managers were away and attending to company business in Dongguan, Hong Kong subordinate personnel were encouraged to take on the additional responsibility of responding immediately rather than waiting and checking with their respective superiors in Dongguan. Developing an extended small clan family culture involving both Hong Kong and China employers was the key in making the successful transition in the management of this geographically separated company.

PERSONALIZED MANAGEMENT STYLE AND DOMINANT CEO

Both firms represented the maintenance and continuity of the personalized communication and coordination system and the dominance of a powerful central individual (in the case of the traditional firm two individuals).

The impact of having two heads in the traditional firm was not investigated intensively but the overall indication is that these individuals spoke through a single voice to the organizational members. The managing partners who were lifelong friends and companions have compatible personalities and behavioral styles. Keeping in constant reach through informal meetings supplemented by telecommunication messages, the partners engaged in an organizational process of harmonizing their behavioral patterns. The extensive use of didactic tactics by the managing partners led to some dysfunctional aspects that threatened to reduce firm efficiency and put a strain on the communication system between Hong Kong and China operations. The two partners of the traditional firm typified the image of the traditional aloof and remote Chinese leader. These individuals communicated entirely with the partner's son or the Chinese production manager while at the Shenzhen plant and have little direct contact with the Chinese personnel. The possible implicit authority inherent in the physical presence of the partners at the Shenzhen may have been magnified by having joint CEOs. One of the owner-managers was more likely to present at the plant at any given point in time.

The progressive firm represented an evolution to a more sophisticated multifaceted communication system that nevertheless still represented personalism and that continued to revolve around a central individual. The personal behavior of the CEO became a model that was emulated throughout the organization. An expanding system of mutual obligations developed between the CEO and staff at all organizational levels in both Hong Kong and China. These personnel became increasingly intertwined with one another in an increasingly integrated and productive organizational culture. The evolving system can be described as being simultaneously centralized and decentralized as all organizational members increasingly committed themselves to mutually influencing decisions that contributed to the achievement of organizational objectives in an increasingly complex and dynamic external environment. The management system remained traditional in the sense that human relationships were guided by the classic Chinese Confucian concepts of humanness of "jen" and politeness or "li" and modern in the sense that the firm made extensive use of the latest telecommunications and computer technology.

TELECOMMUNICATIONS

The installation of telecommunication infrastructure made direct and instantaneous communication possible within the geographical area encompassing Hong Kong and the SEZs. The availability, reliability, and the cost of both wired and cellular telecommunications showed dramatic improvement during the period of time represented by stage 2. Interpersonal communication via reliable and cost efficient telecommunication supplemented and reinforced person-to-person contact.

Continuous contact between Hong Kong and China personnel via telephone and fax took place in both researched firms, but with differing effects. In the progressive firm, Hong Kong personnel from the marketing and purchasing departments, in the course of performing their job duties, communicated with Dongguan personnel on a daily basis and with other functional personnel less frequently. The purchasing manager stated that she always sent faxes in order to keep the cost down, to create a record, and to avoid misunderstandings. Because of the frequency and volume of faxes and telephone contacts, the progressive firm leased its Hong Kong-Dongguan telecommunication lines. Though expensive, this decision allowed efficient cross-border communication that would not have been possible otherwise. With the growth of Hong Kong firms operating in Shenzhen and Dongguan, the expanding public telecommunication lines could not keep up with the expanding demand. To enhance and ensure communication efficiency, the progressive firm created a role in Dongguan titled public relations officer. A former Dongguan public official who occupied this position negotiated contract terms for the leased private lines and also strove to facilitate other company-government relationships. The investment in leased private telecommunication lines easily paid for itself by avoiding time delays and employee frustration.

The traditional firm did not have the same cross-border communication requirements as did the Progressive firm, and utilized lower cost public telephone and fax lines. Although delays in communicating were experienced, the public telecommunication facilities proved adequate. The telephone calls and faxes from Hong Kong were directed to the joint-owner's son, the production manager, or a managing partner who present in Shenzhen.

Cellular phone technology impacted the communication systems of the firms directly and indirectly. In both firms, the use of cellular phones complemented and supplemented the dedicated phone, e-mail, public phone, and fax cross-border and intraprovince communication. The direct impact of information transfer was achieved through cellular calls. The indirect impact was to keep information content confidential. Traditional firm owner-managers utilized cellular phones to convey messages that they wanted to kept from the employed production manager and section heads.

An example of the successful use of telecommunication media in the progressive firm occurred when a sales representative received an urgent cellular phone call on a routine customer visit. This trader requested an urgent small order and offered to pay a premium price. The sales representative called his colleagues at the Hong Kong office who in turn called the manufacturing personnel at the Dongguan plant to see if the order could be inserted in the production schedule. In the meantime, the sales representative went to the office of this trader and, on the way, received a return phone call giving him negotiating alternatives in terms of prices and schedules. Upon arriving at the trader's office he finalized the deal and phoned this information back to the Hong Kong office. The associate in the Hong Kong office then sent a fax order to Dongguan and received an immediate return confirming fax. At his next customer visit, the sales representative received the confirmation and telephoned the trader to finalize the transaction.

LANGUAGE AND CULTURAL LINK-PINS

Language link-pins are individuals who perform the dual functions of the translation of messages between languages and the carrying of culture as they perform their translation tasks (Du-Babcock & Babcock, 1996). The necessity of utilizing language link-pins arises when first language speakers do not share a linking language and yet need to communicate with one another. In the SEZ factories the mainland China work force spoke Mandarin (the national Chinese language) and could not understand Cantonese (the Chinese dialect spoken in Hong Kong). Bilingual Cantonese became language link-pins and Mandarin became the linking language.

Messages inherently reflect the values and attitudes of senders and are imbedded within the content of their transmission. In the process of interacting in their linking roles the bilingual Cantonese were implanting Hong Kong country values and work habits in the Mandarin speaking SEZ work force.

The partner's son in the traditional firm and the production line supervisors and most headquarters personnel on short term visits in the progressive firm spoke fluent Mandarin and consequently linked the Hong Kong headquarters and the SEZ plants. Both firms developed a unified culture based on Hong Kong values and work habits.

Written exchange via fax and regular mail supplemented the oral communication network. This written communication between lower level personnel in Hong Kong and Dongguan was accomplished without language translation. There is only a single written Chinese language and the Hong Kong personnel could write and read simplified characters.

The importance of language link-pins and cultural carriers was magnified because of the difficulty that mainland Chinese had in entering Hong Kong. In the progressive firm, Hong Kong-based language link-pins established direct telephone communication links between the Hong Kong headquarters and Dongguan and maintained direct face-to-face conversations on visits to Dongguan. This verbal exchange provided the framework and context for written communication. Consistent with the Chinese cultural imperative of establishing relationships or "guanxi" in order to have successful business relationships (Hsu, 1971, 1981; Tung, 1987, 1988), these traveling Hong Kong-based language link-pins were engaged in relationship building as well as task activities in their business trips to Dongguan. Without these trips and the presence of fluent Mandarin-speaking Cantonese in the Chinese plants, building a unified company culture would have been more difficult, if not impossible.

CONCURRENT MOVEMENT OF PRODUCTION FACILITIES

The concurrent movement of production facilities to the adjoining SEZs was mutually beneficial to these Chinese family firms. Companies that located in the neighboring province enjoyed more advantages than those moving to inland China or other more distant locations. The first advantage is in line with hot spot theory (Pouder & St. John, 1996). According to Pouder and St. John, simultaneously locating within close geographical proximity allows firms to generate multiple and cumulative operating efficiencies. At the same time, the condition of being surrounded by firms from the same cultural and language background speeds up the learning curves. Hong Kong work values and methods became the basis of the work system in the SEZ plants. Workers from rural provinces throughout China immigrated to the SEZs seeking employment in these plants. These workers were pliable and responsive to Hong Kong style supervision as they were cut off from their families and friends. They were motivated to work hard in order to succeed and send hard currency back home. These workers were integrated in a company wide unified culture based on Hong Kong values and work methods. Through the intercompany grapevine the workers communicated and reinforced their work experiences and solidi-fied their work habits. In the case of the traditional firm, a Taiwanese owned and managed plant occupied an adjoining plot. This overseas Chinese firm used a work system similar to that of Hong Kong overseas Chinese firms. Operatives from the respective companies met in the courthouse after dinner and passed messages and information back and forth.

The possibility of employing skilled Hong Kong professionals was another advantage that accrued to firms moving operations to neighboring SEZs. For example, in progressive firm, the frontline and midlevel who are presently stationed in Dongguan during the weekdays took on these positions only because they could return to Hong Kong for the weekends.

DIFFERING STRATEGIES AND TACTICS

Table 17.4 compares the differing strategies and tactics of the traditional and progressive firms in implementing stage 2 OD activities. Five contrasting factors are discussed in the following sections.

Managerial Strategies

The corporate level strategies of the traditional firm and the progressive firm diverged upon entering stage 2. The traditional firm stressed continuity in maintaining its low cost no-frills generic strategy. This firm

Table 17.4.   Differences in Stage 2 Between Traditional and Progressive Firms

Traditional Chinese Family Firm	*Progressive Chinese Family Firm*
Continuous of low cost no-frills strategy	Introduction of (movement to) differentiation strategy
Noncomputerized information system	Computerized information system
Continuation of and possibility of intensifying didactic tactics	Disbanding of didactic tactics
Restricted Hong Kong-China communication	Unlimited and directed Hong Kong-China communication
Maintenance of job design and authority relationships	Concurrent job redesign (enlargement) and decentralization (especially to lower level Hong Kong roles)

continued to concentrate on its established products and territories while the progressive firm substituted a differentiation strategy and moved to upscale and customize its products. These conditions set the stage for adjusting organizational variables to fit these diverging strategies. The traditional firm faced the challenge of pursuing its unaltered strategy in a more complex exterior environment whereas the progressive firm was implementing a more ambitious strategy under these more challenging conditions.

Organizational variables (see Table 17.4) were adjusted to fit and reinforce the differing strategies of the traditional and progressive firms. For traditional firms the organizational system was modified to fit the Chinese family firm recipe to the new environment. For progressive firms an altered system was developed to reflect the changes necessitated to operationalize an expanded strategy.

INFORMATION SYSTEMS

The traditional firm maintained its non-computed information system whereas progressive firm introduced a computerized information system. The progressive firm's online computer system linked its Hong Kong marketing, planning, and control functions with the Dongguan production plant. This real time MIS and scheduling system made possible a visible and precise method of integrating and implementing marketing and production planning. Personnel in Hong Kong and Dongguan had immediate and unrestricted access to this data bank. Using this system, a sales representative in Hong Kong could instantaneously check the production status of a customer's order. This ready access to information served as a common frame of reference for communication and coordination processes and for identifying areas of exception that required personal coordination and immediate and direct attention.

In contrast the traditional firm relied on a paper-and-pencil information system as the basis and framework for the integration of its Hong Kong and China operations. The technological level of the impersonal coordination techniques were appropriately matched to the two firms. The introduction of a computer based information system in the traditional firm would have unnecessarily increased the operating costs (to install and run the system) and would have required upgrading of management skill levels (to operate and maintain the system). A so-called "old-fashioned" systems was consistent with the low cost strategy and simple technology of the traditional firm.

Didactic Tactics

Silin (1976, p. 39) described the didactic leadership style as "a mechanism used for retaining power by rationing information and assuming the superiority of the teacher." In the progressive firm the rationing of information would have been clearly dysfunctional and also impossible to achieve without restricting access to records contained in the computerized information system. The denial of access to production schedules and inventory records would have, for example, severely impinged on the efficiency of the communication and coordination systems. Rather than rationing information, the objective in progressive firm was to spread and share information. Acting upon the personal example provided by the progressive firm CEO the management staff took on the dual roles of teacher and student and abandoned the automatic assumption of their superiority ability to isolate opportunities and analyze problems. To illustrate, on the van trips conveying Hong Kong personnel between Hong Kong and China in progressive firm, open discussions of company policy were held without any concern that these conversations were being overheard by other traveling company personnel.

The information processing requirements of the traditional firm were significantly lower. In this firm the manufacturing technology was simple; employees used a succession of machines and produced simple products. Access to customers and low-cost production were the keys to success for the company. Because the son of one of the owners was too young to assume the role of production manager in China and since no other family members were available from either ownership family, the traditional firm was forced to hire an experienced Chinese production manager to manage the Shenzhen manufacturing facility.

Top management in the traditional firm chose to maintain its management system in the Hong Kong headquarters and reinforce the systems by the physical presence of a family member in China and by periodic inspection trips to the plant by the two top managers. Lacking trust in the mainland China production manager, the principle duty of this on-site family member was to check on and control this production manager through direct observation. The top management did not completely trust the mainland China production manager at the same time were not ready to turn over the responsibility for running the plant to an inexperienced family member. The premise of this approach was that management felt that they could not afford to hire an experienced Hong Kong manager.

Knowing that the Chinese manager did not have the capital to start a competing firm but still fearing he might defect to a larger sized corporation, the Hong Kong management pursued a didactic strategy of deliberately keeping information pertaining to their customers from him. Even though the intentional withholding of information interfered with the efficient scheduling of production runs, it also increased the perceived security and sense of control of the owner-manager families. For example, finished items were often shipped to middlemen who then redistributed the goods to the final customers. In the specific case of a large hotel order of slippers, the efficient arrangement would have been direct delivery to the hotel, but the firm chose to first deliver the slippers to an intermediary wholesaler who in turn delivered the slippers to the hotel. The management of the traditional firm was willing to incur this additional transaction cost in order to hoard information and thus retain ownership control.

In sum, the continuing presence of authority figures in the China plants of both traditional and progressive firms, as exemplified by the company owners and managers, reinforced the personal rather than bureaucratic control styles of these companies. Personalized control was exercised in both companies but didactic tactics were utilized only in the Traditional firm. The management of the progressive firm having significantly higher information needs in an increasingly and dynamic environment, exercised the Chinese virtue of adaptability and did not employ the dysfunctional tactic of didactic leadership. In addition such didactic tactics would have been inconsistent with the managerial values and tendencies of progressive firm.

HONG KONG-CHINA COMMUNICATION

Restricted Hong Kong-China communication (traditional firm) as opposed to unlimited and direct communication (progressive firm) was a function of the use of didactic tactics. The traditional firm restricted the communication flow between Hong Kong and Shenzhen with the parameters of the continuing and expanding use of didactic tactics. The managing partners and the partner's son stationed in Shenzhen performed the linking roles to connect the Hong Kong and Shenzhen operations. Communication between Hong Kong and Shenzhen flowed through and was restricted to passing information among these individuals.

The information processing requirements of the traditional firm were strained by the move to Shenzhen. The traditional firm did not adequately develop new management structures and communication systems to transfer and process information between Hong Kong headquarters and the Shenzhen manufacturing plant. As a result, the three active managers experienced higher personal anxieties as they extended their working hours in an attempt to personally control the Hong Kong and Shenzhen operations.

The progressive firm went further than simply eliminating the use of didactic tactics to the active promotion of a free flow of information throughout the organization. The experience of the progressive firm also suggests that small Chinese-family firms can escape the related problem of insider-outsider mentality dilemma in the transitional stage of organizational growth. While the CEO continued to be the central figure in managing the company's affairs, the OD strategy of progressive firm was one of expansion and inclusion of all organizational members and did not have the distinction of fostering the development of an in-group and an out-group. There was a movement toward increased intermingling of company personnel as a more interactive coordination system evolved to meet the communication requirements of competing in the fast moving fashion industry as the progressive firm moved its product mix-up scale to higher value added products.

Organizational Design

The traditional and progressive firms followed contrasting patterns of organizational design. The contrasts are captured in the final two comparisons of Table 17.4 that illustrate differing aspects of the organizational design functions. In the Traditional firm, jobs were narrowly defined and authority centralized. Rules and policies remained unwritten and were transmitted through the verbal commands of management. In the progressive firm there were the concurrent movements toward the enlargement of jobs and the decentralization of authority in order to carry the expanded job duties. Written policies and procedures were introduced to provide guidelines for decision-making and guide behavior in repetitive situations.

With top level personnel spending part of the work week in Dongguan, staff in Hong Kong could no longer check with supervisors who used to be easily accessible in the company's open floor plan office. These frontline personnel were left with the option of having to make decisions or to use fax, e-mail or telephone communication to check either with their supervisors or with other management staff. As these Hong Kong personnel gradually made more decisions, this company underwent a process of decentralization and the formulation of policies rules and procedures. With lower level jobs every overspecialized and restricted to specific duties, personnel increasingly found that their jobs were too narrowly defined to make fast decisions. The CEO initiated a program of job redesign with the objective of reducing and eventually eliminating the problems associated with the splintering of authority. The physical distance, together with the increasing complexities of running a competitive global business, triggered a process of organizational change and adaptation in the Progressive firm. Hong Kong jobs were concurrently being enlarged and enriched (Herzberg, 1968) as job functions were consolidated (horizontal integration) and authority for decisions was moved to lower organizational levels (vertical integration).

USE OF MODEL TO GUIDE STRATEGIC OD

In this paper, we present a model that can be used to guide strategic OD in overseas Chinese family firms as they pass through the stages of organizational growth. In this process the inhibitors to growth that are inherent in the traditional Chinese family firms can be avoided and positive features that lead to growth and successful OD can be introduced. Our analysis provides examples of what to include (progressive firm) and what not to include (traditional firm) in strategic OD. In strategic OD, a long-term developmental approach can be adopted so activities in a previous stage support the active activities in a following stage, and can be integrated across stages.

In stage 1, overseas Chinese family firms develop an equilibrium (consisting of or among organizational variables that include the use of didactic tactics). For firms implementing strategic OD, special attention can be paid to avoiding this phenomenon. In strategic OD, stage 2 development becomes a transition stage where careful implementation guides transition over the transitional and developmental stages towards becoming global operation and thereby avoids the crisis predicted in stage theory in moving from one stage to the next. In our case study, the progressive firm gradually developed its administrative, production, and marketing skills so there was a steady progression in skill development through the stages where the ability to compete in the global competitive market was developed.

Progressive Chinese firms have grown and progressed to stage 3 with examples including such firms as Acer and D-Link from Taiwan, Vitasoy from Hong Kong, and Creative Labs from Singapore. In stage 2, manufacturing operations are moved to nearby lower cost locations. Mainland China was the hinterland for Hong Kong firms. Southern Malaysia offered the same advantages for Singaporean firms and southern Taiwan (Hsin Chu Science Industrial Park, Tainan, or Kaohsiung) for Taipei centered firms. Acer is perhaps the best example of an overseas Chinese firm progressing to stage 3. In their case farsighted company policies and programs were formulated to prevent the emergence of didactic tactics as outlined in stage 1. Acer still progressed through equivalent stages with all operations centered in Taipei in stage 1, administration in Taipei and research and development and manufacturing in the Hsin Chu Science Industrial Park in stage 2, followed by widespread dispersed operations in stage 3.

Language competency development is a critical component of strategic OD of overseas Chinese family firms. Strategic OD in stages 2 and 3 require the development of second language communication capabilities and the establishment of language-based communication channels (see Babcock & Du-Babcock, 2001; Du-Babcock & Babcock, 2007). As the overall competency in European language is relatively low and full bilinguals are few in number, the design of link-pin communication channels (see Du-Babcock & Babcock, 1996) and developing language link-pin translators in these channels is a challenge faced by overseas Chinese firms. The Chinese language comes from different language family from European languages, and is more difficult to master (especially the written part of the language) than are European languages. Translation to and from European languages is also more difficult less precise than translation from one European language to another European language. Although Chinese in large number are studying European languages (especially English because of its role as world's dominant business language), there is still a competency gap in that Chinese organizations do not have an adequate supply of fluent second-language speakers to handle coordination needs in transitioning from domestic to international and ultimately global organizations. This language competency gap also poses an additional factor in OD implementation that makes for increased complexity. The progressive firm provides an excellent example of how to illustrate language-competency development in strategic organization development and the language-based communication zones model can be used to diagnose language competency requirement and to provide guidelines for designing language-based organizational communication channel.

In sum, Chinese organizations have the potential to become competitive global organizations but only if they build upon their strengths of a personalized organization with its inherent flexibility, and eliminate features that restrict growth, and build in the necessary capabilities, structures, and systems as they grow through the stages. Strategic OD can guide the growth of overseas Chinese family firms as they transition into international and finally global enterprises.

REFERENCES

Babcock, R., & Du-Babcock, B. (2001). Language-based communication zones in international business communication. *Journal of Business Communication, 38*(4), 372-412.

Du-Babcock, B., & Babcock, R. (1996). Patterns of expatriate-local personnel communication in multinational corporation. *Journal of Business Communication, 33*(2), 141-164.

Du-Babcock, B., & Babcock, R. (2007). Genre Patterns In Language-based Communication Zones. *Journal of Business Communication, 44*, 340-373.

Galbraith, J., & Kazanjian, R. (1986). *Strategy implementation: Structure, systems, and process* (2nd ed.). St. Paul, MN: West.

Herzberg, F. (1968). One more time: How do you motivate employees? *Harvard Business Review, 46*(1), 53–62.

Hsu, F. (1971). Psychological homeostasis and Jen: Conceptual tools of advancing psychological anthropology. *American Anthropologist, 73*, 23–44.

Hsu, F. (1981). *American and Chinese: Passage to differences* (3rd ed.). Honolulu: University of Hawaii Press.

Lewin, K. (1946). Action research and minority problems. *Journal of Social Issues, 2*(4), 34–36. (Reprinted from *The action research reader* (1988). Geelong: Deakin University)

Lewin, K. (1952). Group decision and social change. In G. E. Swanson, T. M. Newcomb., & F. E. Hartley (Eds.), *Reading in social psychology* (pp. 330-344). New York: Holt.

Pouder, R., & St. John, C. (1996). Hot spots and blind spots: Geographical clusters of firms and innovation. *The Academy of Management Review, 21*(4), 1192–1225.

Redding, G. (1990). *The spirit of Chinese capitalism*. New York: Walter de Gruyter.

Silin, R. (1976). *Leadership and values: The organization of large-scale Taiwanese enterprise*. Cambridge, MA: Harvard University Press.

Sjoberg, G., & Nett, R. (1968). *A methodology for social research*. New York: Harper and Row.

Tung, R. (1987). Expatriates assignment: Enhancing success and minimizing failure. *The Academy of Management Executive, 11*(2), 117-125.

Tung, R. (1988). Career issues in international assignments. *The Academy of Management Executive, 11*(3), 241-244.

Weidenbaum, M. (1996). The Chinese family business enterprise. *California Management Review, 38*(4), 141-156.

ABOUT THE AUTHORS

Philip Anderson is the director of leadership development for the YMCA of the United States headquartered in Chicago, Illinois. He is a faculty member at Benedictine University and Chicago School of Professional Psychology. He holds a PhD in organizational development from Benedictine University and a MEd from University of Illinois in human resource development leadership. His work is published in *Training Today Magazine, International Organization Development,* and the *Organization Development Journal.*

Bertha Du-Babcock is an associate professor in the Department of English, at the City University of Hong Kong, Hong Kong.

Richard D. Babcock is an emeritus professor of management in the School of Business and Management at the University of San Francisco, San Francisco, California.

Jimmy Brown is an industrial and organizational psychologist with more than 15 years of applied experience in professional development and executive coaching. Jimmy has a PhD in organization development from Benedictine University, an MA in industrial and organizational psychology, a BA in psychology, and certification in Birkman Method of Coaching. He has worked both independently and through major management consulting firm, and is an adjunct professor in various universities.

Jim Dunn is the chief learning officer for Texas Health Resources, one of the nation's largest faith-based health systems. Prior to joining Texas

Health, Jim served as the national vice president, human resources and talent retention strategy for the National Home Office of the American Cancer Society. Jim holds an undergraduate degree from Howard University, a masters in public health from Emory University, and a PhD in organization development from Benedictine University. His article, "Strategic Human Resources: An Alliance for the Future" was published in the Fall 2006 issue of the *Organization Development Journal*.

Paul Eccher a principal with Corporate Insights, Inc., has more than 15 years experience in competency model development, behavioral assessment, and training needs analysis. Before starting Corporate Insights, Paul led a team of industrial psychologists who designed and implemented behaviorally based assessment tools to assist clients in their selection and development process. He has helped his clients to understand the competencies, which drive performance success. He has conducted numerous studies linking behavioral competencies to bottom-line revenue generation. Paul received his PhD in organization development from Benedictine University.

Barry J. Halm has been a hospital administrator, regional planning agency director and university faculty member. Dr. Halm has 30 years of experience in healthcare systems, multifacility health delivery organizations, and individual hospital environments. His consulting focus is directed toward operational strategy, organizational culture and governance. Presently, Dr. Halm is an assistant professor and program director for the undergraduate health services administrative major at Minnesota State University and teaches courses in health policy, strategy, management theory, healthcare law and finance. He is a fellow in the American College of Healthcare Executives.

Thomas C. Head is a professor of management in the Walter E. Heller College of Business Administration at Roosevelt University. He has worked on projects in a diverse set of organizations, ranging from Fortune 15 and the U.S. Department of Energy to small start-ups and local hospital chains. Tom is a prolific writer with 13 books and over 50 scholarly articles to his credit. Tom is currently serving on the board of Pro-Change International, was the Region 4 president for the Association of Collegiate Business Schools and programs, and the editor of the new electronic journal, *Pro-Change International Journal*. His PhD is in business administration from Texas A&M University.

Mark Holst-Mikkelsen is partner and industrial researcher at the Danish consultancy Strategos. He is specialized in the field of strategy implementation and has been responsible for a thorough industrial research project among 100 Scandinavian companies with more than 10,000 people involved. The results have been published in a bestselling book on sense-making strategies, published in Denmark with Flemming Poulfelt as co-author.

Rob Kjar is associate director of talent development at Astellas Pharmaceuticals, Inc. He is a member of the ODNetwork, the Academy of Management and the Midwest Academy of Management. He has worked internationally and has written and conducted research on issues facing leadership and global organizations for several organizations. He holds a PhD in organization development from Benedictine University.

Flemming Poulfelt is a professor of management and strategy, vice dean of research communicating and director of CBS Leadership Lab at Copenhagen Business School. His research interests are within strategy, professional service firms, change management, and management consulting. He is the author of numerous books and articles. He serves on various corporate boards of national and international companies. He acts as a consultant and is a frequent presenter at seminars and conferences both in Denmark and abroad.

Mary Lou Kotecki has more than 30 years experience in management and leadership positions. She currently manages a worldwide shared services group and leads a multinational initiative for attaining distinctive customer support for Deere & Company. Her educational background includes an undergraduate degree in chemistry and French, a master of science in industrial engineering and management, and a PhD in organization development. Dr. Kotecki served as feature editor for the *Organization Development Journal* and is a member of the editorial review board for the *Organization Development Practitioner*. Her most recent publication appeared in *Managers Learning in Action*, published in 2004. She continues to consult and present internationally.

Roxanne Ray is a senior performance consultant with Advocate Health Care. She is the principle consultant leading the systemwide frontline leader development program linking learning and development to organizational initiatives. She specializes in organizational change, leadership assessment, development coaching and team development. She holds a master's degree in organizational behavior from Benedictine University. Roxanne can be reached at roxanne.ray@advocatehealth.com

Nazneen Razi is executive vice president and chief global human resources officer at Jones Lang LaSalle. She has over 25 years experience leading human resource organizations for national and global firms and has held senior HR officer roles at Comdisco and CNA Insurance Companies. Dr. Razi earned a PhD in organization development and an MBA from Benedictine University in Lisle, Illinois, where she also served as adjunct faculty for the MBA programs. She served as chairman of the board of HRMAC and is on the advisory boards of Menttium, AON Consulting and on the board of the Chicago Sinfonietta.

Eric Sanders started working on this project as a senior account manager for Human Synergistics, and is now an external organization development consultant. He is an expert at showing measurable financial as well as behavioral results from OD initiatives, and specializes in helping leaders drive culture change. He earned a certificate in OD at Benedictine University, has an MA in economics from Northern Illinois University and an MBA from the University of Illinois at Chicago. Eric can be reached at: eric.sanders@ODeconomist.com

Linda Sharkey is executive director, Global Diversity and Inclusion Network, Executive Networks—a worldwide organization that connects key human resource heads from the largest corporations in the world (companies with revenues in excess of $30B).   Most recently, Linda was vice president, People Development at Hewlett Packard, responsible for establishing and driving the company's talent management initiative, performance management processes, career development, executive staffing and diversity and inclusion. Prior to HP, Linda was with GE and held numerous senior human resource and talent management roles. She holds a PhD in organization development from Benedictine University, MPA from Russell Sage College, and a BA in history from Nazareth College.

Peter Sorensen is a professor and director of PhD and masters programs in OD at Benedictine University. He authored over 200 books and articles, including *Academy of Management Journal, Group and Organization Studies, Leadership and Organization Development Journal, Journal of Management Studies*, and *Organization and Administrative Sciences*. He is past chair of the OD&C Division of the Academy of Management. His doctoral degree is from Illinois Institute of Technology.

Susan Sweem is an assistant professor in the College of Business and Health Administration at the University of St. Francis. Her areas of research include talent management, employee engagement and organization consulting. Her publications include *Client-Consultant Collaboration: Coping with Complexity and Change*, Volume 10. In addition, Susan has more than 20 years experience in human resources management working in various industries including healthcare and global manufacturing. She earned a BS in sociology from Iowa State University, MS in industrial relations from Loyola University, and PhD in OD from Benedictine University.

Jason Wolf is an explorer of organizations and a "radical catalyst" for organizational health, effectiveness and performance. He is a sought after speaker and consultant on such topics as sustaining high performance, organization culture and change, leadership, and service having led major initiatives in both internal and external roles. A true scholar-practitioner, Jason is a faculty member of the Beryl Institute and an associate of the Taos Institute. He is an adjunct instructor at American University and served as a lecturer at Vanderbilt University. Jason served on the board of trustees of the Organization Development Network from 1999-2002.

Therese Yaeger is an associate professor, Benedictine University, has served in numerous managerial roles during her 25-year career. She authored over 100 articles including eight books, including *Global Organization Development: Managing Unprecedented Change* with Sorensen and Head. Yaeger served as executive board member of MCD of Academy of Management. She is incoming president of the Midwest Academy of Management. Therese received her PhD from Benedictine University.

LaVergne, TN USA
20 July 2010

190084LV00002B/18/P